easypcprojects

RICHARD WENTK

WHICH?
BOOKS

CONSUMERS' ASSOCIATION

CONTENTS

Introduction   6

BEGINNERS START HERE

1.1   Outside the box   8

1.2   Insides of a PC   10

1.3   Introduction to Windows   12

1.4   Introducing the Windows XP desktop   14

1.5   Windows shortcuts and speed tips   16

1.6   Software   18

1.7   Files, filing and file types   20

1.8   Choosing a printer   22

1.9   Choosing an ISP   24

1.10   Setting up your Internet connection   26

1.11   Introducing email   28

1.12   Introducing web browsing   30

1.13   Improve your web browsing   32

THE FAMILY PC

2.1   Sharing your PC with others   34

2.2   PC security and childproofing   36

2.3   Kids' stuff   38

2.4   Teenage learning   40

2.5   Home makeover – interior design   42

2.6   Home makeover – garden design   44

2.7   Designing a new home   46

2.8   Games and gaming   48

2.9   How to shop online   50

2.10   Essential consumer resources   52

2.11   Holidays, flights and travel   54

2.12   How to eBay   56

2.13   Books, music, videos and gifts   58

2.14   Houses and cars   60

2.15   The desktop supermarket   62

THE CREATIVE PC

3.1   Introducing Windows Media Player   64

3.2   Media and Media Player   66

3.3   Scanners and digital cameras   68

3.4   The digital darkroom   70

3.5   Retouching old photos   72

3.6   MP3 files   74

3.7   Playlists, CDs and MP3 hardware   76

3.8   Speakers and soundcards   78

3.9   MIDI files and digital music   80

3.10   Getting started with video   82

3.11   Creating your own videos   84

3.12   More about video   86

3.13   Publishing your video   88

3.14   Desktop publishing   90

3.15   Fonts and Clip Art   92

3.16   More about printing and archiving   94

3.17   Creating a web page   96

3.18   Web inspiration   98

3.19   Advanced web creation   100

THE HOME OFFICE

4.1	Keeping your PC organised	102
4.2	Backups and safety copies	104
4.3	The digital office	106
4.4	Alternatives to Office XP	108
4.5	The anatomy of Word	110
4.6	Using Word to create a brochure	112
4.7	More about Word	114
4.8	Introducing Excel	116
4.9	Introducing PowerPoint	118
4.10	Contacts and databases	120
4.11	People, places and things	122
4.12	Microsoft Money	124
4.13	Online banking	126
4.14	More about money	128
4.15	Stocks and shares online	130
4.16	Online tax returns and money transfers	132

THE INTERNET EXPERT

5.1	Introducing search engines	134
5.2	Using Google to find what you want	136
5.3	Advanced Internet research	138
5.4	Mailing lists	140
5.5	More ways to communicate	142
5.6	Finding and downloading software from the Internet (I)	144
5.7	Finding and downloading software from the Internet (II)	146
5.8	News and reviews	148
5.9	The world's biggest reference library	150
5.10	Finding people online	152
5.11	Genealogy online	154

NUTS AND BOLTS

6.1	Essential maintenance for Windows	156
6.2	Essential maintenance – keeping Windows up to date	158
6.3	Virus checkers and firewalls	160
6.4	Pests and pop-ups	162
6.5	Customising Windows	164
6.6	Customisation – digging deeper	166
6.7	Customisation – sounds, file types and speed-ups	168
6.8	Installing new hardware	170
6.9	Other upgrades	172
6.10	Building a network	174
6.11	Building a network – advanced options	176
6.12	Advanced Windows (I)	178
6.13	Advanced Windows (II)	180
6.14	Looking backwards, looking forwards	182
6.15	Glossary	184
6.16	Further reading	186

| Index | 188 |

INTRODUCTION

It's perhaps hard to understand now, but the concept of the Personal Computer (PC) was revolutionary when it was invented in the 1970s because at the time, even the smallest computers took up most of a room and needed a number of able-bodied people to transport them. Larger machines needed an entire floor of an office building, air conditioning, and a round-the-clock team of support staff. The idea of having this kind of hardware at home seemed nonsensical. Now, at the start of the 21st century, you can acquire a PC for a few hundred pounds from a supermarket during a weekly grocery run. This machine will be far more powerful and much easier to use than the hugely expensive supercomputers once used to forecast the weather.

But the storming success of PCs among consumers has created its own set of problems. Computers may be almost everywhere, but the knowledge needed to get the best from them is still lagging far behind. Besides, bundles of software that are routinely sold with new machines may not always be the best tools for an individual's needs, but very little unbiased information exists to point consumers in the right direction.

The aim of this book is to provide you with useful hints, suggestions and project outlines that are genuinely helpful and practical. The contents range over some less-well-known but more useful alternatives to standard software packages. There is also plentiful information about how you can research these alternatives for yourself and make a decision about what to use that will suit your own needs. You'll also be introduced to various creative and hobby applications, such as working with sound and video clips, offered expert-level Internet research tips, and supplied with a guide to personalising your PC so that using it is as comfortable, and perhaps also as colourful, an experience as you'd like it to be.

Whatever your skill level and wherever your interests lie, you'll find that the information in this book will help you pay back the investment you've made in your PC many times over – not just in enjoyment, satisfaction and even an enhanced social circle, but also financially in terms of small business opportunities, money saved and bargains found.

How to use this book

Section 1 includes useful, basic information that will help get you started. While it is not a complete beginner's guide, you will find enough here to help you grasp concepts essential to understanding how a PC works.

Section 2 introduces various home-based PC projects, and advice to help you save a fortune when buying anything from your weekly groceries to a house.

Section 3 covers creative possibilities such as working with music and pictures. Their low price and high power make PCs suited to both fun and professional work.

Section 4 showcases the PC in a functional role, as an office tool and as a handy way to manage and enhance your finances.

Section 5 includes information on how to find further information. The Internet is an almost unimaginably powerful resource for all kinds of research. This section introduces the search skills needed to make the best of what the Internet can offer.

Section 6 is a guide to simple PC DIY projects, including upgrades and customisation.

Warnings and caveats
All the websites in this book were checked before printing, but given the fluid nature of the World Wide Web they can't be guaranteed to remain available for the life of this book.

Please note that inclusion of a website does not count as a formal endorsement by Which? Ltd, or Consumers' Association.

Modifications and upgrades
The PC is an electrical device. If you try to open it while it is still switched on, you risk a fatal shock. Also, the static electric charge we all carry in our bodies can ruin the sensitive electronic components within the computer and/or its peripherals. So before you open up a PC, take the following precautions:

- always switch the PC off, and then turn it off at the wall but leave it plugged in so the chassis remains earthed
- buy an anti-static wristband from a PC store.

Never open up the power supply or the monitor.

Always make safety copies of important information before making any changes to a PC.

Any modifications to a PC are done entirely at your own risk.

OUTSIDE THE BOX

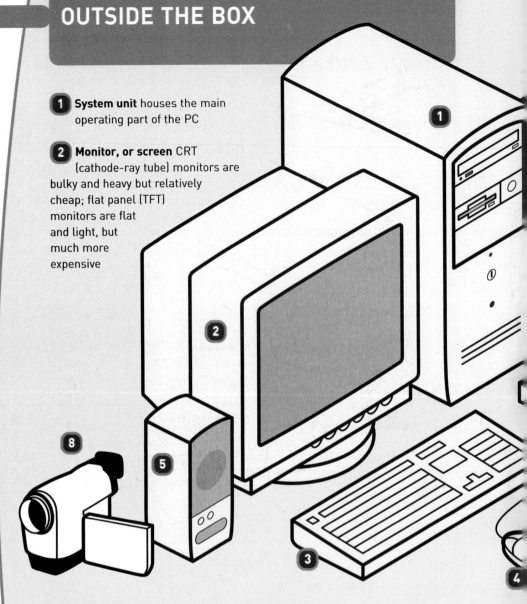

1 **System unit** houses the main operating part of the PC

2 **Monitor, or screen** CRT (cathode-ray tube) monitors are bulky and heavy but relatively cheap; flat panel (TFT) monitors are flat and light, but much more expensive

Other popular extras

Steering wheel for games

Headset and microphone for listening to music and computer dictation

Surround speakers five speakers plus a subwoofer, for games and watching videos on DVD

Music keyboard for composing music

PDA a pocket-sized personal organiser

3 **Keyboard** for typing and controlling software

4 **Mouse** controls a pointer that appears on the screen

5 **Speakers** PCs generally have two speakers; some also have a subwoofer – a special extra speaker for reproducing deep bass rumbles and explosions

6 **Modem** used to connect your PC to the Internet

7 **Digital camera** for taking film-less, electronic pictures

8 **Video camera** for producing moving images

9 **Laser printer** produces high-quality text printing for business use

10 **Colour printer** prints colour copies of photos, posters and other home and school needs

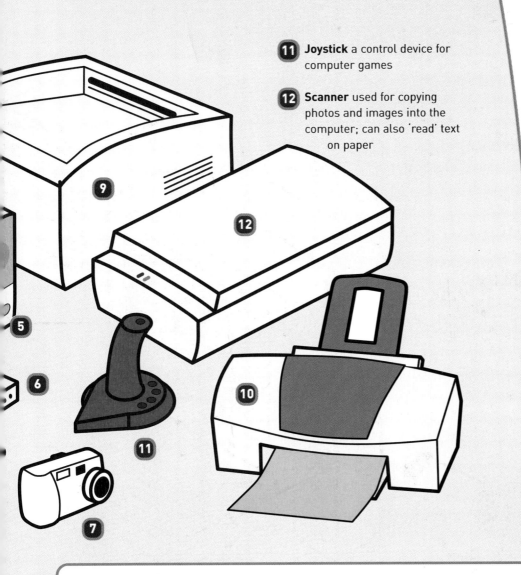

11 **Joystick** a control device for computer games

12 **Scanner** used for copying photos and images into the computer; can also 'read' text on paper

Different types of PCs

Not all PCs look the same. These are the main kinds of machines.

standard desktop PC – the most common choice

slimline desktop PC – attractive looks, but not ideal if you plan to add extras

tower PC – a tall case, with more room for extras inside

tablet – a flat-panel screen with pen input and no keyboard

laptop – small, portable, fold-open PC with a built-in keyboard, mouse pointer and flat screen; popular with business users

INSIDES OF A PC

Power supply
Lots of coloured wires snake out
from this metal box

Motherboard
Holds the processor, memory
and expansion cards

Main processor chip
The brains of the outfit.
Appears in various shapes,
but typically has cooling
fins and perhaps a fan

Graphics card
Connects to the monitor. May also
include video in/out connections

Expansion slots
Extras plug in here. Any connections
will appear in one of the spaces on
the back of the computer

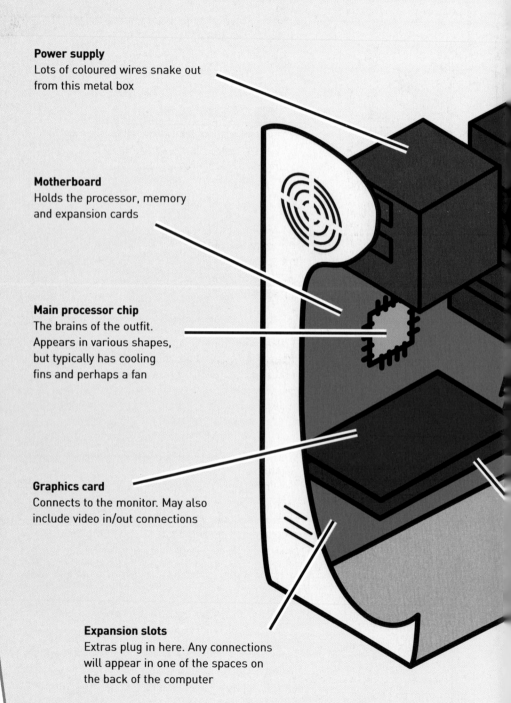

Floppy-disk drive
Used to transfer information from one computer to another; still included on most machines, but hardly ever used now

Hard-disk drive
The filing system. There will probably be only one of these, but you can add more when you run out of space

CD drive
Reads music CDs and software CD-ROMs. If your PC was supplied with a CD-writer, you will also be able to burn your own music and computer CDs

DVD drive
Reads video DVDs and software DVD-ROMs, and also CDs. (DVD-writers are available, but they are an expensive option and not usually sold as standard)

Memory
A temporary working space for calculations. Appears as one or more long, thin cards with small, very thin chips on them. The cards are plugged into slots that are sometimes hidden under the power supply

Cabling (not shown)
Connects all the parts together

Soundcard
The speakers plug in here. Usually also includes a simple music synthesiser, and sockets for an optional microphone and a joystick

Different types of connections

You will find the following types of connection on the back of your PC.

Parallel port – used for printers

Serial ports – used for modems, older/cheaper mice and digital cameras

PS/2 ports – typically there are two, one for the mouse and the other for the keyboard

USB connectors – used for scanners, keyboards, professional digital cameras and assorted other extras

Firewire – also known as IEEE1394, used for video cameras, and professional computing extras such as very fast hard disks and CD writers

INTRODUCTION TO WINDOWS

Windows is an operating system – the software that manages how your PC works. It works like an executive assistant. You tell it what you want to do, it tries to do it for you and reports back if there are any problems. Windows is made by a software company called Microsoft.

Everything that appears on your computer's screen is controlled by Windows, which uses pictures instead of words. This makes it much easier to learn and use than earlier operating systems.

Since its release in 1985, Windows has been through many changes and revisions. This book is based on the latest version, called Windows XP, which is installed on most new PCs. Windows XP is much more reliable than earlier versions. It is compatible with all new software, and most older software. It also includes useful features for hardware items such as digital cameras and video recorders.

Older versions of Windows, such as Windows 95, Windows 98, Windows 98SE or Windows ME, are very much less reliable than Windows XP. They crash (i.e. stop working) much more often. You can sometimes lose work and information when this happens. Internet connections are also slightly slower and less reliable. If you are using any of these versions, you may want to consider upgrading – i.e. replacing your older version of Windows with Windows XP.

To upgrade, you will need to buy a Windows XP upgrade pack, place the CD in your PC and follow the simple installation instructions that appear. (Windows 95 users will need to buy a full version, not the upgrade, because Microsoft does not allow upgrades from that version of Windows.)

There are two versions of Windows XP – Home and Professional. As their names suggest, Home is the suggested choice for home-users; the Professional version has extra features that are useful for more experienced users and those running medium-sized businesses.

Windows history

Windows 16-bit family
Now obsolete; will not work with modern software.
Only 3.1 was commercially successful.
Windows 1.0 1985
Windows 2.0 1987
Windows 3.0 1990
Windows 3.1 1991

Windows 9x family
For home-users, small businesses, computer gamers. Works on most computers; will work with some, but not all, modern software.
Not particularly reliable.
Windows 95 1995
Windows 98 1998
Windows ME 1999

Windows NT family
For larger businesses and 'industrial' use. Designed to be reliable, but not perfectly so.
Works on a restricted range of computers.
Windows NT 3.1 1993
Windows NT 3.5 1994
Windows NT4 1996

Windows 2000 family
Combines the durability and reliability of Windows NT with the ease of use of Windows 9x. Windows 2000 looks like Windows 95, but is different internally. Windows XP has a completely new look.
Windows 2000 2000
Windows XP 2001

INTRODUCING THE WINDOWS XP DESKTOP

These software tools have been 'pinned' – they appear every time you click on the Start button. They are the ones you use most often, including email and Internet software, and word processing. See page 178 for details of how to pin or remove software from this list

The Windows XP working space is called the desktop, because it is based – very loosely – on a desk which has paper and other office tools on it. To make things happen on the desktop, move the mouse to one of the on-screen buttons or other active areas and click with the buttons on the mouse. Different things happen depending on whether you use the left button, right button, or click twice very quickly with the left button (a 'double click').

Your name goes here. If you don't like the picture, click on it to choose a different one

These two options display a list of your documents. The first shows a complete list; the second shows documents you have been working on recently

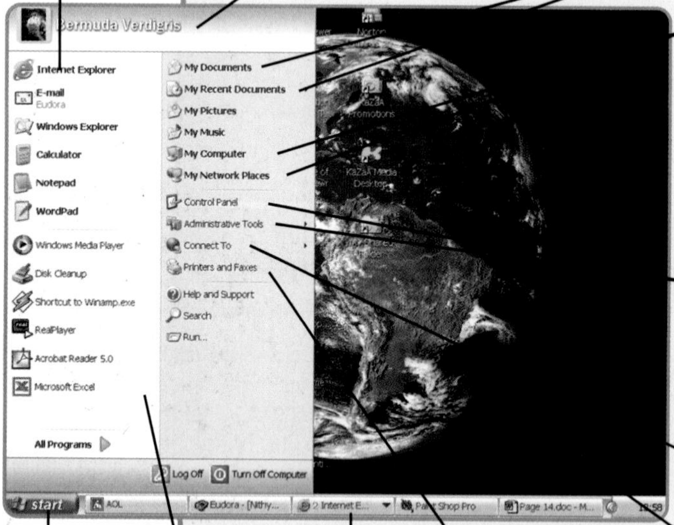

If you want to look at all the documents and software in your computer, double click on 'My Computer'. If you are connected to other computers, you can investigate them in the same way by double clicking on 'My Network Places'. If you are not connected to a network, 'My Network Places' will not appear

These two options are used to set up and maintain your computer, troubleshoot problems and check how well the machine is running. They are not relevant for everyday use

This option lists your Internet connections. Select one (or more if you have more than one ISP) to link to the Internet

Click on the Start button to show the Start bar, which enables you to access your documents, software tools and Internet connection. The tools that appear here are the ones you used most recently. This list is updated automatically, and changes all the time

Use this option to show a list of printers and fax facilities you can use, and to set one as the default choice. Note that printing itself is usually started from within the software you use, and not from here

We've replaced the standard Windows background with something else. You can find out how to do this on page 164

The taskbar shows which software tools you are currently using. Click on a tab to open up each tool's window

Other option

[Search]
This option can help yc find information.

The Start bar displays your favourite software choices

All software tools appear in their own window. Each window is independent – it appears automatically when you start a piece of software, and then vanishes when you stop using it. Only one window is active at a time, and can fill some or all of the screen. If more than one window is open, the active window will appear on top of the others. Windows can also be hidden ('minimised') so that they don't appear at all, in order to avoid desktop clutter.

Windows literally provides a window into a working space. If the information you're looking at won't fit into the window, scroll bars appear at the top and/or sides. You can use these to move the window so that it shows you the part of the information you want to work on.

The title bar shows the name of the document you are working on, and the name of the software tool you are using to work on it. If the window is not filling the screen, you can click and drag anywhere in the bar to pick up the window and move it

These menus show various ways in which you can change a document. Click on each heading to make various sub-options appear

These icons use small graphic reminders to show various ways in which you can change a document. If you hold the mouse over them a small box appears with a word in it explaining what each icon does

This is where you work on a document. Software that lets you work on more than one document at once, such as Microsoft Word, shows each document in its own sub-window. Sometimes you will see special windows that show useful information about a document – for example, a statistics window that shows the number of words

⊠ Click here to close the window and make it disappear completely. If you want to keep your work, you will have to save it first (see page 21)

To make the window fill the screen, click on the ▢ button. To shrink it down to its original size, click on the ⬚ button. ▬ Click here to hide the window. Click on the tab on the taskbar to make it reappear

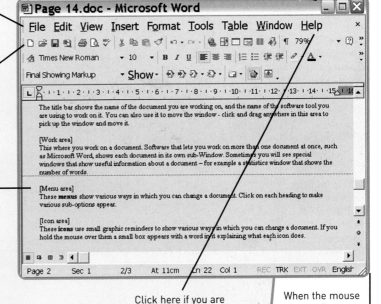

Click here if you are having problems with any part of Windows XP

When the mouse changes to the ↔ or ⬉ shape, click and drag anywhere around the edges to make the window bigger or smaller

un]
r experts only! Gives
u access to special
ftware you won't
rmally need to use.

[Music and pictures folders]
Special folders for storing music and pictures. You can use other folders too, but you may find that these are more convenient.

WINDOWS SHORTCUTS AND SPEED TIPS

Other useful keys

Esc (escape)
Press this if your software starts doing something you don't want, or when a window or message appears and you want to get rid of it.

Num lock
(number lock)
Turn on to type numbers on the keypad. Turn off to duplicate the arrow keys.

Ins (insert)
Using this key allows you to switch between type-over and insertion typing.

PrtScrn (print screen)
This key takes a snapshot of the screen. To save the image, open an image editor (see page 70) and select 'Edit' and 'Paste' or type Ctrl + V.

Some menu options can be selected by pressing the keys in a certain sequence. These are called keyboard shortcuts, and some people find them more convenient than using a mouse.

Your keyboard has some special keys on it. You use these to let Windows know that you are typing a keyboard shortcut, and not ordinary text.

 Shift keys: these keys are used to type text in capitals, but they're also sometimes used in keyboard shortcuts

 Alt key: pronounced 'alt' (as in the first part of 'altitude')

 Alt Gr key: pronounced 'alt gee ar.' Usually used only for obscure and rarely used shortcuts

 Ctrl keys: pronounced 'control'. There are two to make it easier for you to use; both are identical

 Windows key: equivalent to clicking on the start bar

Menu key: usually equivalent to right clicking with the mouse. In some contexts this key will do nothing, whereas a right click would work. Unfortunately this is a 'feature' of Windows

Accessing help
At the top of the keyboard you'll find a row of extra keys labelled with 'F' followed by a number. These are called function keys, and are also used to save time, and make it easier and quicker to operate software.

For example, pressing the F1 key will usually show a page of 'help information' – memory-jogging hints and other instructions that can help you when you are confused or uncertain how to use a piece of software. If you are in front of your PC, try pressing F1 now and see what happens.

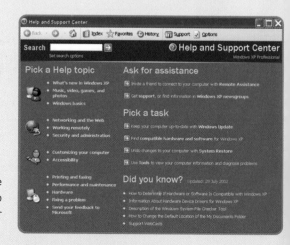

Press F1. . . and you'll see
the built-in Windows help
page appear

How to use keyboard shortcuts

File	Edit	View	Insert	Format	Tools	Table	Window	Help

It's almost impossible to remember all the possible keyboard shortcuts in a piece of software unless you practise them regularly. Fortunately, the shortcuts appear on the menus themselves. The menu shown here is from the Word wordprocessor. You can see that each word includes one letter that is underlined.

Normally you would click on each word to show the menu beneath it. But if you hold down the Alt key and type one of the underlined letters, you'll see its menu details appear under it. Try this now. (Press the Esc key each time to make the menu disappear again.)

The Wordpad Edit menu

The slightly more complicated Edit menu in Word

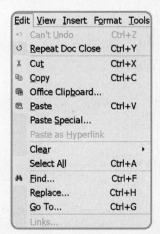

To select items from each menu, use the same system. For example, to select the Cut option in the menu on the right, you'd first hold down Alt and press 'E' to make the Edit menu appear as it does here. Then let go of Alt and press 't'.

Some menu options are labelled 'Ctrl +' followed by a letter. These work slightly differently. They're simpler and quicker two-key shortcuts, and are used for the features in the software you're most likely to use. To use them, hold down the Ctrl key and press the other letter.

Some Ctrl key shortcuts are semi-standardised and will work in most software. For example:
Ctrl + X cuts and remembers a highlighted area
Ctrl + C copies and remembers a highlighted area
Ctrl + A highlights everything that's in the document
Ctrl + V pastes what was last cut or copied at the point where the cursor is
Ctrl + Z undoes the last thing you do. This is an extremely useful option, and one that's well worth taking the time to remember.

Ctrl + Alt + Delete

This brings up a list of all the software you have running. You can kill programs you no longer want to use. You should do this only as a last resort if some software seems to stop working.

Making sense of menus

Throughout the rest of this book, we'll navigate through menus like this:

Insert → Picture → Clip Art

In plain English this means: Find the top menu entry called 'Insert'. Click on it. When the tab with the other menu options appears, move the mouse down to the entry called 'Picture'. Click on that. When the tab appears next to it, select 'Clip Art'.

SOFTWARE

What are drivers?

Drivers are a special kind of software that tell Windows XP how to communicate with a piece of hardware, such as a monitor, printer or scanner. Your manual will explain how to install them. Unlike normal software, you never use drivers directly. Their work is always hidden behind the scenes (for more details see page 170).

A PC is a little like a garden shed – it comes with plenty of space where you can both keep and use tools, but the tools themselves have to be acquired separately. Software is the name given to all the different kinds of tools you can install inside your PC. The full range of available software is huge and consists of hundreds of thousands of different possibilities. Some are sold by shops, some through mail order, some on the Internet for downloading to a PC, and some are entirely free. In spite of this huge range, most PCs use a small subset of the available tools. Some of the most popular ones are listed on the next page.

Installing software

Most software is still sold in boxes that include one or more CDs or DVDs and a manual, installation guide or other reference information. To install this software, all you need to do is insert the disk into your CD or DVD slot and the installation process will start. (If this doesn't happen, or if you buy software from the Internet, or use one of the many free pieces of software that are available there, you will need to start the installation manually. See page 169 for information about what to do.)

The installation process typically asks you some or all of the following:

Whether or not you agree to the licensing terms

This is a legal formality. You will often find that unless you click on an option that explicitly says 'I accept', you won't be able to continue with the installation. (It's worth noting that not all licensing agreements are legally binding whether you accept them or not, so don't worry about this part of the process.)

Your name, company name and perhaps a registration code or serial number

Any serial number will come with the software's packaging, or will be supplied by email for Internet software. If the software was supplied on CD, the name and company name won't matter and can be filled in with anything you want. If the software was downloaded from the Internet, it is sometimes keyed to work only with your personal details, so you will have to enter them correctly here.

Whether you want a 'custom' or 'typical' installation

'Typical' is usually a better choice. 'Custom' is useful for experienced PC users who want to specify in more detail how the software is installed.

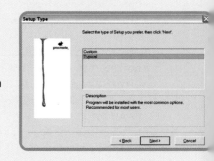

Where inside your PC the software will be installed

Software will usually work wherever you install it. By default, the installation process tries to a pick a sensible location inside your PC – most often the Program Files folder. But you can change this by hand if you want – for example, if one of your hard disks is full and you would prefer to install the software to a spare. (For more information about how folders work and how to specify where information is kept, see page 20.)

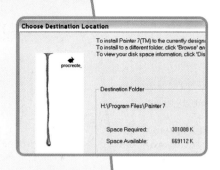

Whether or not you want to register electronically

Registration means letting the manufacturer know that you have bought its software. The company will send you details of special offers and new products. In practice, the time spent registering software rarely makes this worthwhile, unless you plan to call for telephone support. Sometimes there will be an old-fashioned postcard that you can fill in, instead of using the Internet for electronic registration.

Whether or not to read the 'Readme' file

A 'Readme' file includes information that changed after the manual was printed. Any last-minute issues or problems will be included here. It's usually worth selecting this option, just in case, although it's rarely very interesting.

Some popular software choices

System tools
Virus checker: protects from PC viruses
Firewall: keeps Internet hackers out of your computer

Office tools
Word processor: for writing letters, essays and reports
Spreadsheet: for working with figures
Presentation creator: for producing lecture notes and overhead transparencies

Internet tools
Email package: for sending and receiving email
Web browser: for looking at web pages
Web editor: for creating your own web pages
Messaging tools: for typing messages to other Internet users

Creativity tools
Media player: for listening to music and watching video clips
Music sequencer: for composing and recording music
CD and DVD creator: for preparing your own CD or DVD music and video compilations
Video editor: for adding a polished look to your home videos

Fun and education
Games: killing monsters is perennially popular, as are flying and driving simulations
Educational tools: learn to spell, or revise your GCSEs and A Levels

Other useful tools
Route planners: drive from A to B as quickly as possible
Home or garden design: prepare and preview a layout before building starts

FILES, FILING AND FILE TYPES

How big is that file?

File sizes are measured in multiples of bytes – one byte is roughly equal to a single character/letter. Because bytes are so small, they are usually grouped as kilobytes (Kb), Megabytes (Mb) and Gigabytes (Gb) – a thousand, a million and a billion bytes. The numbers aren't exact. Strictly speaking, the multiples are powers of 2 – 1,024, 1,048,576 and 1,073,741,824 respectively – but there are few situations where this matters.

Some typical file sizes:

Short email: 3Kb

Long email: 8Kb

Formatted document: 20Kb

Text of this book: 200Kb

Web page: 70Kb

Small photo: 500Kb

Large photo: 2Mb

MP3 music: 1Mb/minute

Low-quality video clip: 10Mb/minute

High-quality video clip: 200Mb/minute

All the information inside your PC, including your documents, emails, music, photos and also all the software, is stored as files. A file is any single item of information.

Your hard disk is really just an electronic filing cabinet. As with real filing cabinets, your files are placed in folders. These can in turn contain sub-folders. Unlike paper filing, you can have hundreds or even thousands of files, folders and sub-folders on a single hard disk.

To find a specific file you need to know where it is. The filing system as a whole is arranged like an upside-down tree with the trunk at the top. Folders and sub-folders make up the various branches. The 'leaves' are individual files. In computer speak, the path from the trunk to the branches is literally called the 'path' that specifies any particular file. The path is the unique address of each file. If you know it precisely, you can go straight to any file. Fortunately there aren't many situations where you need to do this.

Some folders have standard names that are the same on every PC. They hold the most important and most often accessed information. You can create and delete other folders to suit your own needs and work habits.

The most popular fixed folders are the following.
My Computer – the master folder. Everything is contained inside it.
Windows – the Windows system. You won't usually need to look in here.
Program Files – the software you use. This folder is subdivided by manufacturer name and software name.
My Documents – any letters or other documents you have created.
My Pictures – photos and other artwork.
My Music – music clips.
My Network Places – links to other computers on a network, if you are using one (see section 6.10).
Recycle Bin – when you delete a file, it is moved here. Open the bin to see all your deleted files. You can either empty it to remove them permanently, or restore files to their original folders if you don't want to delete them after all.
Control Panel – a collection of settings for your PC (see section 6.5).

The file selector in Microsoft Word includes extra features to make it easy to find the files you want

Searching...

The search option lets you find a file by name, by creation date, or even by its contents. If you can't remember where you put that letter you wrote last year, searching can help you find it.

This more common file selector is much simpler. Experiment with both to see what the features do

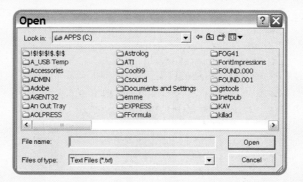

Whenever you use a piece of software, you need to save your work to make any changes permanent. If you need to work on the same information again, you can open it. This will load it into the software you are using. Most software has Save and Open options under the File menu header. Whenever you select either 'Save' or 'Open', you will see a file selector box. This provides a view of the filing system and lets you choose the name of the file that holds your work. Different software uses different file selectors with different features. The one on the top right is very simple. The one on the top left is more complex. Both work in a very similar way.

Apart from a name and a path, files also come in different types. Each type is associated with a piece of software. For example, document files are associated with the Word word-processing tool, music and video files with the Media Player tool (see section 3.1), and so on. These associations appear in file listings as extensions – three letters after a dot. Word files have the .doc extension and music files have .mp3. There are tens or even hundreds of file associations set up in a typical PC. (See the sidebar.)

Windows hides these extensions by default, so you don't need to worry about them. If you want to look at them, you can tell Windows to show them when you are looking through files, but this isn't usually necessary. If you buy a different word processor and want to associate it with document files, you can also change the default file associations. For more information about this, see section 6.7.

Some popular file endings

.exe, **.dll** – a piece of software

.doc, **.txt**, **.rtf** – text

.mp3, **.wav** – music and sounds

.mid – MIDI music

.avi, **.qt**, **.mov** – video clips

.jpg, **.gif**, **.tif**, **.bmp** – pictures and photos

.htm, **.html** – web pages

.xls – a spreadsheet

CHOOSING A PRINTER

Colour laser printing?

Most laser printers print with black ink only, and are designed to work on white copier paper. Colour laser printers are available, but they cost upwards of £1,000 and are expensive to run. For most home and small-business use, inkjet printers are a better way to print in colour.

Ordinary (i.e. non-colour) laser printers are designed for business use. They produce very high quality text in black and white, but photos look poor. Prices vary from £200 to £1,000 depending on print quality and speed. Speed is measured in pages per minute (ppm): 4ppm is slow, 6ppm is moderate, anything faster is very good. Print quality is measured in dots per inch (dpi): 300dpi is adequate, 600dpi is good, and 1,200dpi is equivalent to professional printing. Laser printers are cheap to run, but replacement ink (known as toner) and spare printing parts (usually known as the drum) can be quite expensive.

Inkjet (also known as bubblejet) printers are ideal for home and family use. They print in colour, using a mix of cyan (light blue), magenta, yellow and black inks. Black and white text is not as smooth and crisp as that from a laser printer, but they produce good results when printing posters and cards. Basic models are capable of printing photos, but for better results buy a printer that has 'photo' in the name. This will produce prints that are almost as good as those from a high-street film developer. For best results, you will need high-quality photo-ready printer paper. This can be expensive, but the results are worth it.

Replacement ink cartridges for all inkjet printers can be a major expense. Try to buy a model that uses a separate cartridge for each ink colour rather than an all-in-one cartridge. The former will waste less ink and cost less money. For colour printers, a resolution of 360dpi is poor, 720dpi is adequate and 1,440 dpi is good. For speed, page per minute figures are not a useful guide, as there is no standard colour reference page. If possible, try to see the printer in action to assess speed and print quality for yourself.

Using a printer

Some printing is as easy as click-and-go. But it is useful to understand the various options. Most software has a 'Page Setup' option, which sets margins and page positioning. It also controls portrait (print down the page) or landscape (across the page) modes. There may also be a 'Print Preview' option, which shows a preview of the printed page on the screen. This can be very helpful and will identify potential problems, such as print spilling off the edges of the paper. Some software has more complicated options that will control the number of copies; scale images (make the image larger or smaller and even print it across multiple pages); and define which pages are printed.

It is an excellent idea to familiarise yourself with your printer's abilities, including the less obvious ones. Some experimentation with different software settings, kinds of paper and even different inks will easily repay the time spent.

Printer name: selects which printer to print to

Other options: selects more complicated options (can usually be ignored)

Copies: selects how many copies of each page to print

Printer options: more advanced printer choices

Zoom: selects print scaling

Page range: which pages to print

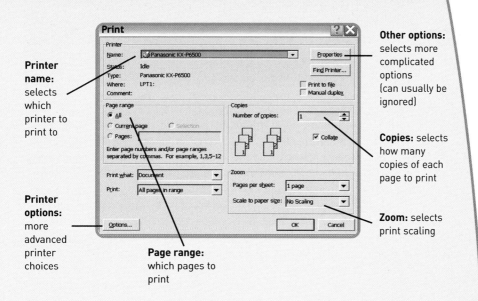

Colour printers add even more choices, so you can vary the colour balance and sharpness and get the best results from the paper you're using.

Print quality options: half-toning controls how fine colours are shaded. The default settings are usually adequate. The other options control the amount of detail

Paper type: select the type of paper you are printing to, and whether to print in colour or black and white

Colour management: there are different ways to attempt to get the best colour balance

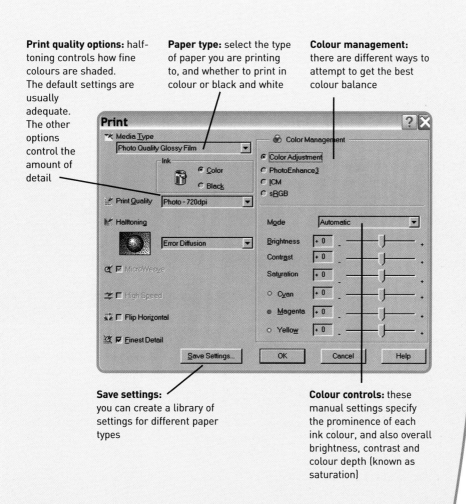

Save settings: you can create a library of settings for different paper types

Colour controls: these manual settings specify the prominence of each ink colour, and also overall brightness, contrast and colour depth (known as saturation)

CHOOSING AN ISP

AOL: ISP, portal, or online service?

AOL isn't a normal ISP. It offers a kind of 'package tour' version of the Internet, including information summaries, chat and other attractions that make it much bigger than a typical portal. It's very easy for beginners to use, but may be frustrating for experienced users. It's also very prone to junk mail. AOL free trial CDs are included in most computer and Internet magazines. The service is worth considering if you want a very basic email service and easy opportunities to socialise and chat online.

To use the Internet you will need to sign up with an Internet service provider (ISP). The ISP will connect your computer to the Internet via an electronic link, look after your email, and provide answers to your technical questions. Some ISPs are very good, while others are very bad. A poor ISP will provide a service that is expensive, slow and unreliable. A good ISP will be cheap, helpful and reliable. Some computer manufacturers sign you up with their choice of ISP by default. This is almost always seen as a money-making venture by both parties. In fact, you can use any ISP with your computer, so shopping for alternatives is a wise move.

To make a choice, look at the reliability and speed league tables published in Internet magazines such as .Net, Internet Magazine and InternetWorks. Even if you don't understand the statistics, you can tell at a glance which ISPs provide a good service, and which ones are middling, mediocre or poor. Long-term performance summaries are especially useful when making a choice.

Other factors to check include the following.
Number of email addresses This ranges from one to an unlimited number.
Free web space 5Mb is a good all-round amount.
Cost of technical support Some ISPs charge £1 a minute or even more for calls to their helpline. Others offer a completely free service.
Useful extras Email virus filtering; spam filtering; electronic chat; newsgroups. (See page 140.)
Monthly cost This is almost always a fixed amount now, perhaps around £15 per month. But you will also find payment plans that make evenings and weekends free, but charge by the minute for Internet use during working hours.
Portals Some ISPs offer a web page that includes the latest news and other information of interest. You don't have to use this facility if you don't want to, but it's useful to know if it's available.

Freeserve offers a simple portal that includes news, weather and other information

Which? Online includes a huge selection of useful consumer reports, tips and other suggestions

How to connect to the Internet

There are two main kinds of Internet connection – dial-up and broadband.

Dial-up uses slow, old telephone technology. The maximum possible connection speed is 56Kb/s (kilobits per second). This is fast enough for email and basic web surfing, but too slow for anything other than downloading very poor quality music or video. It also makes copying software from the Internet slow and clumsy. Large files of 10Mb or more may need to be left to copy overnight.

Broadband is the latest technology. The maximum possible connection speed is up to 1Mb/s – nearly 20 times faster than dial-up. More realistic speeds are between 256Kb/s and 500Kb/s. Accessing video and music clips becomes more practical, and it's even possible to send short video clips in emails (as long as the recipients have broadband too). With broadband, the Internet experience becomes very different, and much more satisfying. A 10Mb file can be copied to your PC in a matter of minutes.

Broadband comes in various types:
ADSL: broadband over a modified phone line
Cable: broadband over a cable TV link (you may also be able to use the link for phone calls)
Satellite: broadband using a special wireless dish (an expensive option, worth considering only in rural areas)
Wireless: broadband over a special radio link.

Unfortunately, broadband is available only in certain areas, mainly larger towns and cities. Current costs are between £20 and £40 per month. Availability is improving rapidly. Satellite and wireless links are becoming increasingly popular and are available in certain rural areas, but can cost £100 per month or more. Check the magazine league tables for details of whether broadband is available in your area.

America Online (AOL) offers a simplified version of the Internet for casual users

Dial-up, ADSL, ISDN or SDSL?

These are all names for different connection types that use a telephone line.

Dial-up: a standard, no-frills phone line. Slow but usable.

ISDN (integrated services digital network): fast dial-up. Runs at roughly twice the speed of normal dial-up, but is usually much more expensive.

ADSL (asymmetrical digital subscriber line): broadband over a telephone line. Around ten times faster than dial-up.

SDSL (symmetrical digital subscriber line): broadband over a phone line for specialised business use. Still experimental.

SETTING UP YOUR INTERNET CONNECTION

Modems

Whether you are using a modem for dial-up or a broadband link, you will need to have it installed before you try to set up an ISP connection. If you bought your PC after 2000, it will almost certainly have a modem already installed. For broadband installation, you will need to talk to your broadband ISP – details vary depending on the service you choose and your location.

Once you have contacted your chosen ISP to sign up for its service, you will usually be sent an introductory information pack that includes a CD. You can set up your connection by putting the CD into your PC. It should start automatically and install the connection for you.

But there are times when you may not want to do this. Setting up an ISP automatically may mean that your PC's settings will be changed to use that ISP exclusively. If you want to change ISPs, or try to use more than one ISP at the same time, the different settings they use may conflict with each other. To keep your PC's settings safe and prevent different ISPs from interfering with each other, you should set up a connection manually. This is also useful if you are trying out an ISP with a free trial and aren't sure if you want to stick with it in the long term.

For a manual connection, you will need three things: the ISP's Internet access phone number (i.e. the one your computer needs to dial to connect to the Internet – not the number you call to get help and support); a 'login name'; and a password. You should be supplied with all of these when you sign up. When they arrive, follow these steps.

1. Click on the 'Start' button and select 'Control Panel'.

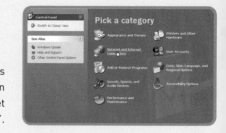

2. The Control Panel shows various settings for your PC. Click on 'Network and Internet Connections'.

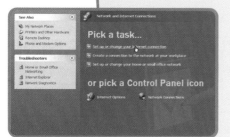

3. The Network and Internet Connections page shows options for setting up Internet connections, and also for connecting PCs together using a network. Click on 'Set up or change your Internet connection'.

4. This will show another Internet set-up page. If you already have any Internet connections you can change them here. Or you can create a new one by clicking on the 'Setup' button at the top right.

5. After an introductory screen (click on 'Next' when you have read it) you will be asked what you are trying to do. Click on the top option and then 'Next'.

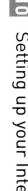

Signing up with AOL

If you sign up with AOL you do not have to follow the steps outlined in this section to set it up. AOL supplies its own software on a CD and doesn't work the same way as other ISPs.

6. Now you can choose from manual installation, selecting an ISP from a list, or installation from disk. If you select the List option, you will see some advertising steering you towards a handful of ISPs. Select the 'Set up my connection manually option' option and then 'Next'.

7. The next step asks you whether you are using a modem or a broadband link. Select the option that applies to you, and click on 'Next'.

8. Now type in your ISP's name. This doesn't have to be the exact name of the ISP. Any memorable name or description will work. As before, click on 'Next'.

9. If you are using a dial-up modem, type in the access phone number here. (Broadband users won't see this step.)

10. Type in your login name here. (Broadband users with an always-on connection won't see this step.) You will also need to type in the password – you have to do this twice to make sure you don't make a typing error. The password you type is hidden for security reasons.

11. Click on 'Finish' and your connection is ready to go. If you go back to the Start menu, you'll see it appear when you select 'Connect to...' Click on your new connection and you will connect to the Internet.

12. If you want to change the telephone number for your connection or remove it altogether, go back to Step 3 and select 'Network connections'. This will show a list of ISPs. Right click on an ISP to show a list of options. Select 'Delete' to remove a connection, or 'Properties' to change the phone number. (For more details about the other options that appear here, see page 176.)

INTRODUCING EMAIL

Smileys and emoticons

Because email uses text but is less formal than a letter, it has evolved its own ways of showing emotions. These extras are sprinkled through email text by many writers. They're not essential, but it is useful to be able to recognise them.

:) or :-) happy, smiling

:(or :-(unhappy, frowning

;-) winking

:-> sarcastic

You will also see phrases such as:

ROFL rolling on floor laughing

j/k just kidding

IMO in my opinion

IME in my experience

This is only a short list. To find out more, use the Internet to search for 'smiley guide' or 'smiley dictionary'.

Over the course of a few years in the late 1990s, email replaced letter post for many business and personal communications. Email is easy to use, free – any charges are included in the cost of using an ISP – and can be sent around the world in seconds.

Windows includes free email software called Outlook Express. If you use Microsoft Office (see section 4.3) you will be able to use a more sophisticated version called Outlook. Outlook Express is very prone to viruses and so you should switch to either Outlook or one of the other alternatives (see section 6.6). Whichever email software you use, the basics are very similar. The guide below applies to Outlook Express.

Mailboxes: the Inbox, Outbox, Draft and Sent Items are grouped here. Click on any of these headings to display a list. You can also create your own mailboxes for keeping email from different sources filed neatly

Main text menu options: these include all the quick options, and other menu items that control send and receive settings and other working details

Quick menu options: create new messages, reply to incoming messages, print, delete and search messages here

Main list: a list of the items in any of the mail boxes. Highlighted items are unread. By clicking on the list headings (From, Subject, Received) you can sort the list according to name, date and subject. Right click on the headings to add more of your own (such as size) from a list that appears

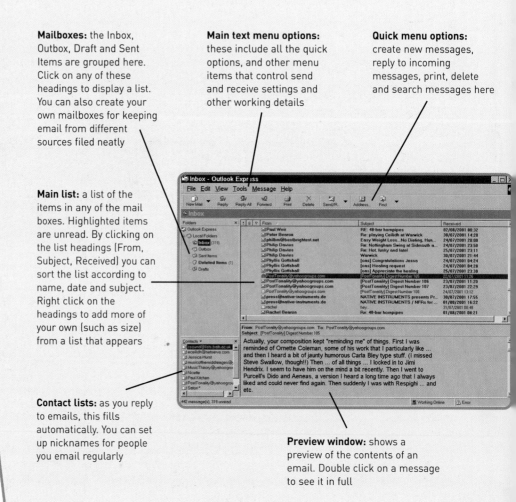

Contact lists: as you reply to emails, this fills automatically. You can set up nicknames for people you email regularly

Preview window: shows a preview of the contents of an email. Double click on a message to see it in full

Send option: sends the email. If you are not connected to the Internet the message will be saved until the next time you connect

Spelling and grammar checker: useful for avoiding misspellings

Attach option: attaches a text file or a picture or sound clip. Click on this button, then select the file. Your attached file will be sent automatically in addition to the rest of the email

Signing and encryption: these are two ways of making sure your email is secure and can't be read. Without them email is vulnerable to copying. However, these features are fairly complex to use properly, and so are usually ignored

From, to and subject: your email address and the recipient's nickname or email address go here. The subject can be anything you like

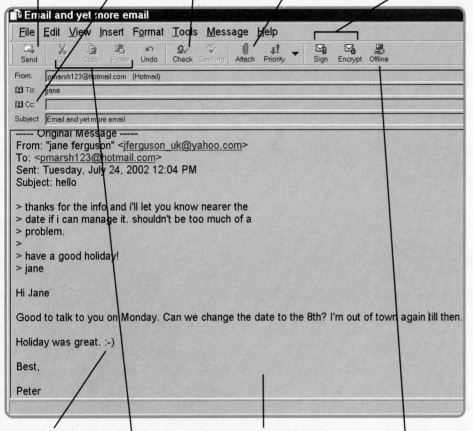

Smiley: shows the writer is smiling. Add these in informal emails as and when you want to (see sidebar)

Cut and paste editing options: these work exactly as they do in other software packages

Message window: when you reply to someone, text from the original message appears with quote marks ('>') on each line. It's considered polite to edit down the original message to its essential lines. Your response can be typed before the quotes, after them, or even between quoted lines to create something that reads more like a spoken conversation

Offline: useful for preparing messages when not connected to the Internet

INTRODUCING WEB BROWSING

Is it a link?

You can tell when a link is present because the mouse pointer changes from an arrow to a pointing finger.

The Internet has billions of World Wide Web pages, each of which is a combination of text and graphics. The vast majority are completely free and can be viewed by anyone with an Internet connection and suitable software. The software needed to view web pages is called a web browser. Windows XP includes a free web browser called Internet Explorer 6.

Web browsing is one of the simplest ways of using the Internet, and also one of the easiest of all types of software to use and understand. Almost everyone seems to pick up the basics of web browsing quite quickly. While there is much more to the Internet than web browsing, the Web includes so much information that some people find it can become almost everything they need.

Title bar: shows the name of the site

Forward: move forward through your browsing steps

Home: return to your starting web page. Use this if you get lost

Media: shows a list of music, video and radio sites. (These are pre-selected by Microsoft and may not be ones you're interested in)

Back: retrace your browsing steps

History: displays a list of all the websites and pages you have seen over the last three weeks

Favorites: shows a list of web pages you have bookmarked for future reference

Refresh: redraw the page. Use if the page is corrupted or garbled or some of the pictures are missing

Links: your favourite pre-set links. You can add to this list just by dragging the address (below) and dropping it on this line

Web address: type in a web address (URL – uniform resource locator) here. Or click on the links that are visible in a page

Stop: stop a page loading before it finishes. Use if you make a mistake or a page takes too long to appear

Features of a web page

All pages look different, but many have similar features to this one. You navigate web pages by clicking on links. These take you to a new page. Links can look like a list of options, a picture, or a single underlined word or phrase. The forward and back buttons on the browser let you move through the trail of links you create. Try it!

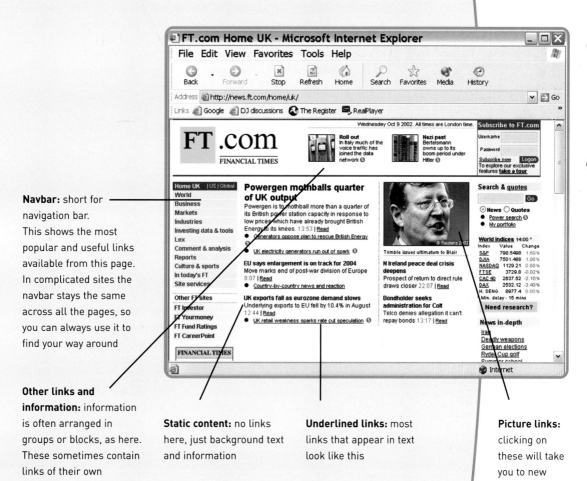

Navbar: short for navigation bar. This shows the most popular and useful links available from this page. In complicated sites the navbar stays the same across all the pages, so you can always use it to find your way around

Other links and information: information is often arranged in groups or blocks, as here. These sometimes contain links of their own

Static content: no links here, just background text and information

Underlined links: most links that appear in text look like this

Picture links: clicking on these will take you to new pages

IMPROVE YOUR WEB BROWSING

Improve your web browsing

1.13

Many people do not appreciate the hidden tools and extras available in a web browser. This guide introduces Internet Explorer's less obvious, but still very useful, hidden features.

Set the default home page

Click on Tools → Internet Options... and this window will appear. You can either type in the URL of the page you would like to mark as 'home', or if you are viewing the page click on 'Use current'. Click on 'OK' to finalise the selection.

Search a web page for a given word or phrase

Click on Edit → Find on this page... or type CTRL + F. Type the word or phrase you want to search for in the box that appears. Click on 'Find next' to start searching.

Create your own collection of interesting sites

When you find a page you want to remember, click on Favorites → Add to favorites. It's a good idea to create folders so that your favourites can be organised into useful categories. To create a folder, click on 'New Folder' and give it a useful name. To remember a page in a folder, select the folder and click on 'Create in...' You may want to change the name of the page to something memorable before you store it like this.

Check your browsing history

When you click on the 'History' quick menu option you will see a list of all the sites and pages you have visited recently. This list is maintained automatically. To see the pages within each site that you visited, click on the site name. If you want to cover your browsing tracks you can delete items by selecting them and hitting the backspace key.

Get plug-ins and extras

Some web pages are more complicated than others, and some can be viewed only with a 'plug-in' – a special software extra that's usually supplied for free. Your browser comes with some plug-ins already installed, but some sites need more. Fortunately, the installation process is often entirely automatic. The site will realise you need a plug-in, and ask you to confirm that you want the plug-in to be copied to your computer. If you agree, the copying process will start and the software will install itself. Over a slow connection it can take perhaps 10–20 minutes for the installation process to complete.

Change the text size

You can change the size of the text that appears on web pages to suit your eyesight and the size of your monitor. Select View → Text size to see a list of options. This trick works on many pages, but unfortunately some pages have fixed text sizes and this won't have any effect on them.

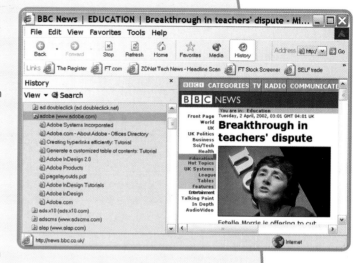

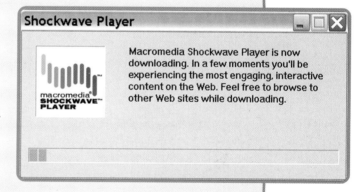

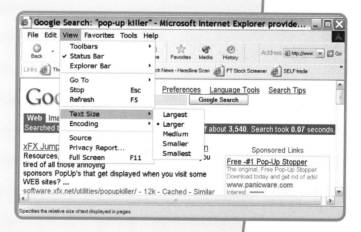

SHARING YOUR PC WITH OTHERS

Advanced user protection with Windows XP Professional

To protect their computers and settings to a higher degree, more advanced users can select 'Run' from the Start bar, type 'gpedit.msc', then select 'User settings' and 'Administrative template'. This will show a window with a list of customisation options. For example, under 'System' you will see 'Run only allowed Windows Applications'; using it will enable you to specify what software your children are allowed to use.

If you want to share your PC with other family members, it's easy to add passwords so that everyone can set up their desktop the way they want. This means they can also keep their own work private and hidden from others in the family. Everyone who wants to use the PC is given an account which creates a separate space for them, and also defines what they are and aren't allowed to do.

Each user is assigned one of three different security levels. The highest level is that of the Administrator, who can do anything on a PC. One level down from this is a user account. Users can use a PC, but they can't make drastic changes to it (e.g. install software, change user accounts, add or delete passwords, or add new hardware). But they can use the Internet, and make their My Documents folder private so no one can read it. At the lowest level are guest accounts. Guests can use software and the Internet and customise their desktop, but do very little else.

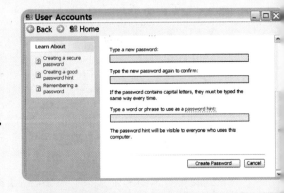

How to create a new user

1. Use the Start menu to show the Control Panel.
2. Click on 'User Accounts'.
3. Click on 'Create a New Account'.
4. Type a name.
5. Choose whether the account is to be Limited or an Administrator.
6. Select 'Create the account' and the new name will be added to the list.

To change an account

1. Go to User Accounts from the Control Panel, and click on 'Change an account'.
2. Select the account you wish to change.
3. Select from the options that appear to change the name, add a password, or change the picture. If you are an Administrator, you can also delete the account.

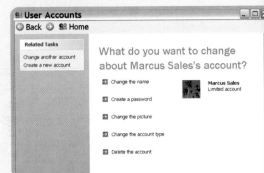

Logging on and off

Signing in to an account is known as logging on. When Windows XP starts, you will see a blue screen with a list of the names of all the family, including the pictures associated with each name. To log on, select a name, and type in the password. Windows XP will then show your chosen desktop layout and graphics, and you can start work.

If someone else wants to use your computer you have two choices.

1. If you log off, all the software you are using will be stopped. You should save all your work first. This is the slow option, recommended for when you have finished a long session and someone else wants to start a long session. To log off, select the 'Log off' option at the bottom of the Start menu, and the 'Log off' option that appears in a box in the middle of the screen.

2. If you switch users, you can keep all your current work intact. This is the fast option. Use it when someone wants to interrupt you for a short period. To do so select 'Switch Users' instead of Log off. There may be a short to medium delay while Windows XP saves the current state of your work. (Note that any Internet connection will remain. You may wish to disconnect from the Internet first.)

Once you have logged off or switched users, Windows XP will show the main blue sign-in screen again. Someone else can now have a turn.

User pictures

A user picture is a small photo or image that is associated with each user account. By default, Windows chooses one of a random selection of cheerful photos that include guitars, tropical scenes, and so on. But you can use the Browse option under Change an account → Change my picture to select a home-made photo or other image as a user picture. Your photo can be as big as you like. It will be resized automatically to fit.

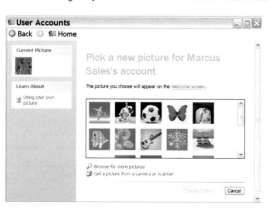

It's impossible to childproof a PC completely. But sensible precautions include:

- having home-made covers for the reset and power buttons, so tiny fingers can't push them

- replacing a standard slide-out tray CD drive with one of those models that uses a slot for the CD

- making sure all cables are connected securely, and that any finger screw connections are tight

- tidying up cables with cable ties (available from most computer stores) so there's no chance of someone tripping over them

- securing the main power cable to the back of the PC. There's not much chance of electrocution, but if the cable is pulled out by accident out you'll lose all your work.

PC SECURITY AND CHILDPROOFING

Choosing a password

By default, Windows XP asks you to change your password at regular intervals. This helps with security, but is also a chore, as not everyone finds it easy to think of new passwords. A useful trick is simply to swap two random words with some digits in between – so, for example, 'random32 word' becomes 'word32 random'.

Windows passwords

You can set up user accounts with or without passwords. If you are working on your own, you can use a null (empty) password. This can save time when signing on, because Windows XP will never ask you for it. Simply leave the password box blank when you set up the account. You can also change an existing password to a null password using the 'Change an account password' option. Delete the existing password and confirm this by leaving the password confirmation box blank as well. Windows will no longer ask you for a password.

In a family, setting passwords is recommended. It's wise to set up a PC so that only the parents have access to an account with Administrator privileges. The best administrator passwords are a combination of two random but memorable words separated by a two-digit number. The names of pets, friends or relatives are not recommended. Nor are obvious words associated with TV or music favourites, hobbies, or other interests.

Protecting files

By default, all the files in your PC will be visible to every user. If your PC has been supplied to you with the disk drives set up to use the NTFS disk system, you can protect each person's My Documents folder with a password. If it hasn't, you can change the disks to use the NTFS system without losing any information (see page 181) and then set up passwords.

How to make sure hidden files remain invisible

If you want to hide information from younger children – and from adults who aren't Windows experts – a possible solution is to use the Hide feature built into Windows. Windows itself uses this to keep you away from files that shouldn't be tinkered with. But you can easily extend it to hide files and folders you don't want others to see. (Unfortunately, this won't hide software. That will still appear in the Start menu of every user, as soon as you install it.)

The Hide feature is turned on by default. To control whether it's on or off, open Windows Explorer, and select Tools → Folder options. In the list that appears you'll see an option called 'Hidden files and folders' and two choices – one to show them, and the other to hide them. For your own use as Administrator, there's no reason to hide these files. But when you are setting up user accounts for children, make sure the Hide option is selected.

Right click on the folder or file you want to hide, and select 'Properties'. At the bottom of the page that appears you'll see three check boxes. Tick the one labelled 'Hidden'. You can make these changes from your Administrator account. Now when your children log in, all the hidden files will be completely invisible to them. You can hide whole blocks or files or folders at the same time. Select the top one in the block, hold down the shift key and select the bottom one. All the files or folders in between will be highlighted. You can change the properties of all of them in one go, just as for a single file.

Internet safety

1. Keep the PC in the main living area, so that you can keep an eye on what your children are doing. This can become a problem with older children, especially those who want to play loud games (don't forget that earphones can be used instead of speakers) or want the privacy to gossip electronically with their friends. There is no perfect solution here, and the line between intrusive surveillance and privacy is something parents will have to tread carefully.

2. If you are using an online service such as AOL, make sure you use the Parental Controls option. This can help eliminate pornographic junk mail, limit children's access to chatrooms and generally control who they can associate with online.

3. Don't assume that Internet Explorer's History feature will provide a reliable guide to what your children are looking at online. Many children from the early teens onwards will be familiar with the History feature and will know how to remove traces of any sites they have visited.

4. To prevent access to inappropriate websites, install a filter tool such as Net Nanny, CyberSitter or CyberPatrol. These can filter sites so that your children can't access pornography and other material you might want to protect them from. Most of these tools have free trial versions, so you can download them all and see which works best for you. One problem with filters is that they can be too enthusiastic, so it's a good idea to be on hand to change settings manually if a legitimate search for information for a school project is tripping over the filtering.

5. If you have good reason to believe that your child is being stalked online by an adult through Instant Messages or Chat (see page 143), it's possible to install a keystroke recorder program that will keep a record of any online conversations. Of course, this is a very intrusive measure and shouldn't be considered except as a very last resort. To find examples of this software, use a search engine to look for 'Keystroke recorder'.

Three web-filtering product websites:
CyberPatrol at www.cyberpatrol.com; Net Nanny at www.netnanny.com; CyberSitter at www.cybersitter.com

It is possible to give each user a separate hard disk with a separate copy of Windows, and then install separate software on each, using Windows XP's 'multiple boot' feature (see page 181). This means you can install and use completely separate copies of XP on separate disks. When the PC is starting up, a message will appear asking you which copy you want to use. This is not a cheap or easy option, but it is the ultimate top-security solution.

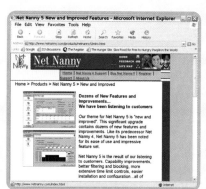

KIDS' STUFF

Kids and future PCs

Some parents buy PCs because they hope to teach their children IT technology for the future job market. This isn't as good an idea as it might appear. PC technology changes very fast, and by the time today's children start work it's unlikely that the technology they'll be working with will look much like Windows XP.

A PC can make a surprisingly effective babysitter, offering exactly the right blend of predictability and surprise to keep kids entertained for at least an hour, and sometimes two or three times that. But it can also be educational. Unlike books and crayons, software works interactively, and can be helpful in developing various key skills. Most kids' software is based on the idea of the 'activity centre', which combines various games and activities into a friendly teaching environment.

Software doesn't usually make any attempt to follow formal Key Stage 1 and Key Stage 2 requirements. Instead, you'll find creative and colourful attempts to teach the same basic concepts, including:

- hand-to-eye co-ordination
- logical reasoning
- listening skills and verbal reasoning
- arithmetic and mathematical understanding

- memory development
- reading comprehension
- writing and literacy
- spelling and other language skills
- artistic and creative skills
- musical development.

If you're looking for software that will stretch your youngsters as well as keep them entertained, it's a good idea to build a collection that covers all of these areas.

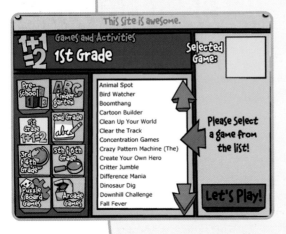

Free games on the web with the Kaboose network...

Where to look, what (not) to buy
Plenty of free games and other resources are available online. Many are written for the US market and could therefore sound American and be geared towards US schooling practices. You'll need to vet these first to make sure they don't confuse your child. Some of these websites offer extra material for a regular subscription, but there's enough available for free to make them well worth visiting.
www.funschool.com
www.kidsdomain.com
www.kidsfreeware.com
www.yourchildlearns.com
www.kaboose.com

...or if you prefer, you can buy software that lets the Mr Men out to play on your PC

Buying software

Unlike general software, which is usually available only from large PC stores and by mail order, you can find software for children at smaller PC stores, supermarkets, and even garages and newsagents. It's often quite cheap compared with other software products.

You won't often see reviews of kids' software in computer magazines. This can make it hard to buy intelligently. Film and TV tie-ins are perennially popular. But unless your child is a particular fan of a character or series, there's no reason to assume that the software will be any better or worse than any other products for children. A good strategy is to buy older, budget-priced software. It's usually just as child-friendly as newer products, but much cheaper.

French program Rayman – budget software without a budget feel

Compatibility issues

Some children's software has been around for quite a few years now, and older software created for earlier versions of Windows won't always work properly with Windows XP. You'll find that the software may not start properly, the colours may be scrambled, or it may crash – stop working – at certain points. If you buy something that does this, all is not lost. Windows XP has a compatibility feature that can fool older software into working reliably.

To use this feature, first use Windows Explorer to find the software's .exe file. Open 'My Program Files' and look through all the folders that appear for the name of the software, or the name of the publisher. Open this folder and you should see a file with the right name (the file type will be 'Application').

Right click on this file and select 'Properties'. Then click on the 'Compatibility' tab, and check the box that says 'Run this program in compatibility mode for...'. The best choice for most software will be Windows 95. The other settings – number of colours, screen size – may be useful if you find the software looks very small on your screen with a huge black border around it.

Making older software compatible with Windows XP is surprisingly simple

39

TEENAGE LEARNING

While software for younger children teaches while pretending to be play, school-age software is much more goal-oriented and tied to specific exams and tests. A PC can play the role of a very effective and affordable private tutor. It is also very useful for helping with the writing of essays and other homework. There are two kinds of educational tools that you may want to consider for your teenager. The first is learning and revision software; the second is the Internet, and especially the immense collection of study materials that are available on the Web.

Software on CD

Most CD-based educational software consists of a summary of the relevant subject with some revision tests. The degree of sophistication of the software varies hugely. Some CDs offer the bare bones of each subject, with simple summaries of each key point, and very basic tests. Others include progress charts and statistics, revision planners, more detailed subject summaries, and timed mini-exams. Some offer the option of keeping track of more than one learner at once, although unless you have twins studying the same subjects, this may not be as useful as it sounds.

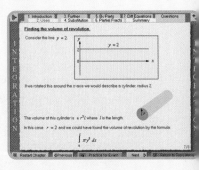

Success Builder's A-Level Physics

Prices for CDs vary between £15 and £30, depending on the content and the cachet of the manufacturer. This is a one-off payment, for each subject. Given that a private tutor can cost at least as much for each lesson, the value-for-money appeal is obvious. When choosing CDs remember two things. The first is to buy a different product from the one that used in school – different presentation of the same material, with different tests, will make for more effective long-term learning. The second is to make sure that the CD you buy matches the syllabus your child is studying. This means that the software has to be current, and it also has to match the requirements of whichever examination board will be setting the final papers. Some products include material for every possible syllabus, so your child may waste time studying the wrong subject areas. If in doubt, you may need to familiarise yourself with the requirements of each syllabus, or perhaps get a suitable summary from the teachers at your school.

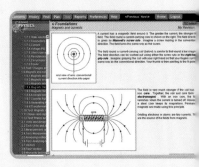

The Oxford Personal Revision Guide to A-Level Physics

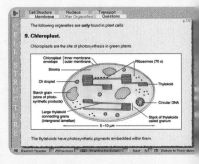

Success Builder's A-Level Biology

Schools and the Web

If you have an Internet connection, you can explore a huge collection of study aids on the Web. A surprising number of these are completely free. In terms of quality, some are less polished and helpful than CD-based software, but others are comparable. You can explore what's available by using a search engine to look for likely keywords. Here is a list of interesting sites to get you started.

http://www.bbc.co.uk/schools/revision/
Free revision help from the BBC. Includes lessons and revision material in Welsh

http://www.schoolzone.co.uk/
A collection of study aids. Includes a huge list of subscription sites for you to explore further

http://www.schoolsnet.com
Not as sophisticated as some sites, but includes lessons and revision aids for GCSE courses

http://www.learn.co.uk/
Lessons for Key Stages 2, 3 and 4 and AS levels. Some material requires a subscription payment

http://www.nc.uk.net/home.html
The definitive National Curriculum site. Each key skill in the curriculum is listed, and links are included to useful sites where available. This isn't a site for pupils, but teachers and interested parents will find it a useful gateway to other resources

http://revisionlink.co.uk/
A list of links to other revision-oriented sites

http://www.schoolshistory.org.uk/
A history-themed site that also includes plenty of links to other resources

http://www.musicatschool.co.uk/index.htm
A music-oriented site with information about the curriculum and simple study aids

Free sites?

How can useful websites like those mentioned in this section be free? Most of them make their money by including advertising. The advertiser pays a small amount to the site host each time the page is viewed. If enough people view a site, the sums involved can become substantial. Education is always of interest to both parents and school pupils, and so these sites can sustain themselves comfortably.

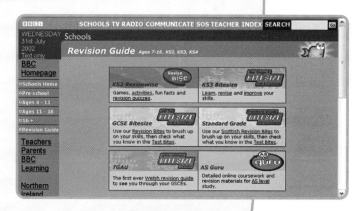

The BBC revision site is an excellent source of bite-sized revision information, and is one of the few resources that is useful for Welsh and Scottish pupils

HOME MAKEOVER – INTERIOR DESIGN

Cameras and lighting

Objects appear different under a blue sky, an orange sunset, and also under orange-tinted filament bulbs and green-tinted fluorescents. Our eyes compensate for these differences automatically so we rarely notice them. But they show up very clearly in photos. Cameras use a feature called white balance to compensate for this. If you're taking photos for an interiors project, make sure that you read and follow your camera's instructions about white balance so that you capture the colours on swatches accurately.

You can find PC software to help with interior design in any large computer store. Such packages make it easy to try out colours, textures and furniture arrangements in a virtual room – sometimes virtual copies of the rooms in your own house – without having to redecorate first.

The first part of the design process involves picking fabric swatches and colour charts and deciding on an attractive combination. Some software packages use a fixed set of textures and colours. This is obviously less useful than being able to add your own. Better software includes the ability to import images you have created with a scanner or digital camera. You can either scan samples at home, or use your digital camera to take photos in a shop. Once imported, they appear as part of a texture library. You don't have to limit yourself to scanning simple shades. You can scan or photograph complicated fabrics, wallpapers and borders just as easily. This makes it easy to create a virtual design using whatever is available at your favourite DIY or home-decorating store. Note that you may need to change the size of your scanned samples. Otherwise you may find that your scanned pattern looks larger than your sofa! Any good paint program can be used for this. Use the sample swatches and textures in your software as a guide size.

Professional designers use a colour board to help them with their work. They arrange combinations of colours and textures to find ones that work. (Any interior design book will include tips on how to do this.) Good software will include a virtual version of this same feature, so that you can preview your colour mix before you start applying it to the walls, floors and furniture.

The final step is to preview your combinations on simulated furniture. Most software includes a set of virtual rooms with their own furniture that you can try out. While these may not mirror your own interiors, they're perfectly capable of producing a vividly photo-realistic simulation of how a design scheme will look in real life. The alternative approach is to use one of the more powerful home-design tools outlined on page 46. With these, you can create your own furniture layout, and then paint in the details as before. In practice, you'll find that the simpler approach is often better and more useful for interior colours, and the latter better for creating furniture arrangements. The simulations in home-design packages rarely look as lifelike as those that are used in interior-design tools. The ideal approach is to use both.

Pick your materials...

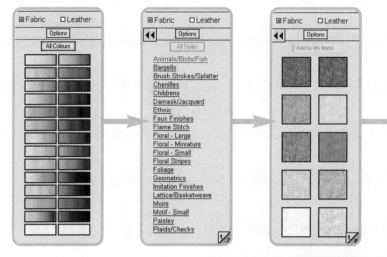

If you have a good paint program, you can simulate many of the features of an interior-design tool. You can use the 'fill' feature to 'paint' furniture, walls and floor with textures and colours, including those you have scanned yourself. Including all perspective effects can be very time-consuming, so ignore them. The results may look a little strange, but they'll be good enough to serve as a preview.

...check how they combine...

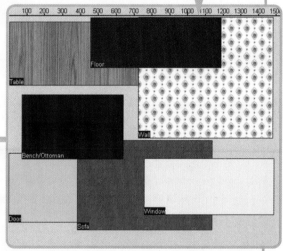

...and then preview them on real furniture

HOME MAKEOVER – GARDEN DESIGN

Knowing what features to look for in garden-design software is crucial to the whole project of giving your garden a makeover. It's true that software can't quite replace the eye and the practical skills of a fully qualified professional garden designer. But the best products will take you much further than you might expect, and with some perseverance you can turn that area of scrub and weeds at the back of the house into an impressively arranged visual delight. These are what good packages offer.

- Probably the most important aspect to look for is inspiration. There's nothing quite like learning from the experts, so choose software that includes a library of suggested layouts and designs, preferably in various styles. You don't, of course, have to follow these exactly or even use them at all. But if you're a newcomer, it's both useful and creative to see how professionals tackle a design, and the kinds of arrangements and techniques they use.

- Because you will need to map your own plot and transfer its physical features to the software, make sure your software can handle real dimensions and include information about the slope and orientation of the land. There should be some way of marking raised and lowered areas as well. Software that can provide only a bird's-eye 2D top-down view is at a disadvantage here. Ideally, you want a tool that can show elevation more clearly.

- For the design itself, you should have access to a large library of plants and the ideal conditions under which they grow, including temperature ranges, light and shade, and soil conditions. It's also useful to be able to choose plants by colour, seasonal variation, height and other criteria such as durability. Surprisingly, even some budget software includes these details. More advanced packages allow you to add customised plant information from a plant encyclopaedia. If you're a very serious gardener, you could even collate all this information into a home-made database. While designing, you should be able to add not just plants, but also water features, garden furniture, ornaments, and other extras and options.

- You should be able to preview your garden as a 3D walkthrough (or rather, mouse-through). This is so that you can see your garden in all its glory in relation to your house and also to the lighting and other local conditions. A useful extra is the ability to change the season so that you can see how your garden varies from spring to autumn. For many people, this is the most enjoyable part of a virtual gardening project – sometimes more than the digging and weeding required to make the project happen in reality.

- Finally, your software should be able to create a planting schedule, and perhaps also a bill of materials and a final estimate. Unfortunately, no software can do the spadework for you, but you will at least be sure that your finished design will be well worth the effort.

Catalogue of Design Styles

One of the best ways to get ideas for your garden is to review what others did with theirs. Browse this sampler of popular styles to start your imagination. Click on a picture below to learn more about it.

A Small City Garden

A Formal Landscape

An Informal Landscape

A Garden for Thoughts

A Terraced Garden

A Cottage Garden

An Italian Landscape

A Modern Landscape

An Asian Landscape

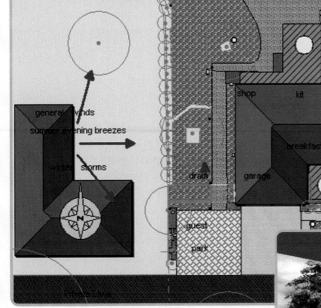

From top to bottom: Get inspired with some design suggestions, plan your garden from the top down... and then take a computer-generated virtual walk through it

DESIGNING A NEW HOME

Wireframe CAD

A **wireframe** CAD drawing shows the bare shape and dimensions of an object, without any further detail. Wireframes are used because they can be drawn very quickly. Once you have a wireframe, you can clothe each object using a texture such as metal or brick. This is known as rendering your object.
Rendering is a slow process. Expect to wait a few minutes, even with a fast PC.

Computer-aided design

All the home projects described so far have been specialised examples of a process known as computer-aided design (CAD). General-purpose CAD can be used to design objects such as furniture and accessories, and even a complete building. If you're used to working with simpler tools, CAD can seem confusing at first. In practice, CAD is just like a drawing board that works in three dimensions. You can create objects, extrude them so that flat shapes become solid (for example, if you extrude a circle it becomes a cylinder), rotate them in three dimensions, stretch and squeeze them, and specify the physical connections between them. If you're an enthusiastic DIY fan, CAD software can be extremely useful. You can design furniture and make sure it looks the way you want it to and fits your requirements, then produce a plan from that, and only then pick up your tools.

Self-build

Any computer store will sell software that includes facilities for creating room plans and blueprints, front and side elevations, and even 3D simulations of your building. These tools are often quite easy to use and typically include design hints and also starter plans. Some include CAD facilities.

But how useful are they? If you can specify both plan and elevation dimensions accurately, a good builder should be able to take your software sketch, provide a costing, and create the building out of bricks and mortar. But there's more to building a real house than specifying where the walls, doors and windows go. Plumbing, heating, wiring, lighting, guttering, drainage and the foundations need to be defined in detail. The final cost, both in time and in building materials, needs to be estimated accurately. There's also no guarantee that a sketched design is structurally sound and doesn't fall foul of local building or planning regulations.

Some builders can handle these details, and so can all architects. An architect can also take your initial sketch and suggest the kinds of flourishes, details and awareness of proportions and use of space that a beginner is likely to miss. In practice, then, it's best to see your sketch as an interesting starting point. Use it to get an overall feel for the look you want, and then get the professionals to fill in the details.

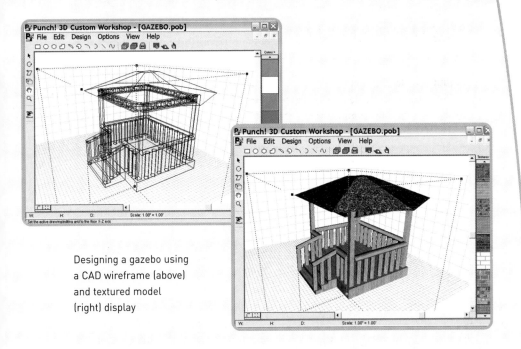

Designing a gazebo using
a CAD wireframe (above)
and textured model
(right) display

Three views of the same building using a
typical home-design package – in this
case Mindscape's Punch! 3D

- accurate dimensions for both room plans and elevations
- a texture mode so that you can preview wallpaper and interior finishes, and also the exterior finish
- the ability to add objects and furniture inside rooms to preview the layout
- walkthroughs and flythroughs so that you can see how well your room layout works
- integrated garden design and landscaping.

GAMES AND GAMING

Free games

Games like Freecell and Solitaire (Start → All programs → Games) are not particularly sophisticated. But they do seem to be unusually good at distracting people from more productive work! You can also play conventional games like chess and draughts on a PC. Many of these more traditional games are available as freeware or shareware.

Cheats

All large games have cheat features built in. To find them, search the Web for the game's name and add the word 'cheat'.

Gaming software

Shoot 'em ups
The most popular category. They are often gory and violent with a strong science fiction element, and users will have to battle hideous, vicious monsters and aliens through buildings and across landscapes. Doom, Quake, Unreal and Half Life are examples of shoot 'em ups. They can be surprisingly scary.

Role playing and fantasy
Based loosely on role-playing games, these usually involve characters who fight with swords or use magic. Some include a quest you have to complete. They can be rather twee compared with the relentless aggression of shoot 'em ups, and are more likely to include puzzles to solve. Examples include Morrowind and the Ultima series.

Puzzles and plotlines
Games like Myst and Riven offer an unlikely but very successful blend of puzzles and a story set in lavishly detailed computer-generated backgrounds. Others, such as Gabriel Knight and Resident Evil, are like animated novels.

Sims
Short for simulators. There are two kinds. 'God games' put you in charge of a virtual world, with the power to influence its development. Cities, civilisations, hospitals, fairgrounds and even relationships have all been simulated. The other sims are accurate simulations of flying or driving cars and trains. You can even, rather bizarrely, simulate a table-top trainset. Some sims include combat elements. Others, like Microsoft's Flight Simulator, are an accurate pilot's-eye view of a long-haul flight, where not much happens except at take-off and landing.

Film and TV tie-ins
Characters such as Harry Potter and James Bond, and films such as Star Trek and Star Wars have been targeted for games spin-offs, which often combine puzzle and shoot 'em up elements.

From left to right – two characters from Myst 3, a strange underground contraption from Unreal, a fighter plane patrols in Microsoft's Combat Flight Simulator, and two characters battle in Sony's Everquest

Gaming hardware

It's perhaps ironic that while you can do serious office work on a mid-price average PC, to get the best from games you'll need the latest and most powerful hardware. Many games are playable even if you don't have the latest hardware – but only up to a point. You may find that the play is jerky, and you may have to use blockier video settings which show less detail and generally look less realistic.

Processor

The faster the better, although it's not usually worth the absolutely fastest and newest chips unless you're a true fanatic. It's especially important for games not to use a cheaper processor family, such as the Celeron or Duron ranges.

Memory and disk space

Games don't usually need extra memory. But they can be demanding of disk space. For maximum speed, many games can be installed to disk, and this can take up whole gigabytes of storage.

Soundcard and speakers

Some cards include special technologies such as EAX which are used only in games. Surround sound audio (also known as 5.1) uses multiple speakers and creates the effect of monsters attacking from behind you – even when they're not visible. Subwoofers are useful for more realistic explosion sounds.

Graphics card

Good graphics cards have two main qualities: speed (to give you detail without jerkiness), and special features (which can create water, fog and other lighting effects). But technology changes so quickly that a full summary of everything a buyer needs to know will be out of date almost immediately. To keep up with the latest developments you'll need to do a lot of background reading in magazines and on the Web.

matrox

- Graphics cards and upgrades
- Digital video solutions
- Imaging hardware and software
- Network solutions

Tom Clancy's Rainbow Six
RAVEN SHIELD
Optimized for graphics by ATI
> play the multiplayer demo

Joysticks and other extras

Joysticks range from basic hand-held units to expensive models which wobble and rattle when there's an explosion. Other game extras include simulated rudder pedals for flight sims, steering wheels for driving sims, and game pads which are similar to those used on stand-alone hardware game boxes such as the Playstation and the Xbox.

3D info

Discussions about graphics card technology is often rather technical, but you can find out the latest news at the following sites.
www.avault.com
www.3daccelerated.com
www.3dchipset.com
www.3dgpu.com
www.bjorn3d.com

Internet gaming

Shoot 'em ups often include an Internet or network element, so you can play against others. Many ISPs and even some games companies include special computers you can connect to, to play against strangers. For details, search for 'games servers'. Sony's Everquest (www.everquest.com) is currently the ultimate Internet game. A huge virtual world populated almost entirely by tens of thousands of players, it's an addictive social-role-playing and fantasy game.

HOW TO SHOP ONLINE

Is your shopping site secure?

Normally, when you fill in a form on a website, the details you type can be intercepted and read by any moderately skilled hacker. Secure sites use an almost unbreakable code to hide credit-card and other personal details. There are two ways of checking if the site you are using is secure: the letters at the start of the address, as shown in your browser, will be 'https://' (as opposed to 'http://'), and you will see a graphic confirming this (for example, Internet Explorer shows an open padlock at the bottom right of the screen to indicate an unsecured site, and a closed padlock for a secure one).

Since the advent of online shopping, most sites offering products or services for sale have moved towards a similar approach. Clearly, there are differences in the presentation of sites, and also in how much product information is available, but the steps involved in shopping online are almost standardised. The example used here is that of the UK branch of Amazon, the well-known online bookstore.

1. Choose your retailer

The best way to find a list of suitable shops is by personal recommendation, from an online directory such as Yahoo (see page 134) or from listings in printed directories or monthly magazines. Search engines are usually best used to search for specific products rather than for stores. When you find a store you like, don't forget to add it to your browser's favourites so you can find it again quickly next time.

2. Find the product you want

Retailers vary in the amount of information they provide – some give plenty of details, and even personal recommendations based on previous shopping choices, while others list very basic facts. Most include category/keyword and directory searches (see page 135) to help you find the products you want.

3. Make your decision

The better sites include customer reviews and ratings, so you can make a more informed decision based on what others have said about a product you are thinking of buying. These reviews can be surprisingly useful, although you need a good selection of them to form an accurate picture. Alternatively, books and CDs sometimes also come with sample pages and music clips.

4. Add your product to the shopping cart

Almost all online shops have a virtual shopping cart or basket. As you move through the store buying items (click on 'Add to order', 'Buy' or 'Order' buttons), they're added to the cart. The basket keeps track of each item, and also works out a running total price. This all happens automatically, so you can focus on which products you want.

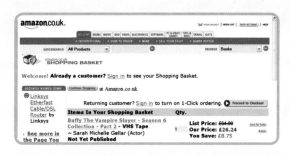

5. Manage your shopping basket

Look out for a link with a name like 'View basket'. This will show you what you've ordered so far. You can also delete items here. Some shops also include 'wish lists' and 'reminders' for shopping at a later date.

6. Sign in and move through the checkout

Click on 'Proceed to checkout', or an equivalent phrase. You will usually need to sign in first. The first time only, the site will ask

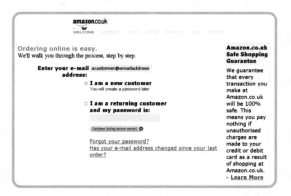

you for your address and other details. You may also be asked to type in your credit-card details. These may be remembered for future orders. On subsequent visits you'll need to use only your name, or perhaps an email address, and a password. Everything else will be remembered.

7. Postage and packing

The checkout screen will show your items, together with postage and packing options, and taxes such as VAT. You'll often be given a choice of delivery options, from slow and cheap or free, to expensive and fast. Don't forget that all of these add to the price. (Be careful - P&P can make a big difference to final prices!)

8. Confirm the order, and receive email and online confirmation

Your order isn't final until you select the final 'Confirm' option. If you change your mind first, close the browser page without confirming and your order will be removed. If you do confirm, expect to wait a while – up to a couple of minutes – while your card details are checked. If successful, you'll see a final confirmation screen with an order number. You'll also be sent a copy by email. Keep this safe in case something goes wrong with the order. For extra security, keep a copy of the confirmation page. (Hit 'PrtScrn', open your favourite image-editing software, and select 'Paste'). Some retailers will also send you email notifications when goods have been despatched, or if delivery has been delayed.

How safe is the use of credit cards online?

No credit-card transaction, electronic or otherwise, is 100% safe. In practice, online shopping is safer than many people realise. Secure sites make it almost impossible for credit-card numbers to be stolen. Most complaints seem to arise with sites that are dubious in the first place, including those that offer online porn or gambling. Straightforward shopping online doesn't appear to be much less safe than handing over your credit card in person in a store.

ESSENTIAL CONSUMER RESOURCES

Comparative price sites

uk.price runner.com
quite possibly the best comparison site

uk.shop smart.com
a limited range, but worth considering

www.book brain.co.uk
for books only

www.123price check.com
books, music and videos

www.check aprice.com
very easy to use

Shopping portals

www.iwantto shop.com
comprehensive

uk.shop smart.com
good bargains, and useful editorial content

www.uk shopping guide.co.uk
another comprehensive UK listing

www.shop.co.uk
dig deep to find some unusual shopping categories

www.intersaver .co.uk
save money by becoming part of a bulk order

Bargain finders

Comparative shopping sites (also known as 'bargain finders') help you compare prices across various shops for items you are looking for. Some sites also include some basic product information. Once you find the cheapest retailer, you can click on a link that takes you to its site, and buy the item in the usual way. You may find, when you get to the site, that the price is higher than that reported on the price-comparison site – this is usually because the retailer is being economical with the truth to attract shoppers. Even so, with a few of the listings you'll often find that you can still save money on prices that are advertised in magazines. You can also use the information when negotiating with local stores that offer a price-match policy.

Sort by: Retailer	Sort by: Added value	Sort by: Rating	Sort by: Delivery	Sort by: Shipping	Sort by: Price	Sort by: Price with shipping	Sort by: Online
iMatters.co.uk Info on retailer		Review retailer		Check with retailer	**£509** Source: Website. 09/11/02	Check with retailer	
Nomatica.co.uk Info on retailer		3.2/5 8 reviews	no units in stock	£8.50	**£509.32** Source: Website. 09/11/02	£517.82	
go2camcorder Info on retailer	2nd Year warranty on all camcorders only £20.	3.9/5 15 reviews		£9.50	£510 Source: Website. 09/11/02	£519.50	Direct link

Using Pricerunner to find a Fuji FinePix S602Z digital camera. The best printed price we could find in various magazines was £539. The best price shown here is £509, but Nomatica doesn't have the cameras in stock. When we visited the iMatters site itself, the price shown was much higher than the £509 shown here. But go2camcorder has stock available at £510. The catch? Delivery in ten days. Even so, it's a very good price

Shopping portals

A step up from the price-comparison sites are shopping portals. These are known for the occasional extreme bargain, and sometimes provide price-comparison facilities as well. Mostly they offer shopping directories, which are an ideal way to start finding shopping sites that might not show up on a search engine. Sometimes you'll even find useful mini-articles about the business of shopping. (See, for example, www.botspot.com/dailybot/shopping_99.html, which has a dated but still interesting summary of various online shopping services.)

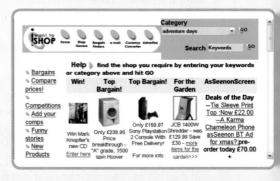

If you want to shop, go to iwanttoshop.com

Customer ratings

A number of sites offer a consumer rating service that's open to the public. If enough people comment about a product or service, you can get a very accurate picture of how good it really is. To encourage contributions, some of these sites even pay their contributors a small amount.

Free ads and second-hand goods

Most free-ad sites are just the electronic versions of the paper weeklies you may be familiar with – *Exchange and Mart*, *Loot* and so on. An interesting variation are the online auction sites, including eBay (see page 56). We've listed some alternatives here.

Amazon's UK site includes UK-specific second-hand goods and traders. The service is an excellent way to track down specific

Find out if you want to, with dooyoo

Buy loot with Loot

second-hand books and music, but it can also be useful for other specialised goods, such as autographed and signed items, and even some antiques.

Ethical trading

Ethical trading is becoming increasingly important to UK shoppers, and some sites are beginning to cater for this. Ethical goods don't harm the environment, and are fairly traded, which means that growers and farmers can expect to be paid a reasonable living wage with some hope of job security.

And finally...

Why not join in yourself? If you have something to sell on a small to medium scale, setting up your own e-commerce operation can be easier than you think. It's possible with some imagination, a little effort and often very little seed investment to start a small online business. A number of sites explain how to do this. We've listed a couple in the sidebar for you.

Customer rating sites

www.dooyoo.co.uk a surprisingly large range of goods and services rated

www.uk.ciao.com very similar to dooyoo

www.consumer reviews.co.uk specialises in computers and technology

Free-ad sites

www.exchange andmart.co.uk wide range of goods

www.loot.com probably the best free-ads site in the UK

Selling online

www.selliton theweb.com very good introduction to e-commerce

www.ishop builder.co.uk an online-shop-building tool

Ethical trading

www.getethical.com an essential read for ethical consumers

www.fairtrade.org.uk a fair-trade organisation

HOLIDAYS, FLIGHTS AND TRAVEL

Road travel

www.via michelin.com includes a route planner to any city in Europe, information about hotels and restaurants, and a live traffic update

www.rac.co.uk free regular traffic news updates, and detailed suggestions about driving in various countries

Travel survival guides

www.flyana .com dry, but also unusually practical and useful, collection of tips on how to (literally) survive air travel

www.tips4 trips .com more than a thousand travel tips contributed by the public

The traveller's Web

The Web already has a reputation as being a useful source of cheap flights and travel. But of course you can do far more with it than hunt for bargains. Whether you're planning a short trip or a long one, you can find everything you need to know about your journey and your destination before you set out.

General information

www.infospace.com/uk.vnetuk/ travel/travelguides.htm Detailed information on resorts, cities and hotels

www.baa.co.uk Essential UK airport information

www.frommers.com The electronic version of the travel guides, with country-by-country info. Particularly good for hotel and restaurant recommendations

www.lonelyplanet.com As friendly and colourful as the printed guides (which you can order online), this site has a wealth of information for aspiring travellers

www.tourist-offices.org.uk Links to all the UK-based tourist offices, with pages of travel advice and suggestions for each country

www.travel.world.co.uk Large directory of travel websites

www.fco.gov.uk Up-to-date travel advice from the UK government for countries around the world

www.masta.org Health advice about jabs, DVT and diseases

With a web full of travel information, at one extreme you can find out about what's available all over the world. At the other, check the traffic flow in London's Marylebone Road

The best prices

You may be surprised to find that it's sometimes possible to haggle online. Sites like the UK Travel Guide include a bid feature where you can name your price, and if a flight is empty an airline may decide to accept your offer.

General holiday and flight bookings

www.ukonlinetravelguide.co.uk
Packed with information and links – and you can bid on flights

www.priceline.co.uk
Another bidding site – make offers on flights and hotel rooms. With the latter, bold bidding can save you more than 50%

www.ebookers.com
A popular site for flight bargains, but prices are perhaps not as absolutely rock bottom as some

www.telmeglobaltraveller.com
A useful site for flexible airfare searching and other travel information

www.virgintravelstore.co.uk
Good for hotel quotes and package holidays

www.holidayautos.co.uk
A choice of car hire rates

www.skydeals.co.uk
Easy-to-use site for booking airfares

www.lastminute.com
One of the more tenacious online stores, Lastminute sells show tickets and other items, as well as flights and hotel bookings

www.opodo.co.uk
Competitive quotes on hotels and flights

www.easyvalue.com
Comparative airfare quotes for no-frills and scheduled airlines

www.skyscanners.com
Comparative airfare quotes for no-frills airlines with good graphics

www.brochurebank.co.uk
Site where you can request brochures for worldwide destinations

Specialist travel

www.skiclub.co.uk
All things ski-related – guides to resorts, snow reports and more

www.thetrainline.com
Online route planner and ticket service for UK rail journeys

www.gapyear.com
Mouth-wateringly tempting travel ideas and booking facilities for gap-year students

www.bunac.co.uk
Working adventures worldwide for students and young people

www.guerba.co.uk
The ethical adventure travel company – minimise environmental damage, and explore countries away from the standard tourist trails

Courier bargains

If you can be flexible about your travel arrangements and want the lowest possible fares, it's worth considering courier travel. There are some restrictions and obligations, but these are usually minimal, and prices are very low (e.g. London to New York return for £150). For details, see these courier websites, or search for '+courier + travel'.

www.courier.org

www.courier travel.org

www.air courier.org

HOW TO EBAY

Using the US version

There's nothing to stop you using the US version of eBay (www.ebay.com). But you will need to let buyers know that delivery will take longer and be more expensive. If you're planning to sell to the USA, it's essential you check delivery choices and get accurate prices before you list your item.

eBay (www.ebay.co.uk) is a popular Internet auction service. Sellers – who could be individuals or companies – can sell anything, ranging from old personal artefacts to brand-new technological items in a time-limited auction (3, 5 or 7 days). Buyers, for whom the service is free, place bids for these items. The seller pays a commission.

eBay doesn't guarantee that fraud will never happen, but it minimises it by including a feedback system for both buyers and sellers. There's also fraud protection for sums between £15 and about £100 (although certain conditions apply). If you send someone a cheque and your goods do not arrive, you can try to claim at least some of the money back. Bidders have to specify credit-card and bank details, which has weeded out some of the more fanciful bids that children and teenagers used to make.

A lot of people seem to have good experiences with eBay. The service is a good way to get rid of junk, old books, CDs, videos, clothes and other items you no longer want or need. But it can also be used more imaginatively. You'll find people selling scanned copies of old magazines, their own music and artwork, home-made Christmas cards, and almost anything else you can imagine. It can pay to get creative!

How to buy

eBay can seem complicated at first. But the basics can be reduced to the following rules.

Signed "Regency" Lidded DERBY Vases NR	£500.00	1	1d 18h 44m
antique childs crib in oak	£300.00	1	2d 00h 55m
victorian chaise lounge	£750.00 £1,000.00 *Buy It Now*	-	2d 03h 54m
HUGE PHENOMENAL VINTAGE FRENCH WINE POSTER RE	£9.75	1	2d 22h 56m
HUGE VINTAGE NUDE MERMAIDS FRENCH POSTER	£9.75	1	3d 22h 21m

Antiques in eBay – a mix of commercial and personal sales

Before bidding
● Shop around to see if similar items are available elsewhere on eBay
● Check products and sellers carefully, using the built-in feedback features and eBay's own published guidelines
● Make sure you understand the delivery options and how much extra you'll pay for each one
● Use a credit card for large purchases

While bidding
Bids can't be retracted!
eBay's proxy system means you can make a very high bid and still pay a low price if no one else wants to get close to your bid.

After bidding

You have three days to contact the seller and arrange payment and the delivery schedule.

If there are problems, you can use eBay's feedback to make a complaint, but your rights are against the seller, not eBay. If you have a serious problem, you could use eBay's own arbitration service.

How to sell

The big appeal of eBay is that you can sell almost anything. You may be amazed at how an item you think of as useless tat may be just what someone else is looking for.

Fees
As the seller, you pay the fees. There's a nominal listing fee for each item listed, and a Final Value Fee, which applies only to items that are sold. Cheap items cost proportionally more to sell.

Delivery and description
If you have a scanner or a digital camera, post a photo or an image on the site. It's also essential to describe accurately the condition of any item you sell.

Auction type and reserve price
You can specify a reserve (i.e. minimum) price. This costs extra, but is worth doing for items whose value you are confident about, or which may be too much trouble to sell cheaply.

Repeat sales
If an item doesn't sell the first time, you can ask eBay to keep repeating an auction automatically until it does sell. It's best not to do this by default.

Accepting payments
eBay owns PayPal (see page 101), which is useful for larger sales. For small and cheap items, a cheque is more practical. Don't forget to wait for it to clear before you make delivery.

Settling your account
eBay expects regular monthly settlement of any commission and listing fees. These will be calculated by eBay and usually debited directly from your credit or debit card. If you don't list anything, there's no fee.

Here's a list of eBay's auction types and options.

Buy it now – specify a target price. If someone bids that price the item is sold to them and the auction ends immediately

Reserve price – specify a price below which you won't sell

Private auction – buyer's email addresses aren't shown

Dutch auction – for multiple items. The highest bidders win the chance to buy, but they pay the lowest bid price. Not, as you might expect, the high bid they made

See all categories in the Category Overview.

shop instantly!

Antiques & Art (16736)	Computers & Gaming (54751)
General (1195)	Books (756)
Antiques 20th Century (926)	Components (8445)
Antiquities (553)	Gaming (26338)
Architectural (334)	Laptop (2783)
Art (4540)	Macintosh (800)
Books, Manuscripts (394)	Networking, IT (1746)
	Other Hardware (483)

Make More Money with eBay

Great music great savings

Free P&P on gadgets

A tiny window on eBay's category list. The full list covers hundreds of different categories

BOOKS, MUSIC, VIDEOS AND GIFTS

Amazon UK *vs* Amazon US

The US site (www.amazon.com) offers easy shipping options to the UK. In theory, the cheapest surface shipping can take up to three months. In practice, it usually seems to take only a month or so, even at busy periods, although this isn't guaranteed. The UK site (www.amazon .co.uk) offers only first-class parcel post. If you're not in a hurry, you could save money because the total cost of a book, including delivery, can be less on the US site than on the UK one.

A typical bargain from Books Online

Books

Amazon

The online bookseller Amazon is very well known, and its sites have become the first port of call for those looking for both popular and hard-to-find books. Amazon is a success because in addition to the discounts it offers on books, it also has ratings and reviews of the books by readers. It sometimes includes sample pages from books. The company also operates an aggressive, although not offensively intrusive, advertising and 'suggestive sale' policy (i.e. it recommends new titles that may be of interest to you, based on the titles you have already bought). The range of books available is remarkable, and almost (but not quite) includes every book in print.

Alternatives to Amazon

Books Online (www.bol.com) offers some of the most significant discounts available anywhere – up to 60% on some titles. Discounted titles are sometimes B-list specials rather than true A-list bestsellers, but the site is still well worth browsing regularly.

Some of the departments on offer at the Foyles online site

Bibliophile (www.bibliophilebooks.com) is another bargain books site, operating on similar principles. It's not unlike the online equivalent of the bargain bookstores you can find in city centres. You may not find anything too mainstream, but there may still be plenty to tempt you. The same company also runs Read By Mail (www.readybymail.com), which offers current full-price titles on a modest 5% discount.

You never know quite what you'll find on Amazon's UK website

Bookbrain (www.bookbrain.com) is an example of a bargain-finder site (see page 52) tailored for book buyers. It compares online booksellers and lists the best (and worst) available prices. Quoted prices include all delivery costs. Truly astounding bargains and discounts are rare, but it's a good starting point for those looking to save money. You can, of course, use Amazon to search for titles on a specific subject and then see if Bookbrain can find the best prices for you.

Of course, many traditional booksellers have their own websites. Waterstones (www.waterstones.co.uk) has taken the easy route and created a site in cooperation with Amazon, with all the familiar Amazon features. Foyles (www.foyles.co.uk) and Blackwells (www.blackwells.co.uk) offer sites with more distinctive and characteristic features.

Music, videos and other gifts

Amazon also sells music, videos, DVDs and software. As with books, these are offered at modest to reasonable discounts. Unlike the US site, you won't find garden furniture and home appliances on offer from the UK store. And the 'gifts' section is really just a collection of re-badged book and music suggestions. Amazon UK's music and video prices aren't outstanding, but again the site has the virtue of comprehensiveness, making it a good choice for more obscure titles that would have to be ordered anyway.

For DVDs, Blackstar (www.blackstar.co.uk) is one of the best and most popular sites. Discounts are reasonable, and you can pre-order titles, so they'll be delivered to you as soon as they go on sale. Worthy competitors include Streets Online (www.streetsonline.co.uk) and DVD World (www.dvdworld.co.uk). The former offers very cheap delivery, the latter slightly better discounts and also a range of electronic goods.

For music, an excellent source is 101CD (www.101cd.com). The CDs on Streets Online and at Disky (www.disky.com) are slightly more expensive, but still cheaper than high-street prices. Also worth investigating is the online used-CD store at Second Sounds (www.secondsounds.com). Not only can you find bargains, but there's also a chance to track down rare recordings you would otherwise miss – and if you're worried about buying used CDs, there's a 30-day refund policy.

The Web has carved a niche for itself as a place to buy gifts and gadgets for all kinds of reasons, and for all occasions. A complete listing of gift sites would fill many pages, but here are some favourites.

www.iwantoneofthose.com
The proverbial toys for boys, including everything from keyrings for a couple of pounds to your own used jet fighter for £150,000
www.find-me-a-gift.co.uk
A selection of his and hers gifts, with fast delivery for last-minute panic buyers
www.innovations.co.uk
The online version of the ubiquitous and definitive gadget selection
www.hard2buy4.co.uk
A compendium summarising gift collections available from other websites, arranged by category with helpful suggestions

You can, of course, find more by using a search engine to look for '+gifts +UK'.

DVD regions

DVDs are coded by region, and matching DVD players are sold to make sure that disks imported from other regions can't be played. Europe is in Region 2, and in theory this means that a UK DVD player won't be able to play disks from the USA, which is in Region 1. In practice, many players are multi-region, or can be set up as multi-region with a small adjustment.

2.13 Books, music, videos and gifts

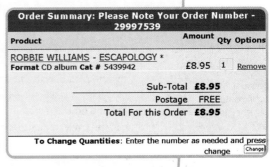

Order Summary: Please Note Your Order Number - 29997539			
Product	Amount	Qty	Options
ROBBIE WILLIAMS - ESCAPOLOGY * Format CD album Cat # 5439942	£8.95	1	Remove
	Sub-Total	£8.95	
	Postage	FREE	
	Total For this Order	£8.95	

To Change Quantities: Enter the number as needed and press change [Change]

Robbie Williams – £11.99 in the high street, £8.95 and free delivery from 101CD

For a stocking filler with a difference...

HOUSES AND CARS

Googling for England

When you're searching for UK properties, you'll need to specify a location and include '+UK'. This will eliminate the locations in other countries that share names with places in the UK.

Property

Buying a house

Before you decide what area of the UK you want to (or have to) move to, you can research it by looking at www.upmystreet.com and entering a postcode. This provides a list of local schools, crime rates, transport, other services and a simple – but useful – snapshot of average house prices. You can find out more about local schools by looking at the listings at www.ofsted.gov.uk and league tables at www.dfes.gov.uk/performancetables.

Local Information
- Conversations (beta)
- Public transport
- Property prices
- Classifieds
- Find My Nearest... ™
- ACORN profile
- Council performance
- Contacting your council
- Childcare
- Education
- Policing and Crime
- Member of Parliament

Do you live in BA1 6BA?
Is high speed BT Openworld Broadband in your area?
To check if it's up your street, click here

Find the best locations with UpMyStreet

Almost all local estate agents and national chains now have websites of their own, but of course you won't be able to search through these unless you can find the URL. Estate Angels (www.estateangels.co.uk) offers a useful, but not quite comprehensive, directory of agents by location. You can also use Google to search for agents.

National property listings include Asserta (www.asserta.com), Fish4Homes (www.fish4homes.co.uk) and Complete Housebuyer (www.complete-housebuyer.co.uk). On all of these you can find buyers selling to you directly. Some sites, such as Property Finder (www.propertyfinder.co.uk), are summaries that list all the properties in an area being sold by estate agents. For alternatives to these suggestions, search for '+UK +property'. Londoners should also see the house sales available on Loot (www.loot.com).

Selling a house

The Internet could also be used to sell your house, whether through an estate agent or by yourself. If you are using an agent, it will arrange for the details (and often photographs) of your property to be put on its site, thus making them accessible to anyone searching on the Net. Alternatively, you could advertise your property on one of the sites listed above, and avoid using an estate agent. Most sites request a nominal listing fee, which is sometimes payable weekly. While the sums may not be small – you can pay anywhere up to £100 – they're much cheaper than using an agent.

Like most online listings, you can search Asserta for price, size and location

For Londoners and those in surrounding counties, Loot remains a favourite

Property abroad

Searching for property abroad used to be difficult, but the Web has made it easy. You can find listings, preview prices, and track down local contact details for agents with very little effort. It's worth knowing that many continental European countries have specialist agents based in the UK, so you can deal with them without having to spend time abroad until you have a property shortlist. (For example, for French property try www.french-property.com.) For countries further afield, you can use a search engine and type in the name of the country and optionally the state, and then 'real estate' or 'property'. This simple exercise will display a huge list of agent contacts and properties in your chosen area. As an alternative, see the FOPDAC (Federation of Overseas Property Developers, Agents and Consultants) website at www.fopdac.com/index1.htm, which lists hundreds of overseas agents by both name and location.

Cars and other items

In spite of campaigns about 'rip off Britain', UK car prices remain far higher than those on the continent. One Swoop (www.oneswoop.com) offers savings of about 9% on standard UK list prices by including imported cars in its listings – higher discounts are sometimes available. Other discount sites to watch include Virgin Cars (www.virgincars.co.uk) and Broadspeed (www.broadspeed.com).

In the UK, one of the best bargain sites is Autobytel (www.autobytel.co.uk). Dealers compete with each other on price, so you can find discounted new trade sales, and also rather less competitive but still interesting used-car sales. (There's the option to sell your car as well, but the prices offered are unspectacular.)

For private sales, try www.autotrader.co.uk, which is the online equivalent of the popular paper version. You can sell your car online for a nominal fee – currently £15 for six weeks of advertising. Also useful are Car Source (www.carsource.co.uk), a sales summary site with useful links, Fish4Cars (www.fish4cars.co.uk), where you can buy and sell second-hand, and Motor Trak (www.motortrak.com), which lets you find specific makes and models in your area.

Car fraud

Worried about fraud? For a fee, Car Watch (www.car watchuk.com) can check to see if the car you're being sold is legal and above board.

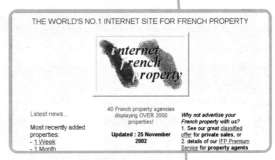

French property, from the aptly named french-property.com

Search by model and price at Fish4Cars

Bargains from abroad, from Oneswoop

THE DESKTOP SUPERMARKET

Supermarkets online

Big stores

If you're in an area supplied by a web-friendly supermarket, you can save an hour or two of driving, trolley-pushing and queuing, in return for a fairly nominal delivery fee. Many of the major supermarket chains have their own services now. All offer postcode checkers, so you can easily find out if your part of the country is covered. But there are two caveats. After signing up, expect an increase in special offers carefully targeted to match your shopping habits. Also, virtual shopping can be slow because some sites are huge and take a long time to download.

The facilities available at the different stores vary. Most will remember a standard shopping list so that you can re-order the same things every time you shop, with optional additions. Prices will usually be the same as in the store, although sometimes you will find special offers online that aren't available to shoppers. If something is out of stock, you'll usually have to do without. But you will be warned of this when you place your order.

www.sainsbury.co.uk
Browse the virtual aisles, enter a shopping list and find out about other services. Delivery is £5.

www.tesco.com
Tesco focuses slightly less on groceries, and more on extras such as electrical goods, clothes, flowers, music and videos. A special free PocketShopper mini-browser is available for users of PocketPCs.

www.asda.co.uk
Delivery is just £3.50, and the virtual store has one of the largest grocery selections of all the supermarkets. There are also special multi-pack shop-and-save deals, and gift selections.

www.waitrose.com
The quality is high, but there's a £50 minimum checkout total. You can pick up your goods from the store or have them delivered. There's a work-address delivery option for companies, and links to John Lewis online.

www.iceland.co.uk
The range is limited by Iceland's emphasis on frozen goods and meats, but prices are low and the coverage area is wide (97% of the UK).

Shop and plan with the Waitrose delivery service

Welcome to the internet grocery service that buys you time

register or sign in
Register or sign in to use WAITROSEdeliver

shop
Want to explore first? Click here to have a look.

enjoy
For lots of recipes, food advice and outstanding offers, click here.

are we in your area?
We are currently operating in a limited area. Click here for further details.

WAITROSE BY INVITATION

Christmas Turkeys
order by 12th Dec for delivery or collection on 22nd, 23rd, 24th December

More food and drink

www.chocexpress.com
Chocexpress offers many terrifyingly tempting pages full of all kinds of chocolates and chocolate selections.

www.hugecheesedirect.co.uk
Huge Cheese Direct certainly sells cheeses, but not necessarily huge ones. Choose from various speciality cheeses, and also chocolates, truffle oils and other gifts.

www.organicsdirect.co.uk
Organics Direct will deliver organic food to anywhere in the UK. Also available are eco-friendly kitchen goods, linens, and other accessories and extras.

www.foodfirst.co.uk
There's no online ordering at Food First, but the site includes a useful directory of quality food shops arranged by county.

www.beersofeurope.co.uk
In spite of the name, Beers of Europe sells beers from all over the world. This is probably the biggest selection of beers online.

www.superplonk.com
Superplonk is wine-writer Malcolm Gluck's online wine magazine. It offers special deals, and also recommendations and features to help you choose a wine.

www.the-home-brew-shop.co.uk
The Home Brew Shop has a rather basic design, but it sells everything for making your own alcoholic entertainment at home, for both beginners and advanced home brewers.

www.gourmet-world.co.uk
Gourmet World offers foods from around the world for gourmet shoppers. Free delivery on orders over £65.

www.virginwines.com
Virgin's wine site lists endless varieties according to various wine qualities – fruity, full bodied, etc. Mixed cases are available, and delivery costs less than £5 anywhere in the UK.

www.madaboutwine.com
There are thousands of varieties at Mad About Wine, including a special virtual cellar of expensive rare wines for the wine connoisseur.

A typical speciality item – a chocolate and champagne gift pack from Choc Express

Champagne & Chocolates

£29.95

Champagne & Chocolate Collections
Smart, boxed presentations to send direct or to hand over yourself. A winning combination. Champagne and chocolates...both are luxurious, hedonistic and celebratory. A box of exquisite hand-piped chocolates with a half-bottle of champagne 37.5cl, 250g.
Free delivery to UK mainland

Beers from all over the world, from Beers of Europe

INTRODUCING WINDOWS MEDIA PLAYER

What are MP3 files?

CD-quality audio takes up a lot of disk space. An hour-long CD would need around 600Mb if you copied it straight to your hard disk. MP3 files are created by an alternative recording system that offers slightly poorer sound quality in return for big space savings. The MP3 version of a one-hour CD would need only 60Mb of storage space. This makes MP3 files a convenient way of storing lots of music inside a PC. It also makes it possible to share music over the Internet. (For more information see page 75).

Your PC can be used as a CD player, music jukebox and DVD player. You can also use it to play home videos, or video CDs. Instead of having separate software for each of these, all versions of Windows that are more recent than Windows 98 include a single music- and video-playback tool called Media Player. (Note that in computer jargon, sound and video are often called 'media', or 'content.') Those with earlier versions of Windows can get Media Player from the cover CDs of most computer magazines.

Types of files Media Player can play

Type	Details	File extension
CDs	Simply insert the CD and Media Player starts automatically	n/a
Home videos	Use File → Open to load these before playing. There may be a delay while the file is scanned before playback starts	mpeg, .mpg, .avi, .wmv
MIDI files	These control a synthesiser built into your PC's soundcard, and typically sound rather crude and music-box-like	.mid
DVDs	The DVD player software (e.g. PowerDVD or WinDVD) supplied with your DVD drive or graphics card will usually be better. (For more about DVD player software, see www.digital-digest.com/dvd/downloads/playback.html)	n/a
MP3 files	Use File → Open and select one of the visualisation options (Tools → Options → Visualisations) to add moving patterns to the music	.mp3
Windows audio files	As with MP3 files	.wma
Internet radio stations	Select 'Radio Tuner' and click on a link	n/a
Streamed video	Click on a web link to start playback. Expect gaps and very poor quality if you are not using a broadband connection	n/a
Playlists	If you have a collection of music tracks, video clips or any other media on your hard disk, you can create a playlist that plays them in the order you want and save it for another time	.asx, .wax., .m3u, .wvx

Setting up Media Player

Media Player's default settings are not ideal, and you will almost certainly want to change these. Select Tools → Options and you will see the following tabbed window.

1. If the Player tab isn't shown, select it. You will want to make the following changes. For privacy, deselect 'Allow Internet sites to uniquely identify your Player'. While this is selected, it's possible for some sites to keep track of the content you are viewing.

2. For convenience, deselect 'Start player in Media Guide'. This will prevent Player from attempting to download a page full of music and video listings every time you start it.

3. Select 'File types' and choose which files you want to play using Player. If you are using an alternative such as Winamp for music (see page 67), deselect all those files that are associated with music and sound, including MP3 files, WAV files, and AIFF files.

Customising Media Player

Skins

Unlike other software, Media Player can have its look customised. This changes the location of the buttons, and the shape and colour of the player itself. This overall look is controlled by its 'skin'. By default, you have three skins to choose from – a standard plain look, a small miniaturised look and a rather extrovert green head. Select between skins by clicking on the 'Skin Chooser' tab, which appears at the bottom of the list of tabs when using the default plain skin. You can download more skins by clicking on the 'More Skins' button. This

takes to you to a page on Microsoft's website which shows a list of skins to choose from. You can add as many skin choices as you like. Designs vary from the pedestrian (variations on the standard look) to the unapologetically strange (pharaohs, flowers, cartoon characters).

Visualisations

Media Player can create a range of moving patterns and shapes when playing music. These are known as 'visualisations'. A reasonable collection is built into Media Player. To change the current visualisation select View → Visualisations and pick one from the list that appears. The small buttons at the bottom right of the Player window (when using the standard skin) will also switch between visualisations.

Using the Options menu choice to show Media Player's set-up options

Here's the mini skin...

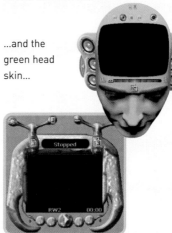

...and the green head skin...

...and a skin with strange tentacles

What is streamed content?

There are two ways to play Internet music and video clips. The first is to copy them to your hard disk. This is the most reliable option. But it is also very slow, especially if you are using dial-up. The alternative is called streaming. Streamed music and video are played directly over your Internet link – much as if there were a CD or video player at the other end of the link. Unlike file copying, streamed playback starts almost immediately. But playback can stutter and stall if the streaming isn't fast enough (and it often isn't). Streaming also means you never acquire a copy of the music or video.

MEDIA AND MEDIA PLAYER

3.2

Media and Media Player

Media competition

Why can't Media Player work with files from Apple and RealMedia? The short answer is competition for advertising. As you may have noticed, when you play or load a file into a player, advertising appears. This advertising is worth substantial sums, so each company has a strong interest in keeping its technology and its player software to itself. While it would be much more convenient for computer users to have a single piece of software that could play anything, this is unlikely to happen any time soon – if ever.

The Media Library

Click on Media Player's 'Media Library' tab and you'll see that it includes a library feature to help you organise your recordings, videos and other content. Every time you load something into Player, its details are added to the library. If you click on the audio or video tabs in the library window, you'll see a list of the files in your collection.

Creating and finding media

You can copy tracks from your CDs to your PC using Media Player's 'ripping' facility. This creates files in Microsoft's own WMA format. You can also create your own MP3 files, although for best results you will need external software to do this. (For more details see page 75.)

You can find a huge amount of music and video for free on the Internet. Many news and information sites include video material. (Note that to get the best results from this material you will need a broadband Internet connection.) When you click on the 'Media Guide' button, you will see some choices. These are usually commercial websites devoted to famous artists. While some people find plenty here to interest them, the Internet also includes more adventurous and less-polished material.
Some sites to explore include the following.

www.mp3.com – the Internet's biggest collection of free music by new artists. Also includes a subscription facility so that you can pay for tracks by commercial artists

www.movieflix.com – a more commercial and mainstream version of atomfilms. For $5.95 it's possible to download bigger-budget, more professional – but still not quite mainstream – releases. Also a good source of old classics

atomfilms.shockwave.com – free films to watch from up-and-coming film-makers, from experimental, to children's cartoons, to adult films

www.vitaminc.com – a smaller-scale UK equivalent of mp3.com

Internet radio

The Internet includes a large number of online radio stations. Instead of broadcasting using radio waves, they stream their programs to the Internet, where you can tune into them using your browser and Media Player. Some radio stations also archive their programmes, so you can catch up on things you may have missed.

www.shoutcast.com: one of the largest collections of small and independent Internet radio stations. It doesn't work with Media Player but with Winamp (see below), although the principle is the same

www.hos.com: Music from the Hearts of Space is an example of a medium-sized radio station devoted to experimental music that archives all of its programmes

Alternatives to Media Player

Media Player has three shortcomings. The first is that it can't handle every kind of media content. For example, it can't play Apple's QuickTime or RealMedia's Real Player files. To access them you will need to use one of the alternatives. The second is that it's not the best choice for working with MP3 files (see sidebar). If you plan to do a lot of recording from CDs to your own MP3 collections, it's a good idea to use something else. The third is that it is not the ideal tool for DVDs. Your DVD player almost certainly includes alternative DVD player software, such as CyberShot's PowerDVD, that works more reliably and has more features.

Winamp

Winamp is the best all-round music player. It's not a glamorous piece of software, but it is simple, easy to use and completely free. It's also very flexible, with support for CDs, Internet radio stations, MP3 files, MIDI files and all other kinds of audio. And it has plenty of customisation options available for free download from the main Winamp site, including skins and visualisations. For more details see www.winamp.com

Real Player

Real Player is a video alternative to Media Player. There are two versions – one free, and another with an improved specification that has to be paid for (about $30). Some websites include both video and audio in the Real format (.ram, .rm files), which can be played only using Real Player. A basic free version is included with all recent versions of Windows. This can be updated to either an improved free version or the paid-for version with a download.

Real Player is an essential extra, but it also advertises itself extremely aggressively. You will regularly see reminders about downloading the latest release and advertisements for its subscription scheme (you don't need this to use Real Player), and the download process strongly encourages you to pay for the more sophisticated version. The free version is adequate for most purposes, although if you watch a very large amount of content with it, it can be worth paying the extra for the upgrade. See www.real.com

Speed tip

The latest versions of RealPlayer, Winamp and QuickTime are often included for free on the CDs given away with computer magazines. You can save yourself the time taken to download from the Internet by installing them from CDs.

Apple Quick-time

Another alternative format you'll need to download and install is Quicktime. It's used on some web sites and to play .qt files. See www.apple.com/quicktime/download

SCANNERS AND DIGITAL CAMERAS

Not just paper. . .

You don't have to limit yourself to scanning photos or papers. If you're feeling creative, you can scan leaves and fabrics, and even small objects. As long as you keep the scanner's glass clean and free from scratches, you can experiment with scanning anything that will fit on it.

Scanners

A scanner is used to copy photos, text and other information from paper into a computer. The scanner literally scans the paper, converts what it sees into a computer-compatible image, and then shows this on the monitor. Most scanners are supplied with Optical Character Recognition (OCR) software, which can read text on a page, so that words on the page can be copied to a word processor for checking (the OCR process is never quite perfect) or editing.

Scanners once cost hundreds of pounds, but are now available for £50. More expensive models are faster and scan colours more accurately. But for casual work a cheap model is adequate. Apart from OCR features, a useful extra to watch for is software with a photocopy mode. This copies a scanned image directly to a printer.

Most scanners are limited to A4 size, and use the flatbed format – rather like a very thin photocopier. Document scanners are more like a bar with a slot in it for the paper to pass through. These can fit in the space in front of a monitor. But they are fiddly to work with and not often used. Slide scanners are designed to work with transparencies. They are used by photo enthusiasts.

The most important features to look for when buying a scanner include the following.

Resolution, measured in dots per inch (dpi)
Although values up to 9,600dpi are sometimes quoted, 2,400dpi is as much as anyone is likely to need in practice. In fact, 300dpi is enough for most work.

Colour depth
Colour depth specifies the scanner's ability to discriminate between similar shades. For casual work, '24-bit colour' is enough. Unless you are a designer or an artist, you are unlikely to need more.

Connection type
USB is the preferred choice. Older scanners use the parallel (printer) port system. These are best avoided now.

A budget scanner for home use

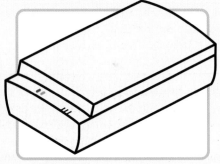

A professional scanner with improved colour accuracy and detail

A slide scanner, used to scan slides instead of printed matter

Digital cameras

The convenience of digital cameras is making them hugely popular. Not having to carry film or pay for development makes them a popular choice for all kinds of work. Prices are coming down, and it's possible to buy an affordable digital camera for holiday snaps, where previously film would have been the best choice. When buying a camera consider the following.

Resolution

This is the most important guide to picture quality. A digital image is made of a grid of dots, called pixels. The more pixels, the finer the image. Resolution is given either as an absolute pixel count horizontally and vertically (e.g. 640 x 480), or as a megapixel rating, which is equivalent to the two dimensions multiplied together and divided by a million (so a 640 x 480 camera has a 0.3 megapixel rating). As a guide, use the following table:

Dimensions	Mega pixels	Printed size (ins)	Typical use
640 x 480	0.3	3 x 2	Website snaps and other online work
1,024 x 768	0.7	5 x 3	Holiday snaps
1,280 x 1,024	1.3	6 x 4	Good holiday snaps
1,600 x 1,200	2	8 x 10	Semi-pro portraits, landscapes, etc.
2,048 x 1,536	3	A4 size	Low-end professional applications
Various	5	A3 or larger	Professional or very serious amateur

Memory

All cameras have limited memory, which can be expanded with extra plug-in cards. These come in three types – compact flash, Smartmedia and Sony's memory stick system, which works only with Sony's own cameras. To work out how much memory you need for each shot, multiply the megapixel rating by three. So a 3MP camera will need 9Mb of memory for each photo. In practice, photos are compressed so that they take up less room, and the real value may be up to one-tenth as much, albeit with some loss of quality. As a rule, the higher the megapixel rating, the more memory you will need and the more expensive this will be. Currently, a 128Mb memory card, which can store up to 100 photos, costs about £35. When buying memory, be sure to shop around for the best price. A fourth memory system, known as an IBM microdrive, uses a tiny disk drive to store photos, and is popular with professionals. This offers near-infinite storage of 1Gb, although it currently costs around £250.

Connection system

Newer cameras use USB, older cameras use serial connections. Note that some new PCs are being made without serial ports, so you may find that your old camera will become obsolete. USB is by far the better choice. Professional cameras use either Firewire or a system known as SCSI ('Scuzzy'). Both need extra hardware that isn't usually installed in a typical PC. Again, check with a dealer what the requirements are. Most cameras are supplied with simple picture-viewing software. Some also include a photo-editing tool such as Adobe Elements (see page 70).

For many people, the convenience of digital trumps the higher picture quality of film, and even the lower cost of cheap film cameras. Some colour printers now have a digital camera connection feature, so you can print your images without a PC. And of course you can have snaps printed from digital shots as easily as from film. However, film remains a better choice if you need the very best image quality.

THE DIGITAL DARKROOM

Popular image editors

Paint Shop Pro 5
Old, but still very useful.
No longer on sale, but occasionally given away free with magazines

Paint Shop Pro 7
The current version, with added features. An excellent all-rounder, and good value (about £50)

Adobe Photoshop Elements
The beginner's budget version of Photoshop (£80)

Adobe Photoshop
The professional's choice. Photoshop takes a long time to master, but does almost everything (£400)

Your digital camera and scanner will include software that copies images to your PC. To work with them you will need image-editing software. Although Windows allows for some very basic image editing, for most work you will need to buy a more powerful package (see sidebar).

Getting organised
When you copy photos or scans to your PC, it's an excellent idea to organise them by date, or in some other familiar and recognisable way. Windows includes a 'My Pictures' folder, in which you can create sub-folders. Most software includes a 'thumbnail' feature which will show you small versions of the images inside a folder to jog your memory.

Tools of the trade
Most editing software includes the same basic tools and features. (Professional software adds more advanced options to these, such as automation for repeated tasks, precise colour control, preparation for printing and desktop publishing, and so on.) Once you learn the basics, you will have mastered most of what there is to know about practical digital photo editing. Tools typically appear on a 'toolbar' like this one from Paint Shop Pro 7.

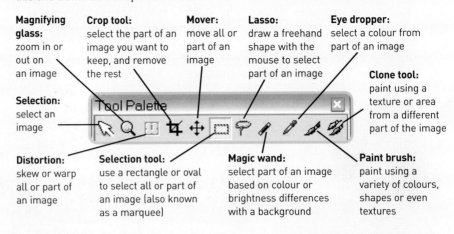

Magnifying glass: zoom in or out on an image

Crop tool: select the part of an image you want to keep, and remove the rest

Mover: move all or part of an image

Lasso: draw a freehand shape with the mouse to select part of an image

Eye dropper: select a colour from part of an image

Clone tool: paint using a texture or area from a different part of the image

Selection: select an image

Distortion: skew or warp all or part of an image

Selection tool: use a rectangle or oval to select all or part of an image (also known as a marquee)

Magic wand: select part of an image based on colour or brightness differences with a background

Paint brush: paint using a variety of colours, shapes or even textures

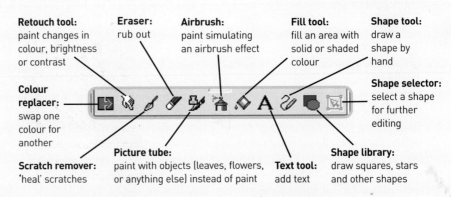

Retouch tool: paint changes in colour, brightness or contrast

Eraser: rub out

Airbrush: paint simulating an airbrush effect

Fill tool: fill an area with solid or shaded colour

Shape tool: draw a shape by hand

Colour replacer: swap one colour for another

Shape selector: select a shape for further editing

Scratch remover: 'heal' scratches

Picture tube: paint with objects (leaves, flowers, or anything else) instead of paint

Text tool: add text

Shape library: draw squares, stars and other shapes

Basic editing

The most obvious changes you can make are very simple. You'll find these options among the menu choices.

Our starting point

Change brightness and contrast

Remove all colour

Intensify and shift the colours

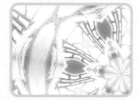
Paint Shop Pro's kaleidoscope filter

Posterisation

But you can also easily aim for far more extreme and creative effects. To produce these you will need to use filters, which come free with your software, and plug-ins, which are available as optional extras (see sidebar). These often have unlikely and even incomprehensible names, so the best way to find out what they do is to experiment.

An ultrasphere effect created with a free plug-in

Photoshop's zoom blur

Paint Shop Pro's unsharp mask filter

Splitting red, green and blue elements with a free plug-in

Photoshop's diffuse glow filter

Instant Pop Art with a free plug-in from the set known as Harry's Filters

What are plug-ins?

Packages such as Paint Shop Pro and Photoshop contain a way of adding extra filters and other facilities to the main program. These 'plug in' to the software. Once installed, they appear as menu choices. There are hundreds of free plug-ins available on the Web. You can also buy commercial examples. Plug-ins vary from simple but useful tools such as colour/contrast/balance/sharpness enhancement, to extremely strange and potentially very creative trans-formations. For more details search the Web for 'free plug-ins' and the name of your software.

RETOUCHING OLD PHOTOS

Retouching old photos 3.5

How does the clone tool work?

Cloning is almost the next best thing to a magic wand for retouching work. Select the 'Cloning' tool, and right click somewhere on a photo. Now hold the left mouse button down and start to draw or paint. The clone tool literally copies the area under your movements from one part of the image to the other. For example, if you have a patch of sky, you can make it bigger by selecting it with a right click, and painting over another part of the photo.

A popular use for photo editing is retouching old photos. Having photos retouched by a professional can be very expensive. With even a basic photo-editing package, such as Paint Shop Pro 7, which was used here, it's possible to produce results of similar quality at home. While it helps to have some artistic skill, effective retouching isn't as difficult as perhaps it seems – even for beginners.

Here's our starting scan of a wedding group from 1914. The picture has faded badly and there's barely any contrast.

The first step is to enhance the brightness and contrast. You can use Paint Shop Pro's Brightness/Contrast menu option (Colors → Adjust → Brightness/Contrast) to make a start. But under Colors → Adjust → Histogram Adjustment, you'll find a histogram tool. This graphs the number of pixels in the image at different brightness levels. Even if you don't understand the theory, you can experiment with the controls to see what they do, and how they stretch the contrast range of the image. Ideally, you want a brightness range with full black at one extreme and any highlights just touching full white at the other.

Tattered edges all around the photo

Scratches and folds at the corners

Scratches and folds on some of the faces

Uneven shape – the whole right-hand side of the photo isn't properly square

Badly damaged area at the bottom of the wedding dress

With the brightness and contrast enhanced, now we can see just how damaged the image is. Blemishes, dirt and marks everywhere

If you zoom in close on an old photo like this one (use the magnifying glass tool) you'll see that it's covered in imperfections and blemishes. Although it's possible to remove every last one, this will take a long time. A better approach is to remove the most obvious faults and leave the rest.

Here's how we've repaired the photo. The most useful tool is the clone tool, which 'paints' a copy from one part of the image over another, like an intelligent brush. It's a great way to fill in textures that look natural but in fact are just copies. The finished photo looks much better, and could easily be printed and framed.

Cloning can look obvious if done too blatantly. It's easy to get an unwanted layered or repeating effect. The solution is to clone from as much of the image as possible, so that textures look random rather than obviously copied. In the example here, it works well with the foliage, because foliage is just a texture and doesn't need detail. It's more of a challenge for the bottom of the dress, because it falls in layers that need to be kept distinct. So here we've been careful to clone only from adjacent areas so that the layers appear clear. Faces are hardest of all. You may need to zoom right in on a face and clone very tiny areas, being careful to make sure the whole face always looks convincing.

Some blemishes have been removed, especially on the faces and the dark suits. The others are left to keep a period feel

You don't have to stop with simple retouching. The original photo has an authentic sepia tone. If you convert it to black and white (known as greyscale), you can then colour in (by hand) tiny areas on faces, hands, clothes and backgrounds. If you find this tricky with the mouse, use the magnifying glass tool to blow up the image so that you can see and colour each pixel individually. Or you can use the lasso tool to draw around each area you want to tint, then use the Colorize option (Colors → Colorize) to add a colour tint to each area. The process can be very time-consuming, but the results can have an appealing antique hand-drawn look – even though they're completely digital.

MP3 FILES

Setting recording quality

The sound quality of MP3 files is expressed as a number of bits/second (b/s). The standard setting for MP3s is 128Kb/s. This offers a good trade-off between sound quality and size, and is also more likely to play properly in a hardware player. You'll find an option to set this rate in every piece of MP3 ripping software that you use. A setting of 256Kbp/s is passably close to CD quality, but 64Kbp/s is noticeably rough and distorted.

MP3 files, which are files used for recording music, have been one of the PC world's great success stories. Ironically, this is largely because they make it convenient for people to flout legal and commercial copyright restrictions. As MP3 files are relatively small, it is easy to record a copy of a song and send it to all of one's friends.

Sending files by email is not always painless, especially for those with a dial-up connection, so MP3 file-sharing services evolved to make it easier to exchange music. To use these sharing services (also known as P2P services – short for 'peer to peer'), you placed all your MP3 files in a special folder on your disk. When you logged on to the service, the files in your folder were added to a huge searchable listing. If people looked through the list and found you had a file they wanted, the service made it easy for them to copy it from your disk to theirs.

Names such as Napster and AudioGalaxy came and went in the space of a couple of years towards the end of the last century. While active, they attracted huge interest from Internet users, who discovered a way to get music for free. But all this copying wasn't legal, and so they were eventually closed down by the world's record companies. A small number of sharing services, such as Kazaa.com, remain, but they are much less active than they once were.

MP3s in action

If file sharing doesn't appeal, what is the attraction of MP3s? The first is that you can buy a hardware MP3 player (a little like a Walkman, but with no moving parts), in which you can store songs by connecting it to your PC and copying your favourite songs across. The second reason is that you can create a store of your favourite songs on hard disk. You can turn your PC into the ultimate jukebox: a typical 40Gb hard disk has room for more than 10,000 three-minute pop songs. By creating your own playlists (see page 76) you can combine your favourite songs into your own compilations. Unlike CDs, which are limited to around 80 minutes of music, a playlist can last for hours (or, indeed, days).

Windows Media Player

Copying music from a CD is known as 'ripping' and this feature is included in Windows Media Player. It's important to realise that when you rip songs to your disk, you're not making a perfect copy; the sound quality always suffers slightly. You won't notice a big change if you are ripping pop music and listening to it on small plastic speakers. But if your tastes run to classical music or playing music through a good hifi, the differences may be more audible. It's possible to make absolutely perfect copies of the music on a CD, but you need special software to do this. (And don't forget that a perfect copy of the music on a CD will need around 650Mb of disk space!)

Practical ripping

Ripping CDs with Media Player is very easy. Here's a step-by-step guide.

1. Insert the CD in your PC's drive, start Media Player if it's not running already, and select 'Copy from CD'. You'll see a list of songs, all of which will be checked. Uncheck the ones you don't want to record. Then click on the 'Copy music' button above the track list. Media Player will rip the tracks.

2. Media Player will add them to the music library. With a modern PC the ripping process is very quick – much faster than the speed at which the music plays. You can even continue to listen to other music while you're ripping.

3. By default, Media Player rips to WMA files. These are Microsoft's own format. They are smaller than MP3s and can sound better. But they're not as easy to share, and not many hardware players can play them. To add MP3 ripping you will need to buy an add-on for Media Player. Click on Tools → Options, select the 'Copy Music' tab and then click on the 'MP3 Information' button. This will take you to a page on Microsoft's site that shows you some MP3 add-on products. Choose one – there's very little difference between them, and they all cost around £10 – and follow the instructions on

how to pay for it, copy it to your PC and install it. (For more about copying and installing software from the Internet see page 144.) The next time you use Media Player, the Copy Music tab will show an option to rip to MP3 files. See also section 3.7.

MP3s and the law

If you copy of a piece of music for your own use at home or in your car, you are within the law. If you share that copy with someone else, you are breaking the law. This applies particularly to sharing your MP3 on a file-sharing service such as Kazaa (for details see www.kazaa.com), but also to making compilations for friends. MP3s are not any more or any less legal than any other music format. It's what you do with them that matters.

Ripping from tape and records

Media Player can't rip from tapes and records directly: you'll need some extra software. Roxio's CD Creator (around £50) and Steinberg's Clean (around £20) are two good choices, but you will find possible alternatives in any large PC store. Ripping from older media is a three-stage process: Record → Clean → Save to disk. The cleaning process can work surprisingly well, but it can't perform miracles, especially with very old recordings. Be sure to allow plenty of disk space for the recording and cleaning process!

PLAYLISTS, CDS AND MP3 HARDWARE

CD protection

Some CDs are now being sold with copy protection. They will play in an ordinary CD player, but the music data has been deliberately tampered with to make it impossible to play them on a PC or copy the music from them. While you can't rip music from these CDs, you can sometimes clone them – i.e. make an exact copy. A product to try is Blindwrite from VSO Software (www.vso-software.fr).

A playlist is a list of your favourite music tracks arranged in the order you want to hear them. Creating a playlist is very much like creating a special running order on a CD player. The difference is that you can make a playlist as long as you like. If you have 200 songs stored on your hard disk, you can create a playlist that will play all of them. With a typical duration of 3 minutes per song, this means more than 11 hours of non-stop music. You can create as many different playlists as you like, to suit different moods and occasions.

Creating playlists

To create a playlist from the library, select the 'Media Library' tab, and then click on the 'New Playlist' button at the top of the window. Type in a name for your new list. You can now add tracks by opening each group of tracks and dragging them to the playlist with the mouse. To rearrange the playlist, drag tracks up and down.

To create a CD version of your playlist, insert a blank CD into the CD drive and click on the tab named 'Copy to CD or Device' at the left. Note that you can do this only if the playlist will fit on to a CD. This means it has to be less than 80 minutes long.

Early versions of Windows XP have a bug (i.e. a problem), which means that if you take out a music CD and replace it with a blank one, Windows doesn't notice. It still thinks that the music CD is in your drive, and complains if you try to burn music to it. Unfortunately, there is only one way to get around this – you will need to restart your PC. Once Windows is ready, select File → Copy to Audio CD, and Windows will write your playlist to a music CD.

Note that you can copy your MP3s and music files to a CD as files. These won't play in most older standard CD players. However, some newer DVD players and CD players include an MP3 file playback feature, which play MP3 files as if they were ordinary CD tracks.

Using the Media Player playlist. Note that Media Player also has a 'tuner presets' option. For those times when you would rather listen to someone else's playlist than create your own, there are many Internet radio stations you can tune into. Select the tuner presets option to be shown some of them

MP3s and WAVs

By default, Media Player uses Microsoft's own Windows Media format. If you'd like to use the more popular MP3 format, you'll have to pay a small amount (about £10) to download and install an extension to Media Player. Links to websites that sell this extension are included within Media Player.

If you want perfect CD copies and the ability to create true CD-quality compilations, you will need to rip tracks to the WAV format. This feature isn't available in Media Player. Two popular alternatives are Nero's Burning ROM and Roxio's CD Creator. These can rip CDs to WAV files, and then arrange these in order on a CD to make a compilation. They are fairly inexpensive (about £60) and easy to use. They also offer other advanced features that are not included in Media Player, such as the ability to edit music and sound, to create DVD safety copies of other information in your PC (see page 104) and to create CDs that can play on both PCs and Macs.

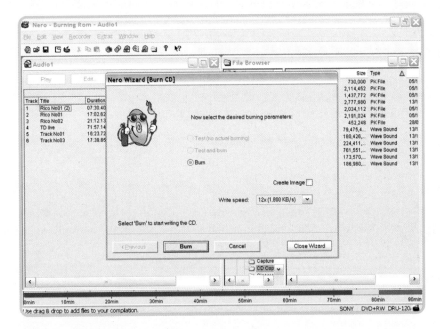

Burning a home-made CD in Nero using ripped tracks. Nero and CD Creator have more sophisticated CD-burning features than Media Player

MP3 hardware

While CDs are good for use in the home and in the car, they're rather bulky to carry. Hardware MP3 players are a better choice for joggers and commuters. Most have no moving parts, and music is copied to them directly from your PC. Some models, such as Apple's iPod, include a small hard disk instead of solid-state memory, and have the capacity to hold an entire CD collection. Some are even key-ring-sized. Media Player includes a feature that will transfer a playlist and the songs in it directly to an MP3 player. Select File → Copy → Copy to portable device.

Over the next few years it will become harder and harder to create your own compilations. Record companies are keen to minimise piracy, and they are putting pressure on manufacturers of PC software and hardware to create technology that makes piracy very hard. A future version of Windows, currently known as Palladium and scheduled for release around 2006, is likely to include some form of DRM. With DRM, it's likely you won't even be able to make safety copies of CDs for your own use.

SPEAKERS AND SOUNDCARDS

Choosing speakers

If you get the chance to listen to speakers before buying them, then do so. Official 'music power' or other ratings you sometimes see in advertising are worthless, and tell you nothing about volume or sound quality. But sound quality does vary, sometimes dramatically. Apart from a simple listening test, it's also worth watching a speaker's power-on light. If this flashes or dims while music is playing at a comfortable volume, there isn't much power to spare, and sound quality suffers.

Speakers

Your PC would almost certainly have come with a pair of budget plastic speakers, and a built-in soundcard. Both will be adequate for casual music listening. Here are some alternatives for better sound.

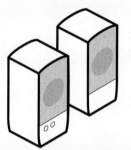

The standard, basic PC set up –
two small budget speakers

The cheapest upgrade – a link to your hifi.
Ask your hifi store which connecting leads you need.
If you use your hifi, you can get some powerful, rich and deep sounds for very little extra money. But be careful with the volume. Some PC sounds (especially the notorious 'ding' used by Windows 95, 98 and ME) are very loud

A better system – two budget speakers and a larger speaker known as a subwoofer for added bass.
This adds depth to music and gives games more impact and presence.
From £25

The ultimate system – five speakers and a subwoofer. With this set-up you can listen to DVDs in surround sound, and get the most from games. But you will need a soundcard designed for '5.1' sound, and also room behind you.
From £50 to £200+ speakers will fit conveniently either side of a monitor

Soundcards

Soundcards vary from simple budget models costing about £10 to professional-quality hardware costing hundreds suitable for use in recording studios. All soundcards include the same basic features.

A microphone input: plug in your microphone here. Recording quality is usually mediocre, but good enough for voice recognition when word processing, and also for Internet-based telephone calls

Line in: Plug in your hifi here. Use a tape output or an AUX output. (Don't connect a turntable directly. You won't damage anything, but it will be too quiet and will sound very tinny and harsh)

Line output: this is where you plug in your speakers

Joystick port: although it doesn't make a noise, if you have an older game joystick it plugs in here. You can also use this connector as a MIDI interface, with a special adaptor

Digital ins and outs: S/PDIF is typically on standard phonos (exactly like on the back of a hifi amp): red for out, white for in, or on mini jacks as shown on the website

Synthesiser: All soundcards include a simple and cheap music synthesiser that can play MIDI files

Optional extras

More expensive soundcards add or replace these basics with extra options. Prices vary from £50 to about £200, depending on sound quality and features.

Optical digital input and output: connect to a CD or minidisk recorder here

Phono S/PDIF digital input and output: connect to a CD player. Also used for semi-professional home-studio recording

Separate 5.1 outputs: an extra stereo output for surround. And perhaps an extra connection for the subwoofer too

Better synthesiser: more expensive cards include more realistic synthesiser sounds

Game support: some cards include special audio-enhancement features for games. These improve the surround effect or give sounds more depth and space

MIDI (musical instrument digital interface) is the way that computers and synthesisers communicate. Think of it as a kind of electronic piano roll – the computer uses MIDI instead of punched paper to tell a synthesiser which notes to play. It can also tell the synthesiser which instruments and sounds to use. MIDI only specifies which notes to play and when. The synthesiser converts that information into sounds.

MIDI FILES AND DIGITAL MUSIC

A better sound?

If you want to improve on the sounds in your soundcard, you can buy and install a better soundcard, install a software synthesiser, or buy a separate keyboard synthesiser. A software synthesiser is the best and cheapest option. This simulates a music synthesiser entirely in software, so you can keep your existing soundcard but improve the sound quality. A good choice is Yamaha's XG range, which is available as a download for about $50. See www.yamaha musicsoft.com for more details.

Using MIDI

MIDI (musical instrument digital interface) is the modern equivalent of player piano technology. A MIDI file creates music by telling a simple synthesiser built into your PC's soundcard which notes to play and when to play them. The synthesiser can simulate the sound of many different instruments. However, some soundcards are better than others. A more expensive soundcard will produce a more recognisable and satisfying rendition of a MIDI file.

MIDI files are often used to provide background music for web pages. The files are tiny – usually no more than 10 or 20Kb – and so can be downloaded very quickly. Web browsers will download and play a MIDI file automatically. If you'd like to experiment further with MIDI files, use a search engine to look for 'MIDI file'. You will find a long list of websites that are MIDI file libraries. You can download the files and then play them using Media Player, or even add them to your own website.

A more creative approach is to compose your own music. To do this you will need a sequencer – a piece of software that lets you edit, arrange and play notes, and define which sounds they will play on your soundcard. The best sequencers show you the notes either on a music staff – which assumes you can read music – or using a simpler piano-roll display. One of the best commercial products is Steinberg's Cubasis, which costs less than £100 and also includes sound recording and editing. It's also worth searching the Web for 'MIDI sequencer' to see some of the less-well-known alternatives.

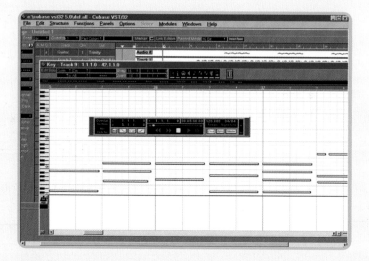

Using piano-roll editing in Cubase, an expensive alternative to Cubasis, to compose a MIDI file. Each bar is like a slot in a piano roll. The whole page scrolls towards the left, and when a bar passes under the keyboard a note plays. The coloured stripes in the background provide an overview of the MIDI information for the other instruments used in this song

Sample-based music

An alternative approach to making music with a PC is to use samples or loops. These are tiny recordings, typically one, two or four bars long. By laying out these samples on a grid, it's possible to compose a very impressive and professional-sounding piece of music. The cheapest software is limited to the tempo and key of the original sample. More advanced products, such as Sonic Foundry's Acid range (see below), can automatically match the tempo of different samples, so that they all play at the same tempo whether or not they were recorded at the same tempo. It's also possible to modify and mix samples using similar techniques to those used in professional recording studios.

In theory, the possibilities of sample-based music are unlimited and it's certainly true that this music-by-numbers approach doesn't need much musical knowledge. Currently, sample-based music can't easily be used on the Web as background music in the way that MIDI files can. Manufacturers of the various sample-based software products have their own websites, where music creators can share their work with others. But there's no simple way to build sample-based music into your website.

Many sample-based music packages are available. Many use the word 'DJ' in the name. (Sample layering is similar to the way that club DJs work.) Products to watch for, in increasing order of cost, include the eJay (www.ejay-uk.com) series, the range of products from Magix (www.magix.com), and Sonic Foundry's Acid range (www.sonicfoundry.com). Most of these include extra features beyond simple sample layering, such as the ability to create your own rhythm loops, process samples in various creative ways, and even to burn your music on to a CD or save it as an MP3 file.

It's important to realise that MIDI files of popular songs and music that use samples from those songs are subject to copyright restrictions. This means that legally speaking, you're not allowed to use these MIDI files or samples on a website without first getting permission from the copyright owner.

And coming up next...?

The MIDI system is slightly dated now. The future MP4 (MPEG4) format can specify sounds as well as notes. In fact, it can create almost any sound imaginable. But it requires expert skills and the format is not yet widely used. A simpler alternative is a sample-based system, such as Beatnik (www.beatnik.com).

Composing a song using HipHop eJay – one of the eJay series which includes HipHop samples and HipHop-style artwork. Each block in the top part of the window is a single sound sample, usually one bar long. Layering the samples and offsetting creates the arrangement. Part of the sample library is shown by the brown blocks at the bottom

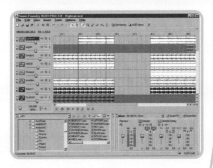

Sonic Foundry's Acid uses a similar approach, but with less creative artwork. The sliders at the left control the volume of each track. Volume changes and other kinds of effects can be automated

GETTING STARTED WITH VIDEO

Adding sounds and music

Video software typically lets you edit sound as well as picture. You can dub music and sound effects, fade sounds in and out, and add special sound distortions – for example, a telephone effect to a voice. The details of how to do this are too involved to explain fully here, but your software's manual will have some examples to get you started.

Many people have video cameras to record clips of their children growing up, school events, carnivals, fêtes and other celebrations, and all kinds of social gatherings. With a computer, any video footage you shoot can be edited at home to create professional results. You can cut out sections that don't work, rearrange sections that do, and use a range of professional tricks to add titles and special effects, and transitions between scenes. When the video is finished, you can save a final production copy in various formats, suitable for distribution on CD, video tape, the Internet or even your own home-made DVDs.

You can therefore create your own mini-documentaries about other hobbies and interests, or about holidays and trips abroad. More ambitious projects include making your own short film or pop video. And if you have a website, you can add video clips of yourself, your family or your pets to it.

While editing videos can be very enjoyable, you will need a fast, modern computer to get the most enjoyment from it. Video editing is one of the few jobs that really does need the best possible hardware, including a speedy processor, and plenty of memory and disk space. While you can work without these, you will spend a lot of time waiting for each edit. Any computer bought since 2000 will be adequate, although the higher its specifications, the faster you will be able to work.

Editing with Adobe Premiere

Transition line:
sets how clips fade into each other

Monitor window:
previews the video

Clip bin:
source material goes here

Transitions list:
a list of video effects and different transitions

Timeline:
video clips go here

Audio line:
audio can be edited as easily as video

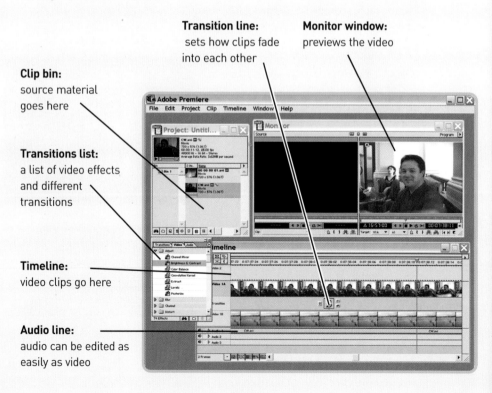

Tools of the trade

A video camera could cost anything between £250 and £2,000, with a reasonable-quality one available from about £600 upwards. Different formats are available, with assorted tape sizes and recording qualities. MiniDV is the best choice for high-quality results. Digital8 is less good; Hi8 even less so. Check for Firewire/iLink connectors, which will copy video directly to and from your PC with no quality loss. Auto-focus, programmed auto-exposure (ProgramAE) and a high-quality glass lens are other features to look out for. Ideally, check for video sharpness and colour accuracy before buying. Size, shape and weight are also very important. Features such as built-in lights, low-light ('0 lux') recording, stop motion, and so on, are useful as extras but are not essential.

A capture card: this pipes video to and from the camera or other recorder. Prices range from £70 for simple Firewire/iLink video in and out to more than £2,000 for advanced editing features and professional software. Some cards include composite video or RGB connectors that are compatible with TVs and VCRs – a useful feature if you want to record your finished video to VHS tape

Windows XP includes a simple video-editing tool called Windows Movie Maker. This is quite basic, but adequate for editing holiday videos and other light use. Budget (about £100) products are available from companies such as Pinnacle, Miro and Ulead. These include some extra features, such as more sophisticated editing tools and the ability to add text titles. Adobe Premiere (about £450) is a good choice for more serious editing, and includes special effects that yield professional results. Recently, affordable DVD-creation tools have begun to appear, which make it possible to burn a simple DVD that will play in most players, if you have a DVD burner.

Options and extras

For more serious video work, a good tripod (from £80 upwards) is a very useful extra. For very serious work, professional lighting makes a huge difference to the quality of recordings. Kits are available from £300 upwards. Most cameras are supplied with cheap, small-capacity rechargeable batteries that will run a camera for perhaps only 20 minutes or so. You may need to spend more than £50 for batteries with higher capacity and a longer running time.

Windows Movie Maker
(see section 3.11)

The need for speed

High-quality video editing is very demanding on your PC's hardware. You will need the fastest PC possible, and plenty of hard-disk space – preferably 20Gb or more free, even for fairly short videos. Even then you can expect to spend a lot of time waiting for edits to finish and the video to be created.

Size and weight

Size and weight are very important when choosing a camera. Camcorders can be heavy and bulky, and for casual holiday use it makes sense to get the smallest and lightest model you can find. For more serious work, the extra weight can help stabilise a camera, especially when used on a tripod.

CREATING YOUR OWN VIDEOS

Fade to black

If you want to fade to black between clips, create a solid black still using a graphics program and import it. Use the transitions feature to fade the surrounding clips into black. Imported stills are stretched or squashed auto-matically so that they will always be the right size for the video.

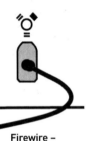

Firewire – records sound and video with digital quality

Analogue – records video with analogue quality. Sound is recorded through your soundcard (see also section 3.13)

Windows XP includes a simple video editor called Windows Movie Maker (All Programs → Accessories → Windows Movie Maker). It has almost everything you need to create and edit your own videos. Creating a video is a five-stage process.

1. Capture – i.e. record – the raw material. Raw, unedited video sequences are called rushes, or raw footage. Connect your computer to the sockets on the back of your video card. Make sure you record the sound too, by connecting the sound out from the camcorder to the line in on your soundcard. It's a good idea to create a special folder for the raw footage to keep it separate from other projects. Movie Maker assumes you have an analogue capture card (see page 83). If you have a Firewire card and a camcorder with an iLink or Firewire connector, you can transfer information digitally – but you'll need to use the software that came with your card to capture the video, because unfortunately Movie Maker can't copy directly via Firewire.

2. Import and edit your material. Select File → Import and load your rushes. Each clip will appear as a collection and will be split into scenes automatically. Windows does this by checking to see if the footage changes suddenly, and copies the footage to a new scene every time it does. Even so, scenes will almost certainly have extra unwanted material at the beginning and end. They may also be in the wrong order. Movie Maker includes tools to solve both these problems. Along the bottom is a filmstrip called the timeline. Drag scenes on to the timeline in the order you want them to appear. To trim the start and end of each scene, click on the tiny filmstrip icon near the bottom left. Move the slider points at the start and end to change the length of a clip.

Clip collections

Preview your clips and the finished video here

Scene trim sliders

The clip shown here only contains a single scene

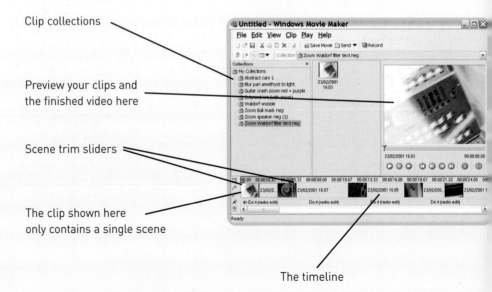

The timeline

3. Add titles and transitions. When you place trimmed scenes on the timeline, by default they'll cut abruptly from one to the next. Movie Maker can create simple fade transitions. Click and drag a clip so that it overlaps the one at the left. You'll see a transition graphic appear, and when you preview the clip (Play → Play Entire Storyboard/Timeline), the new clip will fade in. To add titles, use a graphics editor (see page 70). Microsoft Paint (All Programs → Accessories → Paint) will do if you have nothing else. Create and save a page of text and import the file into Movie Maker. It will appear as a five-second still. To change the length, use the scene trim sliders.

4. Add music or narration. Movie Maker lets you add one layer of background speech or music. You can either import the music from a file or record it yourself live. (File → Record or Record Narration.) Drag the music on to the audio track next to the tiny microphone at the left. Note that music you have ripped from CD using Media Player (see page 74) can't be used for copyright reasons. If you rip the music with other software, or create your own music (see page 81) you should be able to import it easily.

5. Save the finished video. When you have finished creating your video, you can save it to disk, or attach it directly to an email. Go to File → Save movie. (Note: the 'Send to web server' option doesn't currently work in the UK.)

Creating a simple title using Paint and a font copied from the Internet (see page 92). You can, of course, use a different graphics editor if you have one. This title screen will be static. Unlike the titles you see on TV it won't scroll – i.e. move upwards as you watch

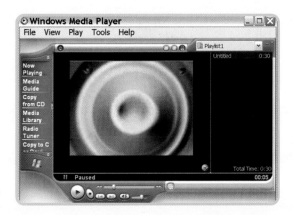

Here's the finished video playing in Media Player. With a suitable video card it's possible to copy this playback to a VCR

As with digital photography, video is recorded using a grid of pixels. For video there is also a frame rate, which is the number of picture frames a second. For emailing or putting up on a website, use the default medium quality 320 pixels x 240 pixels setting at 15 frames a second, which is a good compromise between size and quality.

MORE ABOUT VIDEO

Products to watch for

Pinnacle's Studio Series, Ulead's Video Studio and **Roxio's Video Impression**
At less than £100, all of these offer very useful extra features beyond those provided by Movie Maker.

Sonic Foundry's Vegas Video and **Ulead Media Studio**
At between £300-£400, these are popular alternatives to Premiere.

Adobe Premiere
The standard semi-professional editing package – the video version of Photoshop, about £450.

Adobe AfterEffects
For special effects. Too complicated and expensive for casual video-making, but essential for music videos and serious small films. Between £450 and £1,200.

Windows Movie Maker is a good choice for beginners and for those who want to dabble with editing home and holiday videos. But its features are rather limited, and it's not the best choice for someone who wants to create home-made DVDs, or put up interesting video clips on a website. Paid-for alternatives to Movie Maker include a much richer set of features. While you can pay hundreds or even thousands of pounds for professional packages such as Adobe Premiere or AfterEffects, it's possible to buy editing software with many semi-professional features for less than £100.

Firewire support Being able to record digitally from your camcorder and also control it remotely is very useful. Many packages include a batch-capture feature, which lets you specify which clips you want to record from a long tape. You can of course record the entire tape and edit it down later, but smaller clips are easier to work with and use less disk space.

More transitions Transitions vary from the simple crossfades available in Movie Maker to very complex animated effects where scenes can shatter, rotate and spin in and out of the picture. Between these extremes are relatively simple geometric transitions, including opening barn doors, expanding stars and spirals, and sliding bar effects.

This still from an abstract video sequence was created in Ulead's Media Studio by boosting the intensity of the colours in a deliberately blurred video

Video effects Corrective effects can fix footage that was shot badly, and also create black and white, negative image and other special effects. For creative effects, the sky is the limit. Many of the effects that can be applied to photo stills (see page 71) can also be applied to video. It's also possible to superimpose selectively parts of one video clip on to another. This effect, called chroma keying, is used for the weather forecast on TV.

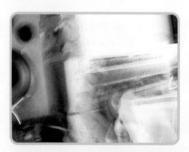

Better sound editing Whereas Movie Maker is limited to a single sound recording, other software makes it easy to add multiple layers. You can therefore record a voiceover and then edit out any fluffed lines or mistakes. You can also get controls for the tone and balance, as well as audio effects like echo.

Better titles Being able to superimpose titles on top of the video is essential for almost any serious video editing. Some packages go much further than this. Adobe's Premiere includes a selection of pre-set title themes which look very sophisticated and professional.

Premiere's titling templates can give a very sophisticated impression

Computer animation

With a computer, you're not limited to videos you've shot with a camcorder. You can also make your own 3D computer animations. Animation software manipulates shapes and backgrounds, controlling their position, colour and texture, and keeping track of all the relationships and connections between the shapes. As you design a virtual scene you can build complex objects out of simple shapes, specify their colour, texture and transparency. You can also add lights to illuminate the scene. The finishing touch is to define an animated virtual camera so that you can look inside your new world. The better the software, the more features it has for working with shapes, and the more shapes it includes. Cheaper software can work only with simple objects such as 3D text, cubes, spheres and cones. More expensive software can easily deal with objects like trees, mountains and human figures.

Simple 3D

Tools like Xara 3D and Ulead's Cool3D offer very simple 3D animations. In Xara 3D you can choose the text you want to animate, pick a font, add some lights, specify colours and textures, and define how you'd like the 3D text to spin. These simple 3D animations and text are often used on web pages.

Animated letters created using Xara 3D. This scene took fewer than five minutes to create. The arrows show virtual lights that light the letters

3D scene design

A more complicated package such as Procreate's Bryce can do very much more. Bryce comes with a library of simple shapes, and some basic tools for designing more complicated shapes. It also includes an impressive range of attractive textures, including metal, glass, fire, clouds and various abstract textures. Skies, waves, clouds, the moon and sun and other astronomical features are also available. Animation is done by using a timeline to specify changes in position, size, rotation and appearance at points called keyframes. The software fills in the gaps between keyframes automatically. Bryce can save animated sequences as video files. It can produce very attractive results, but is better at futuristic science fiction scenes than naturalistic ones.

Speed and power

The Bryce illustration on the bottom left, which is a single frame from a short animation, took 50 seconds to render – i.e. calculate, save and display – on a 2.2GHz PC. Each second of animation requires 25 frames, rendered in sequence. So a one-minute clip will take almost an entire day to render! Even though Bryce is quite slow, it should be obvious that to achieve complicated animations you need both a very fast PC and an almost inexhaustible supply of patience.

In this Bryce scene the metal spheres reflect their neighbours and the sky

Bryce includes a library of built-in textures. You can look at and combine them in this texture editor to create completely new textures of your own design

PUBLISHING YOUR VIDEO

Firewire to VCR?

If you have only a Firewire card and no analogue video outputs in your PC, it would be invaluable to have a camera which works as a Firewire-to-analogue converter, because that makes it easy to record edited video to VHS. As you record a video digitally on your camera, either live or from Firewire, the analogue outputs show a copy that can be connected to a VCR. Sound can be taken from either your soundcard or the sound output connectors on the camera.

Make a tape copy

Not all cards with a video input have a video output as well. If video is important to you, check for this when buying your PC or a new video card. Some cards work in 'dual monitor' or 'dual head' mode, such that there is an independent video output that is separate to the main display and works automatically with software such as Media Player. Others switch into a 'TV out' mode, where you see video directly on your monitor in a flickery video-ready format. VCRs use three types of connector – composite video, S-video and SCART. PCs are likely to use S-video, or possibly composite video. Working out how to connect everything together can be a challenge. If in doubt, find an expert at a larger video or electronics store and ask for help. Once everything is connected, set your VCR to record and play the video on your PC.

SCART socket

Composite
video

S-video

Audio

Video connectors

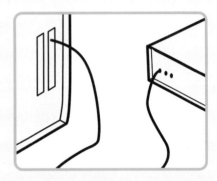

Video recording is easy once you've set up the connection

Copy the video back to your camera

If your camera has only analogue inputs, follow the same procedure as for recording to a VCR. Most cameras come with suitable cables, and most video cards with TV/Video outputs are supplied with suitable leads. Connection details will be explained in the manuals. To copy to a digital camera, use the same Firewire connection you used to capture video into the PC. Media Player doesn't seem to play video out over a Firewire connection, so you will have to use a video-editing package. Most products include a 'Play to video and/or camera' feature built-in.

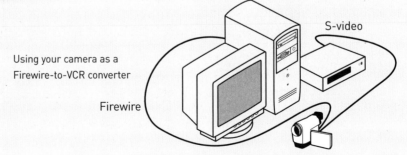

Using your camera as a
Firewire-to-VCR converter

S-video

Firewire

Make a DVD

In the same way that you can buy software to make your own music compilation CDs, you can also buy tools to make DVDs. You'll need a DVD burner for this. Many video-editing packages include DVD-creation features, which can save your video in a DVD-ready format, and also create DVD menus and chapter headings. These won't be as sophisticated as those on a commercial DVD, but you'll be able to add still or moving backgrounds, change the font and colour of chapter titles, and so on. Once a DVD project has been completed, the software will let you burn it directly to a blank DVD. This will probably play in a standard home DVD player. But DVD technology isn't quite reliable enough to guarantee that this will happen, especially if you have an older player.

AVI and other video files can be saved with various **codecs** – drivers for different kinds of video technology. Media Player will be able to play a file only if it has the right codec installed. If it doesn't, you'll see it try to link to Microsoft's site and download a suitable codec. When you are saving a video file, some advanced software gives you a choice of which codec to use. CinePak or one of the Microsoft codecs are good choices.

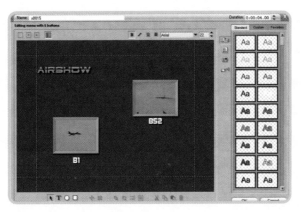

Creating and previewing DVD menus in Pinnacle's Studio 8 budget video editor

Add clips to your website

For a website, use one of the special web-friendly file formats, such as QuickTime (.qt), RealVideo (.rm) and WindowsMedia (.wma). These make relatively tiny files that are very quick to download, with reasonable quality. To save your video in one of these formats, you can often simply follow File → Save as..., then select the format you want.

There are two ways to handle these video files on the Web. You can ask visitors to download them before viewing. To do this, just add a standard link as for an image. Or you can stream them, so that they play live from your site. While setting up streaming isn't hard, the details are too complex to explain here. For more information search the Web for '+streaming +html +"how to"'.

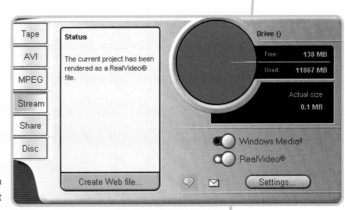

Pinnacle's Studio 8's 'Stream' option saves video in a streamable format

DESKTOP PUBLISHING

Before PC ownership became widespread, it was hard to design posters, cards, newsletters and other small-scale print projects without expensive professional help. With a PC, it's extremely easy to get impressive results with a minimum of time and effort. Indeed, home and small-office desktop publishing (DTP) programs include a wide selection of ready-made templates and page layouts.

At its simplest, DTP now means choosing one of these templates and filling in the text and – optionally – changing the pictures that appear. The example here is a template from Microsoft Publisher, an affordable (about £100) DTP package.

Standard Windows text menu

Standard Microsoft Office icon menus

Task bar

Main title graphic

Business name

Main title

Page selection tools
you can easily create newsletters and brochures with multiple pages, and control the order in which they are laid out and printed

Story headline

Story text

Story graphic

Story graphic caption

Page grid
defines how the blocks of text and their associated graphics are arranged on the page

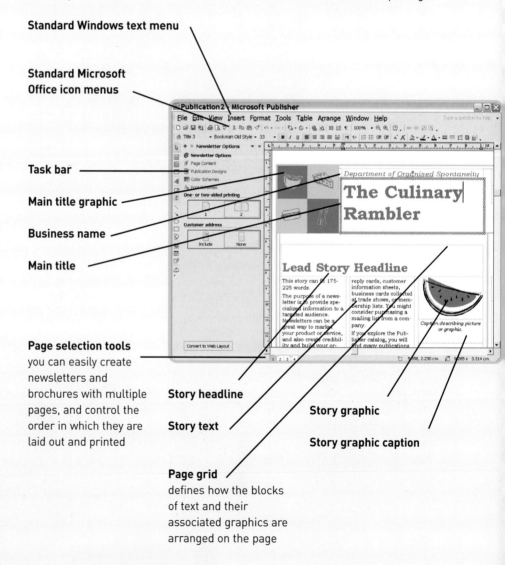

Select a page template

Select a colour scheme

Select a lettering type (font)

If you need a one-off design or a very small print run, it's easy to do your own printing at home on a colour printer. But if you need more than, say, five copies, this can be time-consuming and expensive. Many high-street print shops have colour photocopying machines that can produce adequate copies at reasonable cost. If, however, you need a very large print run (thousands of copies), or if you want to use high-quality ink and paper for a more polished result, you could supply the DTP files to the print shop on CD. For best results, ask your printer what he or she needs before you start your design – the exact requirements do vary. Many printers use Apple Macintosh computers rather than PCs, so you may need to check compatibility.

Select a grid template and add your own photos and text

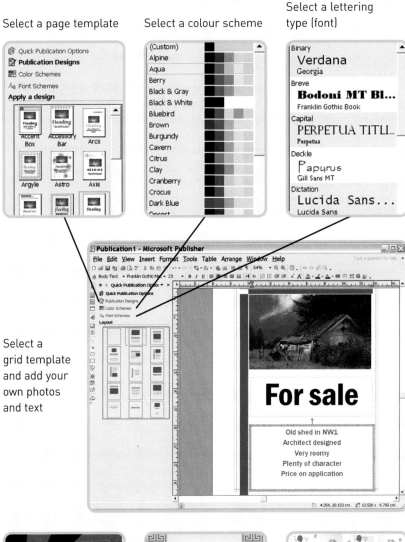

Variation 1

Variation 2

Variation 3

If you don't like the result, you can change any of these elements at any time

FONTS AND CLIP ART

Finding fonts and Clip Art online

Professional fonts

www.fonts.com

www.fontsearch engine.com

www.atomic type.co.uk

Free fonts

(Note that different sites include many of the same fonts. They may also be prone to advertising pop-ups.)

www.larabie fonts.com

www.font garden.com

www.down loadfree fonts.com

www.1001free fonts.com

www.font freak.com

www.freeware fonts.com

Free Clip Art

www.clipart connection.com

webclipart. miningco.com

www.web places.com/search

Fonts and more fonts

If you look at any magazine or newspaper, you will see that lettering is produced in different styles, called fonts. (Professional designers call them typefaces, or sometimes just faces.) There are literally hundreds of thousands of fonts available for PC-users in styles that vary from staid and traditional, to extrovert eccentricity, to copies of famous designs used in advertising, films and TV. Windows uses a font technology called TrueType. A standard Windows XP PC includes a handful of useful but unadventurous TrueType fonts, including Times, Arial and Verdana. Fonts can also include pictures and small illustrations called Dingbats. These are used in place of letters. Windows XP includes a basic set of Dingbats, in a font called WingDings: ❋≋♏✈◆✠♏♍&

All of these are adequate for basic work, but if you are designing posters and websites and would like something more eye-catching, you will need to expand your collection. There are three ways to do this.

Buying a collection

The easiest way is to buy a Clip Art and font collection at your local computer store. This should cost between £10 and £70 depending on the number of fonts included. You can buy thousands of fonts like this, although often you are paying for quantity rather than quality in these collections.

Buying professional fonts

Designers use professional fonts for a more polished result. Traditional fonts are elegantly stylish, and modern designs are exciting and creative. These fonts may also include special features such as ligatures which tie letters together – for example, linking the f and the t in 'left'.

If you buy a professional desk-top publishing package such as Quark Xpress or Adobe InDesign, you will get a small selection of these high-quality fonts. You can also buy them separately from specialist professional design suppliers. Prices are surprisingly high – a single font can cost as much as £100 – but where quality matters the results can be worth the outlay. Some professional fonts use an alternative technology called PostScript, made by Adobe. Unless you are a professional designer, it's best to ignore fonts that use PostScript technology. They may work in Windows, but they're designed to work best with a piece of professional software called Adobe Type Manager. Without this you may get unpredictable results.

left

Verdana   Zapf Dingbats

*Easy*PC **Projects** ☆□❋❋✳▲

Flemish Script   Bauhaus

Buying fonts online

Collections of budget fonts are also available on the Web. These are often produced by amateurs and part-time designers. The quality varies from frankly useless novelty designs to fonts good enough to use professionally. Many are completely free, while others are available at a modest cost.

Using fonts on your PC

Installing a new font isn't a complicated process. Your main Windows folder includes a folder called Fonts. TrueType fonts are supplied in files with a .TTF extension (see page 21). To install a font, copy the relevant file from its original location, such as a CD, to the Fonts folder. It's then ready to use, and will immediately appear in the font selection options available in Word and in other font-sensitive software.

Many fonts available online are supplied as Zip files. To use these, download the file to your PC (see page 144), double click on the Zip file to open it, and then drag any TTF files it contains to the Fonts folder, as usual.

Note that having hundreds or thousands of fonts available at once can slow down your PC. It's a good idea to use only a small selection at any time, and copy the rest to one or more Spare Fonts folders till you need them.

Clip Art

Clip Art is the name given to small pre-drawn illustrations that are used to add colour and interest to a document. For example, a menu can be made to look more interesting with decorative pre-drawn pictures of food. Clip Art is supplied in much the same way as fonts. You can buy collections on CD, or you can download it from the Internet. Professional collections of Clip Art are rare. Designers either use existing collections, or commission an artist to design fresh artwork for them. Microsoft Office comes with a collection of Clip Art, and you can easily expand this by buying a collection from a computer store.

Clip Art suffers from two problems. The first is that when there are thousands of images to choose from, it can take too long to find an image that will suit your document. Office includes an indexing feature that makes it easier to search for art by category. When you buy a collection of art on CD, always check to see if an indexing tool is supplied. A collection of 10,000 images is useless if it takes you a day to find what you want!

The second problem with Clip Art is that it can look cheap and unsophisticated. For casual designs this isn't a problem. But if you ever need to create designs for a professional context where it's important to make a good impression, such as a business card, it can be worth hiring a graphic designer to produce original artwork for you. Make sure you buy the rights to reuse the design, and that it is supplied on CD as well as paper. That way, you can recycle the same artwork on letterheads, compliment slips and even your website.

Some images, such as photos and artwork, are copyrighted. You have to pay the copyright owner a fee if you want to use them, even for small projects. Royalty-free art can be used in any project without worries about copyright and licence fees: one payment is all you need to make. Fonts are always royalty-free; Clip Art usually is. But professionally taken photos may need to be licensed for each project.

MORE ABOUT PRINTING AND ARCHIVING

Giclee and photo printing in the UK

A useful report about giclee printing and printers in the UK is available at:

www.crabfish .com/features /giclee- report.htm

For the latest information about alternative sources, use a search engine to search for '+giclee +UK'.

Digital photo printing:

www.fujifilm. co.uk/fdi/ www.photo box.co.uk

Alternatives to using standard printers

Standard colour printers are capable of producing perfectly adequate posters, flyers, simple greetings cards and basic photo printing, especially if you use high-quality papers and archival inks to make sure that the printing doesn't fade in sunlight. But if you plan to exhibit work professionally or are looking for photographic prints that are closer to the quality available from a professional film developer, there are alternatives that are worth considering.

Dye sublimation printing

Dye sublimation (sometimes known as 'dye sub') is a high-quality professional printing process. Full-page dye-sub printers cost thousands of pounds. But small-format specialised photo printers are available from photo stores and cost £300–400. These produce results that are much higher quality than those from an inkjet. No special skills are needed to use a dye-sub printer. Some can even print directly from a camera's memory card, so no PC connection is required.

Large format and specialised printing

Standard printers can print up to A4. For more sophisticated or professional work, it's possible to buy A3 format printers from companies such as HP and Epson. Some of these can print on to continuous rolls of paper for banners or wide-format landscape prints. Many can also print directly on to CD blanks. Most include six- or even seven-colour printing for more accurate colour balance. Some, such as the Epson 2200, use specially designed long-lasting inks that are unlikely to fade for decades. If you plan to exhibit photo prints or other artwork semi-professionally, and need a way to create prints to order, it is worth investigating these models.

Professional photo printing

A number of services offer a print service for users of digital cameras. Yahoogroups and MSN's groups offer this facility on their community websites. Camera-maker and film specialist Fuji also offers its own service. You may find that your local film developer can also turn photos on CD into prints for you. More printing options are available from specialists such as PhotoBox. They can create very high-quality large-format professional prints, as well copying your images on to calendars, mugs, mousemats and T-shirts.

Iris Giclee printing

The giclee (pronounced 'jee-clay') process creates very high-quality prints for fine-art and photographic use. The printers cost many thousands of pounds and are far too expensive for home use. But if you create digital artwork and would like to be able to sell prints, a giclee bureau can print out and optionally also frame and mount your work. At up to £100 per print, prices can be high. But the process currently offers the best print quality available.

Archiving your artwork

Archiving artwork can be more complicated than just creating standard backups (see page 104). It's more useful to keep separate records of each piece of art, website and photo collection you create. This may not be as easy as it sounds. Whereas paintings, film negatives and drawings are physical objects that are easy to store, any digital art project is more likely to be made up of a collection of interrelated files. While it's possible to save just the final step, it can be very useful to also save all the stages along the way just in case you want to go back and rework them later. If you're collecting only family snaps, this won't matter. But for more creative projects you'll find that there will be folders full of intermediate steps, offcuts and related work. You may also need to include any Clip Art and fonts you use. As a good rule of thumb, it's wise to assume that an archive isn't complete unless it is fully self-contained, and can recreate the original work in its entirety. While professional publishing tools such as Quark Xpress can manage this kind of archiving automatically, and even Word has an option which lets you save all the fonts included in a document, for other kinds of creative projects you'll have to manage this kind of archiving by hand.

The second issue is the backup format used. Whereas paper lasts for centuries, computer storage rarely lasts more than a decade or two – not because of technical problems, but because technology evolves so quickly. Someone who stored the text of a book on a floppy disk in 1994 will find that by 2004 the disk may be unreadable on the computers of the day because they lack a floppy-disk slot. The archive is useless without special hardware that may be difficult to find. By 2010 floppy-disk drives will be almost impossible to buy.

Archiving solutions

Two things need to be done for effective digital archiving. The first is to make sure that your work is always organised in a way that makes it easy to create safety copies. If your website needs photos and images that are scattered through assorted folders all over your hard disk, it's going to be next to impossible to recreate the site if your ISP loses all the files from its web server. Keeping projects organised and filed, complete with all the relevant files involved, can save you a lot of trouble later.

The second is being sure to keep multiple copies of work, both on your PC and away from it. For very important projects it's a good idea to make two safety copies, and keep one near your PC and the other at a safe location elsewhere.

Unlike most photo-editing tools, Microsoft's PictureIt!, sometimes included within Works (see page 108), includes easy-to-use calendar-creation tools, and also other special print projects.

The archives for this book - currently stored on a DVD

CREATING A WEB PAGE

Ingredients of a website

A website is just a collection of files. Files with the .htm or .html extension are the core of the site and include all the layout and the text for each page. Those with a .jpg extension add illustrations that slot into each page layout. In a complicated site, these files will be arranged in various folders. You may also see .css files. These control the fonts used and various advanced page layout possibilities.

Easy web design

The easiest way to create a web page needs no tools, no specialised skills and very little time. Many of the online services such as AOL and MSN include simple web-creation tools that are based on ready-made templates. These are usually found in an area called Hometown, Homestead, Homegroups or some similar variation. To create a page, you pick a theme from one of those listed, add some text and perhaps a picture or two, choose which graphics you want to use from a small selection, and your page will be ready to go almost instantly. As an example, here is how AOL's 1-2-3 Publish tool works.

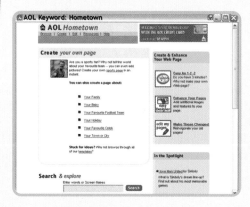

Pick a theme.
Here we've chosen holidays

Choose from the design possibilities.
Select each option with the mouse. Out of sight here are options to add a picture and more text

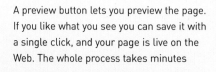

A preview button lets you preview the page. If you like what you see you can save it with a single click, and your page is live on the Web. The whole process takes minutes

More advanced designs

Some of these simple sites include more advanced design tools. AOL offers EasyDesigner, a piece of software written using the Java language (see page 101), which automatically appears within your web browser. (It takes a while to load.) With EasyDesigner, you can change the graphics that are used, and the page subdivisions and section headers that appear on your page. It's still quite limited, but it does make it possible to customise your pages to an extent.

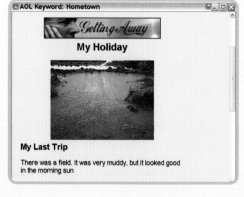

The easy approach is perfect for quick and simple designs. But it means that you are forced to use someone else's template. If you want to create a more customised look, you need a freeform web-page editor. Here we've used Namo's Web Editor, an affordable but powerful piece of web-editing software (see www.namo.com). Like other software, Namo's Web Editor includes plenty of easy-to-use design templates. The simplest way to design a site is to pick one of these and fill in the blanks. You can also create completely customised designs from scratch.

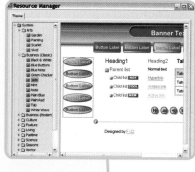

Namo's main editing page is 'What You See Is What You Get'. It's very easy to add and remove elements, change the format of a page, and make other alterations to the basic template. It's also simple to add your own web links, both to outside sites and to other pages in your own site.

As you work, Namo keeps track of how all the files in a website are related. You don't need to worry about this for a simple site, but if you're trying to create a large site with plenty of pages, you can use a block diagram like this one to help you keep track of all the links so that when you test the site you can be sure they all work properly.

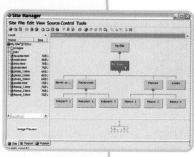

Namo includes a built-in preview feature which shows how the page will look when it goes live. It's also easy to load pages directly into your browser for testing. For very fine tuning, you can alter the raw HTML (hypertext markup language). This is the language used to define how pages appear on the Web. If you're not an expert, you can ignore this feature. It's easy to design pages without referring to it.

When you have finished your site, you will need to copy it to your web space using a process called FTP (file transfer protocol). FTP is a way of telling one computer to copy files to another, and is built into the Namo Web Editor. To use FTP you will need to fill in some information about the ISP's web space. Your ISP should be able to tell you exactly what to type here. Once you have entered the details, click on the 'Publish' tab that appears at the bottom of the main editing page. It can take up to a few hours to copy an entire site from your PC to your ISP. Once there, your page will go 'live' immediately.

WEB INSPIRATION

Free resources

www.bravenet .com

A huge collection of tips and various plug-in tools to spice up your site

www.abcgiant .com

A Clip Art collection aimed at web designers. Ad-heavy, but potentially useful

www.123web master.com

A sprawling collection of links to web-design know-how. Comprehensive, but perhaps a touch intimidating for beginners

As with any medium, the most important aspect of a website is the message it conveys. Clearly, design plays a big part in this, but deciding what you want your site to say and aiming it at the kinds of visitors you are trying to attract is crucial. Here are some ideas.

Friends and family

For those with an extended family, the Web is an ideal way to share family news and events such as holidays, births, deaths and other changes. You can make your site a common contact point, perhaps with a discussion board that's open to everyone.

Hobby and lifestyle sharing

Whatever your hobbies or personal, religious, spiritual or creative interests, the Web is a good way to share them and make contact with like-minded people. Samples of your work or ideas always work well on a site you set up.

Fun, humour and entertainment

There are plenty of online joke collections already, but some sites have made a name for themselves by creating new kinds of humour, especially with photographs and animations.

Work experience and CV

Not many jobs expect or allow a web CV, but there's no harm in a concise listing of your professional accomplishments and interests. This is an especially popular option with academics and researchers, and also anyone who works freelance and finds themselves regularly being asked who else they have worked for.

Some other USP

USP is business-speak for unique selling proposition (or point). If you have something that makes your site special in a way that's either entertaining or useful, you can expect a steady stream of visitors. The key here is to provide a unique resource. Anything will do the job, whether it's unusually amusing film reviews written by you, or essential information about dog breeding.

An example of elegant web design. The design is very clean and clear, the menu options are well presented and easy to understand, the choice of colours is strong without being overbearing, and the whole is very legible and straightforward

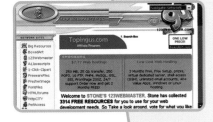

A less impressive design. The blinking advertising is distracting, the menu options are confusing, and the whole thing looks very messy and daunting

Bad web design: common gremlins and horrors

Pop-ups
Visitors will hate you for them. Avoid them if you can.

Long page syndrome
Never put everything on a single page. Always use themed sections.

Unreadable text
Make text large enough to see, with good but not garish colour and brightness contrast between text and background.

Pointless special effects
Don't use animated GIFs – tiny repeating animations – or Javascript (see page 101) unless they really do contribute something essential to a site.

Bad MIDI music
If you want to include music, add it as an optional link and download.

Others
Guest books and hit counters which count visitors are distracting, and 'Under Construction' graphics are now out of date. Don't use them.

Choices for a good website

Consistent menus and a visual theme
Even a tiny site benefits from links to themed sections. Duplicate what professional sites do by reusing the same links to these sections on every page.

Photo galleries
These can be time-consuming to create by hand, so use special software. Search for 'web gallery' and 'shareware' to find some options.

Web logs
'Blogs' – online diaries – are a popular part of online culture. If you want to slot a blog into your site you can use a blog 'plug-in' tool such as Moveable Type or Blogger. If you just want to keep an online diary, use a site like Free Open Diary or Dear Diary.

Discussion boards
These are web spaces where visitors can talk and debate with each other. They're very popular once your site reaches a certain critical mass. Try a product called Snitz, which is easy to add to your site, and completely free.

Favourite links
If you include a well-organised list of favourite links, this can be useful to visitors. But this does of course steer a visitor away from your site, so use this feature with care.

Diary sites

www.deardiary.net
www.freeopen
diary.com

Blog plug-in tools

www.movable
type.org
www.blogger.com

Discussion boards

www.ezboard.com
forum.snitz.com
www.conforums
.com/index.html

(note: conforums is paid for by advertising pop-ups – the others are free)

3.18

Web inspiration

ADVANCED WEB CREATION

Hosted website jargon-buster

Perl, CGI-BIN, PHP4

These acronyms mean you can add more complicated features to your site, including shopping carts and e-commerce facilities.

MySQL, Microsoft SQL

You can keep a database of goods and items on the hosting company's computers. Again, useful for shopping sites.

SSL server

Takes secure credit-card payments – once again, for online shopping

Front Page Extensions

Take advantage of special features offered by Microsoft's Front Page web-design tool.

Getting more serious

Web hosting

For a more professional web presence, you can rent web space from a web-hosting company. With this, you can create a huge site that you have almost total control over, free from pop-ups and other annoyances. Prices can be as low as £20 a year. Any Internet magazine will have a list of hundreds of hosting companies competing for your custom. You'll see immediately that prices vary hugely, and it's a fact of life that you don't necessarily get what you pay for. The most important feature is uptime – reliability – and how much web space you get. You can tell a lot about the quality of a company by the speed and efficiency with which it deals with any initial queries. And do shop around – it can make a huge difference to what you pay.

Domains and domain names

These are the personalised number plates of the online world. Normally with an ISP both your web space and your email include the ISP's name. With your own customised domain you can change that to a name of your choosing – for example, your website could be called www.myname.com and your email would be me@myname.com.

The most useful domain-name extensions – .org for charities, non-profit projects and personal websites, .co.uk for UK businesses, and .com for international businesses – have been available for nearly a decade now. So the most popular names are already taken. Most registration services include search tools so that you can see which names are already in use (try www.netbenefit.com).

The services offered by a typical web-hosting company

> **What we offer**
> - Register your domain name
> - Manage your e-mail
> - Build a web site
> - Choose a shared hosting package
> - Choose a dedicated hosting package
>
> **Domain Name Search**
>
> [   ] go
>
> Type in the domain name you require and select GO! We will check availability of the following suffixes: .com .net .org .info .biz .co.uk .org.uk

Once you find a free name you like, you'll have to pay two sums – a one-off payment to your hosting company to handle the registration paperwork, and another regular annual payment to the Internet's central registration service for continuing use of the name. The former sum should be as little as possible, and the service may even be free. The latter is about £25 a year. You may also have to pay extra for email forwarding, which acts as a kind of PO box between your real email box – the one maintained by your ISP – and your named email. However, sometimes this is included within the cost of the hosting.

Beyond simple sites

It's perfectly possible to use nothing more than simple HTML to create an effective and attractive site. For the majority of sites, it's the content that matters the most. As long as the presentation and design are competent and not a distraction, the content will speak for itself. But it's worth being aware of what's possible with other tools.

Java and Javascript

Java special effects are supplied as applets – tiny pieces of software that are loaded and installed automatically. Javascript is an extension to basic HTML. Thousands of pre-written effects and tools are available online on various sites devoted to these extras. You can easily add these to your site. Examples include animations, colour effects, clocks and quote generators, simple chat tools, games, and roll-overs – menu buttons that change their appearance when you move a mouse over them. While a little up-front learning is needed to begin to use Java and Javascript, they provide a relatively simple way to add some visual spice to your site.

Some flash effects created with Flash

Javascript is much simpler to use, but also rather less exciting

Macromedia Flash

Flash is a piece of commercial software (about £300, from many computer mail-order stores) capable of truly eye-popping visual effects which combine animation, sound, music and sometimes also video in creative ways. It's very popular with professional web designers, and is often used on commercial websites. It's not easy to learn but, as with Javascript, there are various sites which can provide quick Flash gratification for your own pages.

PayPal

PayPal is a simple money-transfer tool which makes it possible for you to collect payments without the confusion and expense involved in taking credit cards directly. While it's not quite perfect – costs are higher for UK and European Union users than for those based in the USA – it's proving very successful with small-scale entrepreneurs and others who want to sell something from their site.

Java and Javascript sites

www.freeware
java.com

www.dynamic
drive.com

javascriptkit.com

Flash sites

www.fake
pilot.com

www.mini
clip.com

www.orisinal
.com

Flash help sites

www.flash
kit.com

graphics
soft.about
.com/cs/flash/

www.free
flash.nu/

Paypal

www.paypal.com

KEEPING YOUR PC ORGANISED

Why drive C:?

The floppy-disk drives in a PC (there's room for two, for historical reasons, but only one is ever used today) are labelled A: and B:. The hard disk is the first drive after this, and labelled C:. If you add more hard drives, these will become D:, E: and so on. Your CD or DVD drive is always the last in the list. Letters are available up to Z:.

Even though information stored in a PC uses disk space instead of paper, it's just as easy to lose it inside a disorganised PC as it is in a disorganised office. To make life easier for you, Windows XP includes features that can help you stay organised. You don't have to use them if you don't want to, but it's a good idea to do so, especially if you are new to PCs.

My Documents

As explained on page 20, the hard disk in your PC is the electronic equivalent of a filing cabinet. If you add more disks, you are adding more filing space in extra cabinets. But the basics of staying organised remain the same. The most important folder in your PC is called My Documents. By default, Windows is set up so that this folder holds all of your work, including all the letters you write, posters you design, and so on. My Documents is so important that when you open Windows Explorer it's the first thing you see. It's considered even more important than your main disk drive, which appears below it. (This can confuse people, because in reality My Documents is stored just like any other folder on your main drive. But Windows gives it special prominence in Windows Explorer.)

My Documents includes other sub-folders. The most important ones are My Pictures and My Music. Other sub-folders you may see include My eBooks (see page 150), My Photos and My Videos. In fact, you can add as many other folders you like here. Folder names don't need to start with the word 'My' – you can use any name you like. Other possibilities include My Downloads for when you're copying software from the Internet, and Archive for information or work you want to keep but no longer use regularly.

Inside My Documents

Windows XP has My Documents to encourage you to keep all your information in one place. The main advantage of following this suggested approach is that it

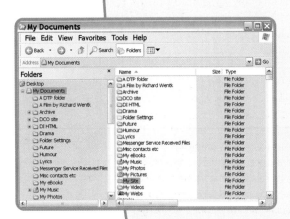

makes it relatively quick and easy to find whatever you want. The disadvantage is that it's not ideal for more advanced work. For example, if you work with sound or video, it's a better idea to use a different disk drive altogether for the files. Also, you still have to remember to create sub-folders. Filling the My Photos folder with hundreds or thousands of digital photos is less convenient than keeping them in sub-folders arranged by the date they were taken. You could even create two main sub-folders, one holding folders of raw full-sized photos arranged by date, and another holding copies that have been retouched and perhaps resized, and then grouped into separate folders to make themed albums.

Other important folders

Desktop
This is rather like a folder that contains everything in your PC. In Windows Explorer, all the information is contained in the Desktop. When you double click on Desktop to open it, you'll see My Documents, My Computer, which contains all the disk drives in your PC, and some other extras.

My Computer
My Computer contains the various disk drives, and their folders. Like Desktop, it's not really a true folder. It appears in Windows Explorer with its own special picture of a PC, so that you can recognise it easily.

Program Files and Windows
Your main disk drive is usually called the 'C:' drive (see the sidebar). Because most of your work will stay within My Documents, you're less likely to need to look into what's stored here. But it's useful to know what there is and how it's organised. If you double click on C: you'll see all the folders stored on your C: drive. The two most important are Program Files and Windows. (The latter may be called 'WinXP', or some other variation on the theme of 'Win' or 'Windows.')

Program Files holds all the software you have installed in sub-folders. By default, most software looks for this folder and tries to install itself here. The Windows folder (or whatever it's called on your PC) holds Windows itself. Windows tries to hide these folders from you in two ways. The first is a warning message that appears when you open them in Windows Explorer. The second is by literally making some files invisible. This is wise because if you change the contents of these folders or remove the hidden files, your PC may stop working. But there are times, such as when you're copying fonts (see page 92), that you need access to them. Don't let the warning message put you off. Unless you start deleting or moving files at random, it's unlikely that you'll do any serious damage here.

Shared Documents
Normally My Documents is protected so that other people can't read the contents unless they log in using your password. (Note: this is true only if your PC has been set up using the NTFS system – see page 181). To share information, copy it to the Shared Documents folder. Any files you copy here will be visible to everyone who uses your PC. They'll also be visible to everyone on your network.

My Network Places
If your PC is connected to other PCs, you can see the information they contain by double clicking here. For more details see page 174.

Beyond C:?

If you add an extra disk drive (see page 172) because you have run out of space on the first one, you have two choices about how you use it. The first is to treat the first disk as full, and to install software and keep new information on the new disk. A better solution is to 'clone' the original disk using a tool like Partition Magic (see page 181), and then either physically swap it with your old disk, or use Partition Magic's Boot Manager to swap it virtually (also page 180).

Overview of a large PC. This one has five disk drives. The CD drive appears as H: There are two users, each with their own version of My Documents. Note that when they are logged in, these folders appear to them as My Documents, even though in fact Windows calls them something different when they are not

BACKUPS AND SAFETY COPIES

The DVD maze

There are two kinds of DVD technologies: DVD+R/RW ('DVD plus') and DVD-R/RW ('DVD minus'). The two are not compatible. We suggest you use +R/RW technology, because blank disks are cheaper and it has other technological advantages. To create disks for a home DVD player, use +R instead of rewritable +RW blanks. Note that there's still a 10% chance – owing to a limitation of the technology – that your disks may not work in an older DVD player.

Hard-disk drives are never completely reliable. When a disk drive fails, all the information on it disappears completely. If the internals are still intact it's sometimes possible to pay a specialist company to retrieve the information, but this can be extremely expensive and time-consuming. In the meantime, you'll be left with a PC that doesn't work. And sometimes a disk literally falls apart physically, so there's absolutely no way to rescue your files and settings.

As ever, prevention is better than cure, and the best way to avoid a PC crisis is to create safety copies. These are often known as backups. There are three ways to create backups. System backups create a copy of everything, including all your software, work and Windows settings. Project or document backups copy just the work created for a particular project or document. Incremental backups are used as supplements to system backups. Instead of copying everything, they copy only the files that have been changed since the last backup.

Backup hardware

Floppy-disk drive

Capacity:	1.4Mb
Cost of drive:	£15
Cost of media:	Pennies
Good for:	Small notes, a Windows start-up disk
Bad for:	Everything else
Notes:	Floppy-disk technology is all-but obsolete now. Future PCs may no longer include floppy-disk drives at all

CD drive

Capacity:	700Mb
Cost of drive:	£50–£100
Cost of media:	About £1
Good for:	Letters, documents and emails, MP3 collections, photo albums, website design
Bad for:	Complete system backups, video and audio projects
Notes:	A good choice for document and folder backups. CD-R disks can be written to only once, and the information is permanent. CD-RW disks can be altered and re-used, but are also slightly more fragile

DVD drive

Capacity:	4.7Gb
Cost of drive:	£200 upwards
Cost of media:	£5–£10
Good for:	Audio collections, video projects, small-scale system backups
Bad for:	Nothing
Notes:	Watch out for the different DVD formats (see sidebar)

Travan tape drive

Capacity:	4Gb to 30Gb
Cost of drive:	£200–£400
Cost of media:	£10–£40
Good for:	System backups
Bad for:	Project backups
Notes:	Travan tape drives are rather slow and can be noisy. Because of the nature of tape, it's a bad idea to keep multiple projects on a single tape. You'll waste a lot of time waiting for it to fast-forward and rewind

AIT/DLT/DAT tape drive

Capacity:	20Gb to 100Gb
Cost of drive:	£40–£1,500
Cost of media:	£20–£50
Good for:	Professional system backups
Bad for:	Project backups
Notes:	These three different tape drive types are aimed at serious and professional users. They are much faster than Travan drives, but also much more expensive

Spare hard-disk drive

Capacity:	40Gb to 250Gb
Cost of drive:	£60–£300
Cost of media:	n/a
Good for:	Everything
Bad for:	Nothing
Notes:	While fast and convenient, this option is not easy to use unless you're confident in fitting and removing hard drives. An alternative is to buy an external Firewire drive (£200–£300). This plugs in outside the PC, and offers all the same advantages. Not cheap, but perhaps the most effective all-round solution

Backup software

For backing up simple projects on to CD or a spare hard disk you don't need to use any special software at all. You can simply use Windows Explorer to copy the files and folders you want. Windows XP doesn't support copying to DVDs yet, so for DVD backups you will need a DVD-compatible product such as Roxio's DirectCD (www.roxio.com – and also available over the counter in large PC stores).

Windows includes its own simple backup tool (All Programs → Accessories → System tools → Backup). It's very easy to use, and gives you a choice between saving everything that exists in the My Documents folder or in your PC. One useful feature is its ability to create a Windows rescue disk. If your disk drive dies, this will make it easy to restore all of your Windows settings after you have reinstalled Windows. Unfortunately, it lacks any tools for incremental backups.

For more advanced backup options, you'll need to buy backup software. Some popular options include Stomp Backup MyPC (www.stompinc.com) and Dantz Retrospect (www.dantz.com), available in Full and Express versions. Iomega's QuickSync (www.iomega.co.uk) is designed to create backups while you get on with other work. Prices vary from about £50 to £250, and free trial versions of these products are often available.

Microsoft's backup tool is simple but can save your entire Windows system

For disk backups, the best choice is a tool such as PowerQuest's DriveImage. This is specifically designed to 'clone' disk drives very easily, and can also create compressed copies. Note that if you are making a backup of your main Windows hard disk, just copying the files to another drive won't be enough. Some important files are inaccessible to normal copying, so you will need to clone the entire drive. PowerQuest's Partition Magic offers more advanced features, such as the ability to clone a drive to one of a different size (www.powerquest.com).

PowerQuest's PartitionMagic has a quick drive-copying feature built-in

Scheduling backups

It's more convenient to schedule backups so that they happen automatically. This makes sure your files are up to date whether or not you remember to back them up manually. Windows XP includes a simple scheduling program that can start software automatically (All Programs → Accessories → System tools → Scheduled Tasks). Double click on the 'Add new scheduled task' option and add your backup task here. You can then specify how regularly you want it to run, and at what time.

The Windows Task Scheduler, set up here to start a backup every Friday evening

Help! I deleted a file by accident!

Solution 1: Look in the Recycle bin. Windows stores files here before it deletes them. To recover a file, select it and use File → Restore.

Solution 2: Use a third-party file-recovery tool, such as Norton Systemworks or OnTrack's SystemSuite. If you've just lost a file and don't have a recovery tool yet, don't install the tool on your disk – in fact, try not to change anything on your hard disk. Run the tool from the CD instead. After you get your file back, you can install the tool to disk.

THE DIGITAL OFFICE

Different versions of Office XP

Not every item here is included in every version of Office XP. The standard version includes Word, Excel, Outlook and PowerPoint. The Professional version comes with Access. The Professional Special Edition also includes FrontPage and Publisher. A Developer version includes yet more features, but is designed for software designers rather than home or business users. Each separate program is also sold individually.

Whether you plan to use your PC to run a small business, keep track of home finances, or make other financial chores less burdensome, you'll need to use extra software. Microsoft has produced a software package called Office XP, which includes all the most widely used business and office tools, and is very capable and powerful. The next few pages offer you an introduction to Office, and also give you some alternatives to Office which may suit your needs better. Office comes in various versions which contain some or all of the following pieces of software.

Word

A word-processing package. You can type text on to the screen from your keyboard and make changes to it, then email or print the results, or just save them for later. Word also includes features for working with tables and lists, producing diagrams and scientific equations, checking spelling and grammar, and creating a professional and polished look by using special lettering, simple graphics, and so on. Also available are facilities for working with form letters and mail outs, and very simple web page designs.

Excel

A spreadsheet, which is a grid of cells, a little like that used in a game of Battleships. Each cell contains either a fixed number or a formula that calculates a result based on the numbers in other cells. The result from one cell can be used in a formula in any other, so formulae can be chained. For example, ten columns of figures can each be added together to produce ten subtotals, and then the subtotals added to produce a final total. If any of the figures is changed, all the sums are recalculated. Spreadsheets aren't limited to numbers or simple arithmetic. Cells can contain dates, scientific data, words, or almost any other information.

Access

A database, which is an electronic version of a card index, with the difference that you can define sub-cards so that (for example) if you are keeping track of addresses and a group of people all work for the same company, you can make the company address a single entry and have each person's contact details refer to that entry. If the company moves, updating that one entry will change the address details in everyone's records automatically. Databases are useful for keeping employee records and price lists in a business. But they're rather complicated if all you want to do is maintain an address book, or index your CD and DVD collection.

PowerPoint

A tool for preparing office presentations. You'll almost certainly have seen slides at lectures and conferences prepared with colourful backgrounds, bullet points and large text, and perhaps also graphs and other extras. PowerPoint is the tool used to create these. It's very easy to use, and can produce slides ready for printing on overhead transparencies, or for a live

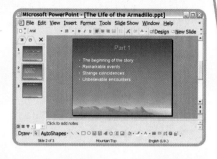

'performance' with music, sound effects, and animated transitions between slides. The features are very useful for office workers, but you're unlikely to need PowerPoint at home.

Publisher

A desktop publishing (DTP) tool. Publisher is used to create posters, cards and newsletters. It is fairly easy to use and includes a useful range of template designs that look good and can be customised. Or you can create your own designs completely from scratch. Publisher is affordable, and although it lacks some of the features available in more expensive DTP software, you won't miss them for simple poster and card designs. But if you want to create professional-looking newsletters, you may find that Publisher isn't quite sophisticated enough.

FrontPage

A web-page design tool. Like Publisher, FrontPage offers a range of pre-set designs in which you fill in the blanks with your own text, and the software does the rest. Unlike Publisher, FrontPage isn't quite as easy to use as it could be. Some of it is quite technical, and it may leave beginners confused. Although it is capable of good results, it may be worth considering an alternative product.

Outlook

Email tool and diary. Outlook is the more sophisticated version of Outlook Express, which is included with Windows XP. Outlook Express includes email, an address book, and support for reading newsgroups. Outlook adds a desk diary, appointment calendar and space for general-purpose notes. Although both programs are easy to use and include all the features you're likely to want, they have also been heavily implicated in most of the email virus disasters suffered by companies and individuals in the last few years. Virus protection in both programs is almost non-existent. Both also default to sending email in a web-readable format. This makes messages bigger, and means that anyone who pays for their Internet access by the minute will be wasting money. (Messages that are pure text, without any pictures, borders or other trimmings are preferred by most Internet users.) Unless you have an extremely good reason for using Outlook or Outlook Express, it would be best if you switched to one of the alternatives.

An educational edition of Office XP, identical to Office XP Standard but costing less than half as much, is available. Originally this version was meant only for students and teachers who could prove conclusively that they qualified for an educational discount. But it is now sold over the counter to anyone who wants it. Strictly speaking, non-educational users are breaking the terms of the licence agreement. But if you have children at school or college and wish to buy on their behalf, or are yourself doing any full- or part-time educational course, you qualify for the discounted price.

ALTERNATIVES TO OFFICE XP

The Works upgrade option

If your PC comes with Works installed, you can buy an upgrade to the full version of Office. The upgrade version is about £100 cheaper than the full version, and upgrades are available to Office Standard or Office Professional. When you try to install the upgrade, it checks to see if you have suitable software on your disk. Word is considered suitable software, and the rest of Office is installed around it.

Office Suites

Microsoft Works

Also known as WorkSuite, Works is a family-oriented package. Instead of including serious office tools, it comes with alternative software that's likely to be more immediately useful and will also take less time to learn and use. It includes the full version of Word – the application that is the most useful. Also included is the Money manager and budget planner (see page 124), the Encarta digital encyclopaedia, Picture It! image editing and photo archiving, and Autoroute route planning. Picture It! is a budget alternative to Paint Shop Pro. Taken together, Works represents very good value.

Lotus SmartSuite

During the mid-1990s, SmartSuite was considered a serious alternative to MS Office, but for various reasons it lost out and came to be thought of as an also-ran. Technically, the latest version of SmartSuite, known as SmartSuite Millennium, lags slightly behind Office. (Avoid SmartSuite 97 as it's completely obsolete now.) But it includes its own professional-standard word processor, spreadsheet, database and presentation creator. SmartSuite typically costs about £35 (Office Professional will set you back £350), so it is to be recommended if you are on a tight budget and are looking for a full set of professional office tools for your own use. It's not a good choice if you plan to exchange office documents with other people via email, because SmartSuite isn't compatible with Office – and most people use Office, which means that they may not be able to make sense of your files. SmartSuite is now hard to get hold of – it's typically sold by small software sellers who advertise in magazines like MicroMart – and is also sometimes given away free by magazines on their cover disks.

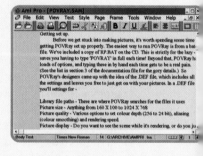

Software 602 PC Suite

PC Suite is an entirely free alternative to Office that includes a Word-compatible word processor, an Excel-compatible spreadsheet, plus photo editing, and photo filing and organising. An expanded version called PC Suite Plus costs $29.95 and adds a small selection of extra features, including a thesaurus. There's no database or presentation software. Both versions are available as downloads from the Internet (www.software602.com), and can be tried out at no charge. (The trial version of PC Suite Plus turns off some of its features after the trial period is over.)

Sun StarOffice

StarOffice is the most convincing serious alternative to Office for business use. Like Office, it includes a word processor, a spreadsheet, a database and a presentation creator. These are fully compatible with those in Office, and so files can be interchanged with ease. It lacks some of

Another completely free Office clone can be found at the OpenOffice project (www.openoffice .org). Be warned though, it's a 50Mb download!

the polish of Office, and some features are less well developed. However, at $75.95 it is much cheaper, and will be almost as productive. More information, with the option to buy the software, is available at wwws.sun.com/software/star/staroffice/6.0/

Email alternatives

Eudora

Qualcomm Eudora is a good alternative to Outlook Express. It is more secure and less prone to viruses, and can also be easier to use. The latest version (5.1 at the time of writing) includes some gimmicky features, such as proofreading for obscenities, but otherwise is a reliable and solidly useful email tool. There are three versions. The Lite version is free, and lacks some of the more useful features.

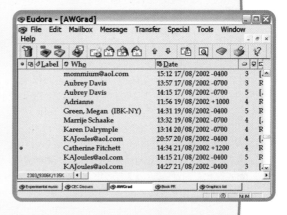

The Pro version includes all these features, and costs $39.95. An intermediate version includes all the features of Pro and is free, but continually downloads and displays advertising – a major annoyance, especially when using a dial-up connection. For details see www.eudora.com.

PocoMail

Unlike Eudora and Outlook, PocoMail can be tuned and customised by users. The look, feel and even some of the features can be modified to taste. This makes it a good choice for more experienced and advanced email users who are looking for extra tools for general email management, and to help eliminate spam. While it's not particularly difficult to use, it's perhaps not the ideal choice for complete beginners. It comes with a 30-day trial period, and the software can be downloaded from www.pocomail.com. The cost is $25.

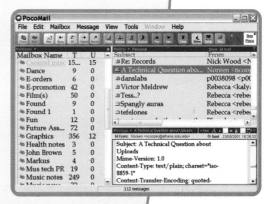

THE ANATOMY OF WORD

Translation

Word includes some simple translation features which attempt to convert English text into Spanish or French. While it's useful to have the option, don't expect too much from it. It is rather crude and is unlikely to impress a native!

Word is a complicated piece of software with many options. But the basic elements are very simple.

Your document appears in a window, in either normal or print layout mode. (Switch between them with View → Normal, Print Layout or Web Layout.) Draft mode shows plain text without any formatting (i.e. without information about the page layout.) There's also a print preview and a web preview option. These show your document exactly as it will appear on the printed page or on a website.

You can use the zoom tool (View → Zoom) to make the document bigger and easier to read, or smaller so that you can see more text at once. Zooming affects only what appears on the screen, and not what the document looks like when printed.

Main menu

A standard Windows-style list of drop-down text menus. Menus are shortened so that only the options you are most likely to want are visible. To see the rest, click on the double down arrow.

Toolbar menus

Toolbars are like menu options, but use pictures instead of words. They're quicker to use than menus, because you can do what you want with a single click. You can create your own toolbars which include the tools you personally use the most. Or you can use the ready-made toolbars that are included with Word. This toolbar collection shows the main text editing toolbar, file saving and printing options, and change tracking. Other toolbars are used for working with tables, adding pictures and images, and so on. If you want to see a list, right click on any toolbar and select a different one from the list that appears, shown here on the left. To create your own toolbar go to Tools → Customize and select the 'Toolbars' tab. Select 'New', then command. Now drag the tools you want from the lists that appear. Be careful – the new toolbar will be small, and will appear (rather confusingly) in the middle of the page, rather than grouped with the existing toolbars.

Taskbar

The taskbar is an alternative to the toolbar system, used for more complex tasks. It can be set up to show a list of recently edited documents, options for creating a new document and also more complex features such as mail merge, which merges a list of names and addresses with a form letter template.

Basic text editing

Here's a closer look at the toolbar used for basic text editing.

Paragraph styles: Combine all the choices listed below to create pre-set styles that can be applied to titles and paragraphs in a document.

Fonts: Choose what kind of lettering you want to use. All the possible lettering types, known as fonts, appear here in a menu that drops down when you click on this triangle. The default shown here is Times New Roman. (For information about how to add more fonts, see page 92.)

Text size: From small to large. (In fact, you can make a single letter large enough to fill an entire page.)

Text effects: You can make text bold, italic, underlined. Other options, including superscript, subscript, strikethrough, outlined and shadowed, are available under Format → Font.

Text colours: You can highlight text or change its colour.

Justification: Align text to the left, right or middle of the page, or stretch it so that lines are always tidy at both edges. You can also set the spacing between lines.

Show paragraph markers (only rarely useful). Set the amount by which paragraphs are indented. Useful to help make pages look neater.

Numbering and bullet points: These buttons add numbers and large marker dots or other shapes known as bullets, that are used to add visual emphasis to lists.

Borders: Add a border to a sentence, paragraph, or the entire page.

Drag and Drop editing

Word uses a kind of editing called Drag and Drop. You can cut, copy and paste text using either the Edit menu or the related keyboard shortcuts. But it's often easier and quicker to move a block of text with the mouse. Click the left button and drag the mouse over the text you want to move. The text will be highlighted. Then click with the left button again and drag the text to its new location. When you release the mouse, the text will reappear at the marker shown by the mouse pointer.

USING WORD TO CREATE A BROCHURE

Printing colours in black and white

If you create a document that uses colours and try to print it on a black and white printer, such as a laser printer, the colours will be replaced with shaded dots. This almost always looks terrible. You can get better results by converting images to just two colours, full black and full white, with no shades in between. Paint Shop Pro (see page 70) has a feature that will do this. Select Colors → Decrease color depth → 2 colors (1 bit).

Word can be used for more than just writing letters: you can use it to design reports, brochures, faxes and simple newsletters. But setting up styles and templates for these documents is time-consuming. And the best results need practice and a good eye for page design. Since people often lack time and the skills to do a good job, Word includes a number of document templates that can be used 'off the peg'. Here's how to create a simple single-sheet advertising brochure and flyer, starting from one of Word's templates.

1. Select File → New to create a new document. This will show the new document taskbar. When you want a completely blank document, select New/Blank Document from the list that appears. In this example we'll use a template. Click on 'New from Template/General Templates'.

2. A box will appear showing which templates are available. If you click on the tabs that are shown you can explore all the templates. As you do this, previews appear in the small window at the right. Select the 'Publications' tab, and then 'Brochure'. (You may discover that this template isn't installed. If so, you'll need to find your Office XP installation disk and go through a short, simple installation process. Word will explain what you need to do.)

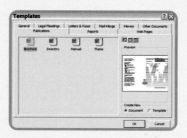

3. The brochure template appears. Notice that it's arranged in three columns, with the paper positioned horizontally (this is known as 'landscape') instead of vertically ('portrait'). The template includes two pages, one for each side of the paper. When the brochure is finished you'll be able to fold it into thirds, just like real printed brochures.

4. Even on the biggest monitors, you won't be able to see all of the brochure at once. To get an overview, select View → Zoom and click on the 'Many pages' option in the box that appears. Then set the zoom factor to a low value, perhaps 20% to 30%. (The exact factor you need depends on the resolution of your monitor.) If there's room on the screen, Word will display both pages next to each other instead of one on top of the other. This makes it easy to look at the overall design.

5. Set the zoom back to 100% and start making changes to the text of the brochure. It's a good idea to keep the format – the positioning of the lettering – unchanged when you're experimenting. When you have more experience you'll begin to feel confident about changing anything and everything. Let's begin here by changing the company name and slogan to something less official.

THE HAPPY PLAICE

THE BEST CHIPSHOP
IN ANYSHIRE

The freshest fish, every day

6. The graphic under the new company name also needs to be changed. Instead of the world logo, we'll insert a piece of Clip Art (see page 92). Office comes with a collection of Clip Art on CD. Select Insert → Picture → Clip Art from the main menu. The taskbar will switch to show the Clip Art selection. Type 'Fish' into the search box, and click on the 'Search' button under it. After a while, you'll see a collection of possible art appear at the right. (Note that Word can be extremely slow here. If this is the first time you have tried to use Clip Art, Word will literally search your entire disk to create a library of art for you. If it starts this search – you'll see some warning messages appear – you'll have time to make some tea or even cook and eat a whole meal before it has finished!)

7. Delete the world graphic by selecting it with the mouse – a border will appear around it – and hitting the backspace key. Pick a suitable fishy graphic and double click on it. It will appear in the space left by the old graphic. But it won't be the same size, so you'll need to resize it to fit. This is very easy to do. Click on the lower edge and drag it down. You'll see the graphic expand. If you go too far, select Edit → Undo or type CTRL + Z and try again. As an exercise, see if you can replace the '&' graphic in the middle panel of the page with another copy of your Clip Art fish.

THE HAPPY PLAICE

THE BEST CHIPSHOP
IN ANYSHIRE

The freshest fish, every day

8. Now change the rest of the text in the brochure. Select each section to highlight it, and type in your new text. You'll notice that the layout may appear scrambled when the new text isn't the same length as the original. You can solve this problem by typing blank lines (use the Enter key) to pad out the gaps. If you're feeling adventurous, you can try changing fonts and text styles at this point. When you are done, your brochure will be ready to print. If you want to make hundreds of copies, burn the finished Word file to a CD and hand it to a professional printer. You may be able to send the file to the printer as an email attachment.

Word-processor or desktop publishing tool?

As you can see, Word is very versatile. If you already have Word, you may be wondering whether or not you need a more sophisticated desktop publishing (DTP) package as well, such as Microsoft Publisher (see page 90).

The advantages of using a DTP package are that page layouts can be more sophisticated. A package such as Publisher also includes a huge selection of prepared project templates to experiment with. These can save you hours of time. However, if you do very occasional design work or need a simple design tool for a one-off project, Word will almost certainly be adequate.

MORE ABOUT WORD

Working with tables

The Table menu header includes a wealth of useful features. Apart from creating tables in the form of headings and column entries, you can also use this feature to sort text, for example, when you are creating a glossary or index. There are too many table options to describe in detail here. The best way to learn about these features is to experiment with them. For more information, refer to the Help feature (press F1 or select the Help menu header).

Word has many features which can be useful for standard letter writing, preparing reports and even creating more complicated documents. Here are details of some of them.

Word count (Alt + T + W)

Hold down the Alt key, hit T and W. To count the words in an area, highlight it first by clicking and dragging with the mouse.

Undo (Ctrl + Z)

Hold down Ctrl and hit Z to undo the last change you made. Word can undo multiple actions, stepping back through your changes. Note that Undo can't be undone. (A Repeat Typing feature – Ctrl + Y – repeats the last words you typed. But this won't necessarily replace something if you hit Undo accidentally.)

Find (Ctrl + F) and replace (Ctrl + H)

The standard search is a simple word-match tool, but if you click on the 'More' button you'll see a selection of more powerful matching options. 'Replace' replaces found words with another word of your choice. You can also replace punctuation marks.

The clipboard

When you cut or copy some text, it's transferred to a holding area called the clipboard. Word offers a multi-clip clipboard. Select Edit → Office Clipboard to see it. Every clip you cut or copy appears here. Select individual clips as you want, and paste them into your document.

Grammar and spelling (F7)

Select Tools → Options and then the Spelling/Grammar tab to see the automatic spell-check options. It's useful to have words replaced automatically. Turn off checking for words in capitals if you use a lot of acronyms. To check a document manually and add words to a custom dictionary, use Select Tools → Grammar and spelling. Grammar-checking is best left turned off. It's not particularly useful.

Autocorrect

If you find yourself regularly mistyping a word in the same way (for example 'teh' instead of 'the'), add it to the list shown in Autocorrect (Tools → Autocorrect options), and Word will correct it as you type. You can control other substitutions, such as smileys, arrows and symbols.

Autosave and recovery

Select Tools → Options and then the 'Save' tab. Make sure the 'Save autorecovery info' item is ticked, and specify a short interval of a few minutes in the box to the right of it. Now if your PC suffers a power failure or other problem, Word will have enough information to recover any documents you were working on.

Return to editing position (Shift + F5)

As it says – use this keyboard shortcut to take you back to the position of the last edit you made.

Thesaurus (Shift + F7)

Word includes a built-in thesaurus. It's not quite Roget, but very useful all the same.

Speech recognition

You can install it by clicking on Tools → Speech. Speech lets you dictate to Word. The technology used is slightly old now, and not as accurate as that available in more recent alternatives such as IBM's Via Voice and Dragon Dictate. Word is much less intelligent than a human secretary. But this feature can speed up some typing tasks.

Symbols and special characters

Select Insert → Symbol to display a box full of special characters, including accents, characters from Greek and other alphabets, and symbols such as © and ™. Note that these will work properly only if they are part of the font you are using. The standard Times New Roman and Arial fonts include most of these characters, but fonts you buy or download probably won't.

Change and version tracking (Ctrl + Shift + E)

It's sometimes useful to be able to keep track of changes as you make them. Select Tools → Track Changes and any changes you make to your document will be underlined and shown in blue. Deleted sections are shown with a strikethrough. Change this colour scheme and the way that changes are shown by going to Tools → Options and 'Track changes'.

Mail merge

If you have a form letter and want to merge in a list of names and addresses, you can use Word's mail-merge feature. If you select Tools → Letters and Mailings → Mail Merge Wizard, you'll be taken step-by-step through the process.

Repeating actions

If you find yourself repeating the same action or sequence of actions over and over, use a feature called a macro recorder, which can record and then repeat a set of actions. Go to Tools → Macro → Record New Macro. See the sidebar for more information about macros.

Selective cut and copy

Hold down Alt as you drag the mouse. Instead of highlighting sentences and paragraphs, you can highlight a square block of text. This is very useful when you have columns of text and want to select one.

Headers and footers

View → Header and footer will make a box appear from which you can select various bits of information that appear at the top and/or the bottom of a page – for example, chapter headings and page numbers.

Save as HTML

A cheap and simple way to create a page of web-ready information. This feature doesn't quite work perfectly, but it's adequate for simple pages.

Customised toolbars

Toolbars are the icon collections that appear under the main menu. There are many options here. Use Tools → Customise to show a list. Using the other tabs on this page, you can control which icons and shortcuts you want to see. You can even use Word with no toolbars at all.

Creating advanced macros

Word includes a complete programming system called Visual Basic. When you record a macro, it's stored as a short Visual Basic program. You can also write Visual Basic programs without recording them first. If you ever need a specialised tool in Word, you can use Visual Basic to create it. You can also use it for advanced projects which link information in Word with a database or spreadsheet. For more details, see one of the many printed Visual Basic manuals that are sold in PC stores.

INTRODUCING EXCEL

Graphs and charts in Excel

The default chart shown here is a simple one. Excel can draw many other types. Select Insert → Chart and then click on the various options that appear. To show each graph, click on 'Finish'. To remove it, hit the Backspace key. Note that some charts need two columns of data instead of just the one we're using here. If you select one of these, Excel will show a warning message.

Excel is a complicated, versatile piece of software that's most at home in a professional setting. To get the best from it, you'll need to be reasonably good at maths, have some problem-solving ability, and be prepared to learn simple programming skills. This is why Excel isn't recommended for home budgeting, or anything more complicated than simple bookkeeping.

But Excel does have some features that are useful to beginners. To illustrate this, we've created a two-stage example. The first stage shows how to produce a simple graph. The second and more complicated stage on the next page is a demonstration of how to convert metric measurements to imperial.

1. When you start Excel, you'll see this blank grid of cells. Each cell in the grid can contain a number – which can be a date, a price, or almost anything else – or a formula. We'll start with dates. Select the cell at the top left (it should be labelled A1) and type in the date as shown.

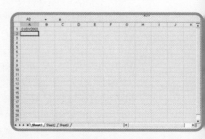

2. Click on the cell underneath it (A2), and type in your first formula like this: =A1+1. The '=' sign tells Excel that what follows is a formula. 'A1+1' means 'take the contents of cell A1 and add 1 to it.' When you hit Return, you'll see this cell now shows the day after the one above it. Try changing the date in A1. You'll see that A2 automatically always shows the day after.

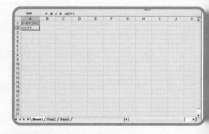

3. Select A2, and type Ctrl + C to copy. Click on A3 and drag the mouse downwards till you get to A31. You'll see the area highlighted in dark grey. Type Ctrl + V to paste. Excel will now do something impressive – it fills all the A column down to A31 with dates, in calendar order. If you change the date in A1, you'll see that all the cells will again follow the change.

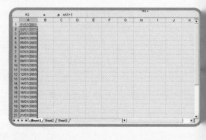

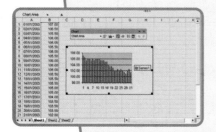

4. Type two different numbers into B1 and B2. (We'll pretend these are daily weight measurements from your bathroom scales – you can use real measurements if you want to!) Highlight column B by clicking on the 'B' column header. Then select Insert → Chart, and click on 'Finish'. You'll see a graph of your measurements appear. Add some more numbers to the B column. For each one, the graph will be instantly updated. You could extend the period by repeating the copy and paste at the bottom of column A, and then adding more entries into the B column.

5. So far we have weight in kilos. What if we're old fashioned and would prefer it in stones and pounds? While Excel has built-in conversion facilities, they're not intelligent enough to do this, so we'll have to do it ourselves. The first step is to convert kilos to stone (1kg = 0.45359lb; 1st = 14lb). So the formula for C1 that converts stones from kilos is '=B1/0.45359/14'. If we copy and paste the whole column as before, we now get a list of kilo equivalents of column A in stones in column B.

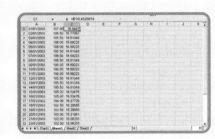

6. But something isn't right. We'd rather have stones and pounds, not the decimal fractions of stones we're seeing here. Excel includes an integer part (whole number) calculation feature called 'Int'. To eliminate the decimals, we use '=INT(B1/0.45359/14)'. Now we just get whole numbers of stones. (We could simplify this formula to '=INT(B1/0.032)', but we'll leave it for now as a reminder of where the formula comes from.)

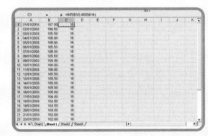

7. This is an improvement, but pounds are still missing. The way to calculate the pounds in each stone is to divide by 14 and take the remainder. Excel includes a remainder division tool called 'Mod.' So our formula is '=INT(MOD((B1/0.45359),14))'. Note that a tiny tag appears in yellow showing the MOD function. Click on this and you'll see help information for the MOD feature.

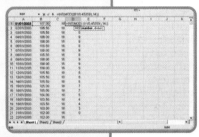

8. We're nearly done. Now all we have to do is combine stones and pounds into a single number. The way to do this is to divide the pounds by 100, to force them to appear after the decimal point, and add them to stones – and so our formula here is '=C1+D1/100'.

The important thing to remember isn't the details of the formulas we've used, but how you can use Excel to create relationships between cells, formulae, and its built-in calculation tools. It's really just a huge and complicated desk calculator, with some automatic features.

In Excel you can create multiple worksheets, and still make connections between the cells in the same way as you do on a single sheet. Use your mouse to select the cells. For more details see the Excel help feature, available if you hit the F1 key.

INTRODUCING POWERPOINT

Why use Power-Point?

You're unlikely to find a good use for PowerPoint at home, unless you need to give a lecture or talk to a club or society. If you have a colour printer, you can print PowerPoint slides directly on to overhead projector transparencies (which you can buy at any good office supplies store). PowerPoint will also produce black and white handouts, although you'll need to choose backgrounds and colour schemes wisely to get the best results.

PowerPoint is a powerful piece of software. Originally it was designed to print attractive slides for handouts and overhead projectors. Many business users now use their laptop to show their presentation live. So PowerPoint includes features for working with music, video and animations. In spite of its sophistication it's still surprisingly easy to use. Here's a step-by-step guided tour.

1. When you start PowerPoint, this is what appears. In the middle is the first slide of your presentation. Around it are various editing options. It's possible to design your own slides completely from scratch, with your own artwork, lettering and layouts. But the built-in designs are so good there's very little reason to do this. For now, we'll start simply.

2. As the prompts say, click on the various parts of the slide to add your own text: it really is this straightforward. Just type the text you want to appear on your slide. To add a new slide, click on Insert → New Slide. When you do, it's added to the list of slides that appears at the left.

3. The slides in PowerPoint have various possible formats. If you can't see these options, click the 'Design' button at the right. Then select Slide Design → Slide Layout. You'll see a list of the available formats. Experiment with these to see what they do. The slide shown here is another simple slide with a title and some bulleted sub-headings.

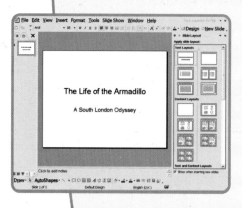

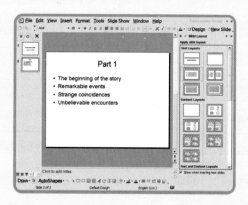

4. So far, the visual impact of our slides perhaps leaves something to be desired. This can easily be changed. Select Slide Design → Design Templates. You'll see a list of different designs, each of which adds a different background and a different lettering style. Click on each of these to see how it changes the look of your slides. If you click towards the right of each design preview in the taskbar, you'll see an arrow appear. Click on this and you'll be given the option to change the design of the current slide, or of all the slides in your presentation.

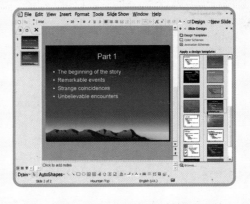

5. Each design is available in a range of colours. If the Color Schemes link is showing in the taskbar, click on it. If not, select Slide Design → Color Schemes. This time, you'll see a list of colour previews. Experiment with these to find one you like. Again, you can apply it to all the slides, or just the current one.

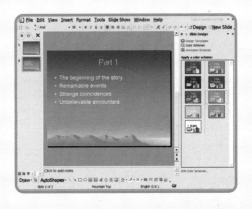

6. There are two ways to make your presentation more interesting. The first is to add sound and video. Select Slide Design → Slide Layout. Now choose one of the 'content templates' – perhaps one with a title. You'll see a graphic representing the content. You can fill this space with a sound or video file, set up either to play when the slide appears or when you select the content. The other option is to add animation to each slide. Select Slide Show → Animation schemes, and experiment with the list that appears. You can also add transitions between slides. Select the taskbar menu again, and choose 'Slide transitions'. Again, experiment with the list that appears. When you are done, you can preview the whole slideshow by hitting F5.

Introducing PowerPoint

PowerPoint's other features

This simple introduction is enough to help you create your own presentations. But PowerPoint can do far more than what we've shown here. You can work with organisational charts and block diagrams, financial and other charts – you can import these directly from Excel – and slide show timing, so that you can create automated slide shows. In fact, there are too many features to list here in detail. While you can buy expensive books that explain how PowerPoint can be used, it's easier and cheaper to simply experiment with all the menu options, and resort to the built-in F1 help if something isn't clear.

CONTACTS AND DATABASES

The PDA option

Microsoft's Pocket PC system, the Palm hand-held organiser and Nokia's Communicator series of mobile phones are all pocket-sized (albeit jacket-pocket) ways of managing contacts. They're most often used as an electronic version of a paper organiser, but with added email and sometimes web facilities. They can all be expanded to do other kinds of work with additional software. Some, such as Nokia's 9210i Communicator, include a built-in mobile phone.

Contacts

Managing contacts and addresses on a PC can be both frustrating and gratifying at the same time. The obvious advantage is the simplicity of it: when a friend or business contact moves, all you have to do is retype his or her details to keep them on your system. The frustrating part comes from trying to find software that organises information the way you want it to be organised. Everyone uses contacts differently, and keeps different kinds of information about the people they know.

Outlook and Outlook Express

Outlook Express, included free with Windows XP, includes some simple contact features. It's comprehensive but in practice it's rather fiddly to work with. Outlook, which is included in Microsoft Office, is more business oriented. It's one of the few contact managers that can keep track of almost all the contact information you'll ever need, including home, mobile and various work numbers, the numbers and names of an individual's boss and any assistants, their website URL, and so on. It's slightly easier to use than Outlook Express, and unlike Express it includes a mail merge feature for contacts (select a contact, then Tools → Mail Merge), which can print to address labels, or link easily to Word for producing form letters.

Other alternatives

Lotus Organizer is a popular alternative to the various versions of Outlook. Its presentation is very simple and familiar – it looks and works very much like a paper organiser – and it includes diary and appointment features, special date reminders, email and links to other software. Once part of Lotus SmartSuite, which was a competitor to Microsoft Office, it's now sometimes given away for free with magazines.

Act! (www.act.com) is another popular choice for business use. It includes a free-form organisation which lets you specify what kind of information you want to include with each contact. You can also make copious notes for each contact, which is useful for sales work.

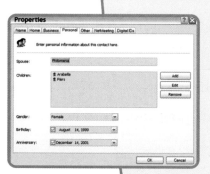

Outlook Express can remember birthdays and other useful personal information

Lotus Organizer isn't the most visually appealing contact application, but it is one of the easiest to use and most productive

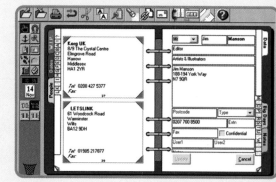

Databases

The ultimate tool for managing contacts, or any other kind of information, is the database. Microsoft Works Suite includes a simple database, and the professional versions of Office include a more complex package called Access. With a database you can specify exactly which information you want to keep, and how you want to organise it. You can also sort and summarise information to order.

While you could use a database to keep details of your video collection or to manage recipes, in practice it's often easier to use some other method – perhaps even an old-fashioned but convenient tool like a card box. As a rule of thumb, databases come into their own only when you need to cross-reference or summarise the information they contain.

So, for home cooking, for example, it's just as convenient to store recipes in simple text files in a folder, or even on paper in a card index. It's only if you entertain on a lavish scale or run a restaurant that the features in a database can become truly useful. Access is too complicated to describe in detail here. But, for example, you could use it to cross-reference a list of ingredients – which you would update with the latest price information – with a menu plan based on various recipes that use those ingredients. The summary tools could then provide the total quantities for each ingredient for a given menu plan, and also the total cost. For a job like this, a database would be more convenient than a spreadsheet, because it would make it possible to pick and choose from the various possible recipes. It would take a while to set up such a project. But the investment could easily be worth the time, and once done your database would carry on being useful and saving you time indefinitely.

The database included in Works is supplied with templates for various simple database projects

PEOPLE, PLACES AND THINGS

Never get lost

For those who can afford the hefty price, it's possible to buy GPS (global positioning system) receivers that plug into your PC. If your PC is a laptop, you can use a combination of Autoroute and GPS to track where you are on the map. Garmin has the largest range of GPS receivers. Some include maps and a large screen of their own, so you don't need to use a PC at all.

Finding places, going places

If you've ever tried planning a driving holiday, you'll know that getting from A to B by a certain time requires a lot of guesswork and often a little luck. Route-planner software can eliminate the guesswork. You can specify start points and destinations using addresses, post codes or zip codes, and sometimes even latitude and longitude. The PC will then guess journey time and even fuel consumption based on estimates you give. You can print maps at various scales, and also create directions which list all the roads used and approximate journey timings.

Microsoft's Autoroute (about £40) is a popular route planner, available in versions that cover either Europe or the USA. (There's no worldwide version yet.) Alternatives include Route 66 Pro (£55), which includes a remarkable 4.75 million streets across Europe, and a live link to traffic information when you are online. Map & Travel's Route Planner (£30) is rather simpler and also cheaper. (You may also want to look at the various free online route planners listed on page 54.)

Explore the streets around the seafront of Naples from the comfort of your keyboard with Microsoft Autoroute

Maps for everyone

The Ordnance Survey sells and licenses its information to various digital mapmakers. You can find tourist quality (1:600,000) and road maps (1:250,000) in almost any computer store. If you need more detail, Memory Map (www.memory-map.co.uk) sells the familiar and detailed 1:50,000 range of OS maps. A set of 12 CDs (each CD costs £24.95) covers the whole of the UK. Memory Map also sells its own hike planner and navigation tool, and digital versions of the A–Z range of street maps. All of these can be connected to a GPS receiver (see sidebar). Most will also work in a more limited way on a hand-held pocket PC, so they can be used outdoors without a laptop.

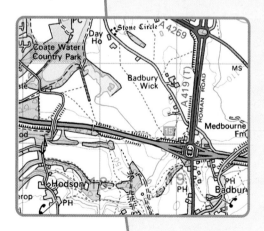

If you've never learned how to re-fold an OS map , Memory Map's digital maps may be just the thing for you

Finding people

Apart from the friend-finders and other resources that are available online (see page 152), it's possible to buy a database of UK names, addresses and phone numbers. The UK Info product range from 192 (www.192.com) combines information from the UK phonebook and the electoral register. It can be quite frighteningly effective at finding addresses and phone numbers if given a name and an optional geographical location. Those worried about privacy can rest assured that if someone is ex-directory, no phone number is included.

A professional version (about £200) includes business contact information, which the personal version (about £50) lacks. Continental European versions are available for £10 extra. There's also a historical version, which includes the last ten years of records for about £250. The UK Info desk even has a simple route-planner feature, and a facility for online phone calls – similar to voice chat (see page 143) and free, albeit not quite as convenient as using a real phone.

Finding out about things

Microsoft's Encarta digital encyclopaedia has become a bestseller. It's not outstandingly comprehensive, but it is very easy to use, and is supplied with online links that provide news and extra information when you are connected to the Internet. A basic version of Encarta is included in the Works Suite (see page 108). You can buy a more advanced version for about £35.

For a more detailed alternative, it's worth considering the CD/DVD versions of Encyclopaedia Britannica. For between £20 and £60 depending on the edition, you get the impressively comprehensive complete text of the 32-volume print version, and some rather less-convincing multimedia sound and video enhancements. There are various optional extras including student editions, an atlas, a thesaurus and other useful reference material. The software comes on between 2 and 5 CDs, depending which package of extras you buy.

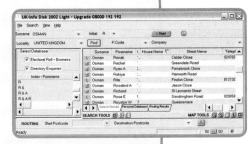

The Hindu festival of lights, Diwali, as described in Microsoft's Encarta encyclopaedia

Big data? Big disks

Autoroute, Encarta, Britannica and the UK Info disk can all be run from CDs. But disk swapping can be inconvenient, and they become much easier to use when all the information they include is copied to hard disk. The catch? You'll need to allow around 500Mb for each program.

4.11 People, places and things

Not quite the entire population of the UK, but surprisingly close – UK Info disk from 192.com

MICROSOFT MONEY

Money *vs* Quicken

Intuit's Quicken is Money's main competitor. The two programs are very similar, with directly comparable features, and both seem to satisfy consumers' needs. However, the consensus among users and independent software reviewers is that Money is slightly more flexible for home finance, and Quicken is better for those who spend a lot of time maintaining a stock portfolio. It's rare for people to switch midstream. But if you're thinking about buying one of them, it's worth investigating both in detail.

Microsoft's Money is a budgeting tool and financial planner specially designed for use at home. It includes powerful cash-flow and budgeting tools, and also the useful ability to download bank statements from most, if not quite all, of the UK's online banking services. (You should check with your online banker to see whether or not Money is supported. See the next section.) This automated facility makes reconciliations and accurate record-keeping much more straightforward. For those with longer-term strategic interests, Money also includes hints and planners that help with saving for various goals, and facilities for creating and managing portfolios for both immediate and retirement investment aims.

Setting up Money is rather tedious. It has a slightly quirky design which looks and works half like a web browser, and half like a standard piece of software. To begin with, you have to specify your own and your partner's account details, and also list every regular bill payment. Creating a full financial picture, with all possible income and every last bill and outgoing, can take an hour or two. But this has to be done only once.

Once Money is ready, you'll find it makes budgeting much easier and quicker. There's a 'background banking' facility so that your accounts will be updated automatically while you are doing something else. Moreover, it's possible to link the prices of shares to the real market price and set up warnings so you can sell or buy according to live trading conditions (although these are delayed by about 20 minutes, and there's no option for live Level 2 prices – see page 130).

Other useful features include loan-repayment calculators (so that you can check how much you still owe), payment summaries for budgeting (so that you can see in advance if a month is going to be difficult), and various other kinds of reports and calculations, including useful extras such as VAT and capital gains tax. It also provides a summary graph that tells you whether or not your finances in general are getting healthier overall.

There are no particular tips to remember with Money, because its biggest strength is that it includes so many tips of its own. While you can budget with a pen and paper (or a spreadsheet – see the sidebar), Money will force you to think about the bigger financial picture – which is a powerful and useful feature in itself.

By using a spreadsheet like Excel, you could do almost everything that Money does. You won't be able to synchronise your finances with your bank or download the latest stock prices, but basic budgeting is certainly possible. So which is better? We'd recommend Excel for very simple budgeting. But Money is a better choice for more general use. You are unlikely to use all the features, but their presence can nudge you to think about aspects of your finances you might otherwise miss.

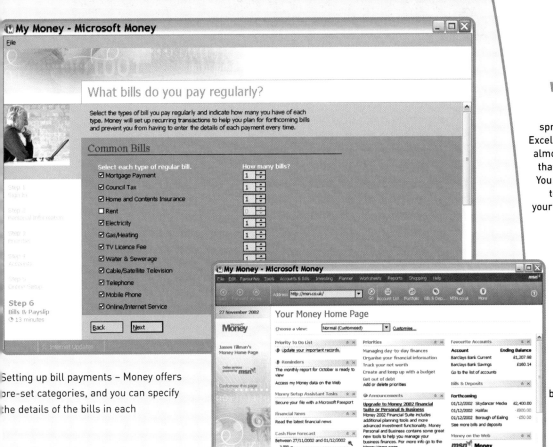

Setting up bill payments – Money offers pre-set categories, and you can specify the details of the bills in each

The home page at the centre of Money is designed to work like a web page, and includes internal links that work like menus, and external links to Microsoft's MSN web service

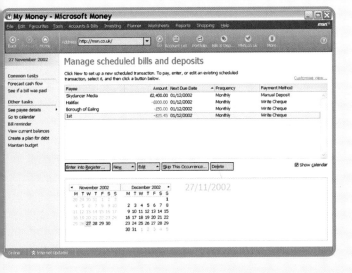

You can add bill payments at any time, either as regular outgoings (by month, day, week, etc.), or as one-off payments. This summary shows your payment calendar

ONLINE BANKING

Email and the banks

Banks don't like email because it's not secure. So you can bank online, but you won't be able to email your manager or your branch directly!

Not many people appreciate just how flexible web banking can be. You can use most of your bank's services at any time of day – without joining a queue. You can bank in your local library, in a teashop with a laptop and a mobile, or in an Internet café anywhere in the world. (However, be careful about using public PCs, where spyware may have been installed, and where people or even CCTV cameras can be watching.)

A common misperception is that there's little more to online banking than using your PC and a website to check balances, arrange transfers and pay bills. In practice, even the Big Four banks offer much more than this online. Newer banking companies have taken a more adventurous approach, and offer a more comprehensive service than you'll find in a typical branch bank.

Banking securely

A big part of online banking's appeal is that it's very easy to use and doesn't need advanced web skills. The biggest complication is remembering passcodes and registration numbers. For security reasons, you shouldn't write them down or keep them in a file. But a useful trick is to write down the numbers modified in some simple way – for example, with every pair of digits swapped, or with some other more memorable number added. This keeps the codes safe, even if someone sees them. Once connected, web pages are displayed using secure hacker-proof Internet technology – but check for the secure 'https://' indicator at the start of the URL to be sure.

Comparing banks

All the online banks offer the same basic services. You can check your balance, transfer money between accounts, pay bills and set up regular bill payments. You'll also find invitations to explore the kinds of services you'll find in a typical branch, including loans, ISAs, mortgages, home and car insurance and, share dealing and so on.

The main comparison points include access to more advanced services such as fast transfers, interactive payments via satellite TV (a service offered by HSBC and Egg), higher current-account interest rates, and – perhaps most importantly – lower credit-card and loan rates, especially for those with good credit ratings. The older, Big Four high-street banks tend to be rather more formal and rather less generous in this area. While this isn't always true, it means that the newer services (see facing page) are well worth investigating.

Online newcomers

The newcomers – Smile, Egg, Cahoot, Intelligent Finance (IF) – are all owned by existing large financial institutions, but have been created specially for Internet users, and so have a slightly more adventurous style. For example, Goldfish includes consumer buying guides on its site, and Cahoot's credit card offers very low transfer rates and an exceptionally low interest rate.

Virgin One pioneered the all-in-one account, which links mortgages, savings and a current account into a single account, and saves you money on your mortgage payments over the long term. Other banks, such as IF and Direct Line, offer similar products now. All these services are subtly different, and the rates on offer vary too. Doing some online research can literally save you thousands of pounds. To find out how, see Section 4.14.

The Barclays online banking service offers few frills

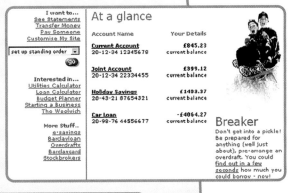

Barclays
www.personal.barclays.co.uk

LloydsTSB
www.lloydstsb.com

Natwest
www.natwest.com

HSBC
www.ukpersonalhsbc.com

Royal Bank of Scotland
www.rbs.co.uk

Cahoot
www.cahoot.com

Virgin One
www.virginone.com

Direct Line
uk.directline.com

Smile
www.smile.co.uk

Egg
www.egg.co.uk

Cahoot
www.cahoot.com

Intelligent Finance
www.if.com

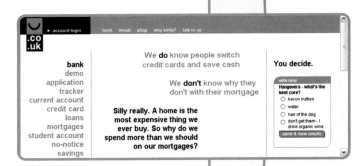

Smile's site goes for a friendly approach

Egg includes TV banking via Sky

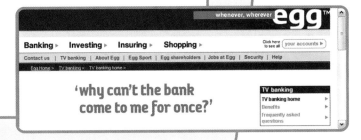

MORE ABOUT MONEY

Comparison and listing services

It would take hours to find and compare all the possible rates and services available online. You can avoid that by trying these comparison and listing services. An hour or two of research here can literally save you hundreds or even thousands of pounds. Apart from familiar services such as loans, mortgages and credit cards, you'll also find health and critical illness insurance, dental insurance, pet insurance, offshore accounts, and other more obscure financial products that you may not have considered but could find useful. One word of warning – some of these sites are funded by advertising and use sponsored pop-ups aggressively. This doesn't affect the quality of the information, but you should consider installing an ad pop-up stopper (see page 163).

Financelink – a comprehensive financial website directory

Financial advice and comparison sites
Blays (www.blays.co.uk)
Moneyfacts (www.moneyfacts.co.uk)
Moneyextra (www.moneyextra.co.uk)
Moneysupermarket
(www.moneysupermarket.co.uk)

Use these sites to find financial services, and to compare the rates and financial products on offer. Blays is comprehensive but a little more terse than the rest. The others include various comparison tools and listings. Moneyextra and Moneysupermarket feature automated product selection, so you can enter your requirements and personal circumstances and find the best rates and deals online. Moneysupermarket even includes a mortgage auction feature, where mortgage companies can compete to offer you their most competitive bids.

A few of the services available on MoneyExtra

Financial listings
www.financelink.co.uk   www.find.co.uk

These listings sites can provide you with a jumping-off point for further research. You'll find quick links to thousands of financial websites covering savings, investments, loans and also business finance.

Financial advisor listings
www.sofa.org   www.unbiased.co.uk
www.ifadirectory.co.uk   www.financialplanning.org.uk

Explore these sites if you're looking for a consultation with a financial advisor. SOFA is the professional organisation for financial advisors. The other sites can help you find an advisor based on your location, the fees or commission charged, the product areas covered, and even by whether the person is male or female.

More general help

Although personal finance is now part of the school curriculum, it's still possible to leave school ready for university or employment with only a very sketchy understanding of important financial essentials. Whether you're a complete financial beginner or an expert looking to consolidate and streamline your incomings and outgoings, help is at hand at the following sites.

www.bbc.co.uk/yourmoney
Recovering spendaholic Alvin Hall takes you carefully through the sometimes painful process of looking at your finances honestly, creating a plan to get out of debt, and managing your savings and financial future.

www.moneycentral.co.uk
Microsoft's own financial pages. There's plenty of advertising (some of it useful), but also unique services such as a tax-code calculator and payslip checker, and simplified best-buy tables for current and deposit accounts, and also mortgages.

www.thisismoney.com
Possibly the most comprehensive range of price-comparison tools available in the UK. You can compare banks, insurers and other services, and also gas, electricity and water rates, and even TV and home phone payments. There's also a vice-o-meter, which shows how much the government makes from your weekly alcohol and cigarette bill.

www.about-mortgages.co.uk
A huge list of all the UK lenders, with links to sources of online mortgages. It also includes information about online conveyancing. For other loans, there's a companion site at www.about-personal-loans.co.uk.

www.eiris.org
Information about financial services specially targeted at ethical investors. A useful section answers questions for those new to the process of asking for financial advice.

You can find news as well as price comparisons at This Is Money

Investigate your mortgage options at About-Mortgages

Mortgages

- Fixed Rates *(with no extended redemption tie-ins)*
- Fixed Rates *(with extended redemption tie-ins)*
- Capped Rates
- Discounted Variable Rates
- 100% Mortgages
- Self Certification Rates
- First Time Buyer Discounted Variable Rates
- Variable Rates
- Buy to Let Rates
- Current Account & Offset Mortgages

STOCKS AND SHARES ONLINE

Useful dealer listing sites

www.funds-sp.com

www.trust net.co.uk

www.gomez.com

www.bluesky ratings.com

www.apcims. co.uk

Cheap share trades

Citydeal
www.city deal.co.uk

Nothing Ventured
www.nothing-ventured.com

Hargreaves Lansdown
www.h-l.co.uk

iDealing
www.idealing.com

Saga
www.saga.co.uk

MyBroker
www.mybroker.com

Share
www.share.com

Traders and trading

In a typical trade, you pick a listed share, specify how many shares you would like or how much you want to spend/sell, and then confirm the trade. You only rarely receive paper share certificates, although you can sometimes ask for them at extra cost. Usually trades are confirmed electronically.

At first glance, the handful of online brokers that advertise widely all offer similar services. Experienced traders can tell the good from the bad according to the following.

Trading fees A fixed fee of less than £10 is typical for small trades. Some traders such as Halifax Sharebuilder (www.halifax.co.uk/sharebuilder) charge as little as £1.50. Others charge a commission. Some also charge an annual subscription fee.

Payment You won't usually be allowed to pay by credit card, although debit cards may be accepted. Many dealers run an account system where you have to keep a certain amount of money ready for trading. If you need to keep a lot in this account ready for trades, make sure you are getting a fair rate of interest on the balance.

Price information When you buy or sell, you always see up-to-the-minute prices for a single share. But for a market overview, prices will be delayed by 20 minutes. You can sometimes pay extra to see prices that change in real time (known as Level 2 prices), but this isn't recommended for dabblers or casual traders. Some dealers offer special portfolio-management software. This can summarise your portfolio on a single screen.

Charts and graphs You can pick shares according to 'fundamentals' – basic business indicators – or by referring to charts that summarise movements. Not all investors use these charts, but if you master the basics and decide that they work for you it's important to choose a dealer that offers them.

Special features Stop loss trades will automatically limit your losses if your favourite stocks start heading south. Trading on foreign exchanges, including the Dow and NASDAQ, is another option. Online ISAs are also popular, and a good way to avoid paying tax on income and gains from many investments. Most dealers can create a 'self-select' share ISA for you into which you can put your own choice of shares. You will probably pay a small sum for it to be managed.

A typical online portfolio, managed by dealers SelfTrade

Getting advice

Many dealers will send you regular trading tips by email. For reasons that should be obvious, it's perhaps best not to take these too seriously. If you're looking for more objective trading advice and suggestions, the weekly magazines Investors Chronicle, Shares Weekly and Growth Company Investor, and services such Hemscott (www.hemscott.net) can provide alternative perspectives. Messageboards and chatrooms are a popular way to exchange share tips, but you should be wary of advice you receive. At worst they can be examples of the criminally minded leading the blind. The FSA consumer website (www.fsa.gov.uk/consumer) includes a good overview of more general trading information, and also lists regular consumer alerts.

Advanced trading

Many online dealing houses offer other financial products such as CFDs (contracts for differences), covered warrants, and traded futures and options. These can seem like magic to novice investors, because they make it possible to trade more shares than you can afford to buy. Some can also be used to 'go short', which means you can make money even if the market falls. They may even be free of stamp duty and capital gains tax. Dealing commissions can also be lower – in some cases trades are entirely free.

However, a reputable broker will deal in these only if he or she is satisfied that you are a sophisticated investor who understands the risks. You will usually be asked to provide an initial investment of thousands of pounds – in some cases, tens or hundreds of thousands. In practice, all of these products are very sensitive to market movements, so the risks are far higher than even for normal shares. With some products, your potential loss is literally unlimited. So although these options are available and may be widely advertised, you shouldn't consider them unless you understand them fully. At the very least, this means good market intelligence and a much better grasp of what moves the markets than will be available to a casual investor. **They are definitely not suitable for beginners or casual traders.**

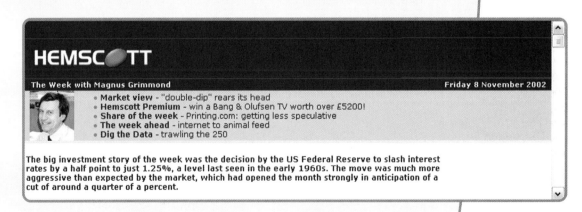

Advice online – Hemscott's regular newsletter is a staple among some investors

ONLINE TAX RETURNS AND MONEY TRANSFERS

Digital certificates

A digital certificate is an electronic ID card that's occasionally used for secure online transactions and other business. It's more convenient than a PIN number because you don't have to remember the details. While interesting in theory, certificates are expensive and rather clumsy in practice. To get a certificate you have to fill in an online form, send off an application that includes copies of various forms of physical identification, and pay just over £50. For now, we suggest that the PIN option is more convenient.

Government services online

The government is keen to eliminate as much paperwork as possible as soon as possible, and replace paperwork collection with online services. The eventual plan is to make all transactions electronic, although it's hard to see how this is going to be possible in practice. As part of this process, various services are now available online including VAT returns, income tax returns, corporation tax, tax credit applications, PAYE returns, child benefit claims and job-centre listings.

Also available, but of rather less interest to most people, are export permit applications and applications for aid for farmers.

Signing up for all of these is a two-stage process. First, you need to apply through the central government gateway at www.gateway.gov.uk. This will give you a PIN number, which is sent to you through the post, or a chance to buy a digital certificate (see the sidebar). Once you have signed in, you then have to go to the websites of the government service you want. Unfortunately, direct links aren't provided, so we've listed them here.

How to sign up for electronic services, the government way

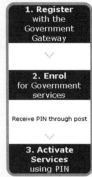

Links to self-assessment returns, corporation tax, PAYE and tax credits
www.inlandrevenue.gov.uk/index.htm
VAT returns
www.hmce.gov.uk/business/electronic/evr.htm
Links to child benefit online
www.dwp.gov.uk
Job-centre listings
www.jobcentreplus.gov.uk

Resources on the Inland Revenue Site

Get a job online. This query found a job in Belgium

Once you've found the office you want, the remainder of the process is self-explanatory. Filling in a tax return online is no harder (and no easier) than filling in a paper one. The advantage is the convenience of not having to deal with paper and of being sure that your return is delivered on time. (Make sure you apply for the service well in advance – if you leave it to the last minute, you may miss the deadline anyway.)

It's worth knowing that unlike local job-centre searches, online job-centre listings now cover the whole of the EU. Clearly, not everyone is happy to travel, but for those who are prepared to look outside the UK, the listings can provide leads to some surprisingly interesting and potentially lucrative work.

Money transfers

An interesting new way of transferring money is Yahoo's Pay Direct, managed by HSBC. Fees are reasonable – 50p to pay by debit card, 50p plus 2% for credit-card payments. You can also fund payments by making a transfer beforehand, although this takes up to five days. Payments by card are completed within one day. For more details see uk.paydirect.hsbc.com.

Another option is PayPal (see page 101). It's not a free service, and your recipient will have to sign up for it before he or she can receive your money. He or she will also have to wait until PayPal does a payment run before he or she can receive the money.

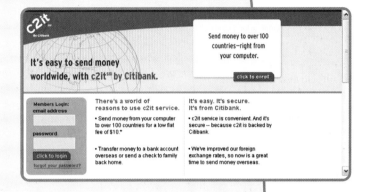

Otherwise, there are no direct transfer facilities available from the UK. For transfers to the UK from the USA, a good choice is c2it (www.c2it.com). The user pays a flat $10 fee. The service also allows fast free transfers within the USA.

Western Union (www.westernunion.com) doesn't allow direct transfers on its website, but it does provide telephone links and postal addresses for its agents in the UK, who can arrange wire transfers to other countries for a reasonable fee. Although the money is wired electronically, it can't be transferred to a bank account directly. Instead, the recipient has to visit the local Western Union agent and receive payment in cash and/or a cheque.

BACS and CHAPS
If you need a fast transfer of money from your bank account, you can use the banks' own BACS (three-working days) and CHAPS (same day) payment services. Businesses that require regular payments to be made, for example, for an employee payroll, can ask their bank about PC software that will automate these payments. But this isn't available to the public for one-off payments. In fact, there's no direct open access to the BACS or CHAPS systems online. Unfortunately, if you want to use these services, you'll have to talk to someone at your bank about them.

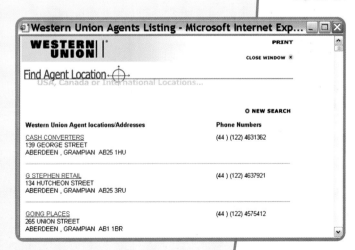

Citibank's wire transfer service – available for transfers only *to* the UK

Western Union's site lists hundreds of agents all over the UK

INTRODUCING SEARCH ENGINES

What does indexing mean?

Search engines 'crawl' the entire Web using software 'spiders'. In plain English this means they automatically follow the links on every page for as far as they lead. As they do this, they keep notes about the information they find on each page. This information is compiled into an index. When you run a search, you are really searching the index, not the whole of the Web! The index is updated regularly – perhaps daily for information on popular sites, and monthly for less popular ones.

According to some estimates, there are about 10 billion pages of information on the Internet – far more than are in print form in the world's largest libraries. A big part of the Internet's power comes from this huge, ever-changing pool of knowledge. But this size is also the Internet's biggest weakness: without some way of ordering the data, it is too unwieldy to be of use.

Search engines are part of the answer. They attempt to index about 2 billion pages, and provide a kind of telephone-directory service that makes it possible to find interesting and useful pages with some simple search skills.

There are over 100 search engines available, but at any one time only a handful will be popular and heavily used. Each of these may be superseded at any time as engines with more advanced technology become available. Older engines will still work, but may not give the widest or most useful selection of results.

Search engines are not intelligent. They index pages simply by checking which words are included in the text on each page. They don't understand English and they have no ability to make sense of context or meaning. In spite of this they can be surprisingly useful and effective.

News sites such as the BBC site and some shopping sites often have small search engines of their own built into the site. These are sometimes limited to pages on that site. Again, they are a useful way to find information you are looking for.

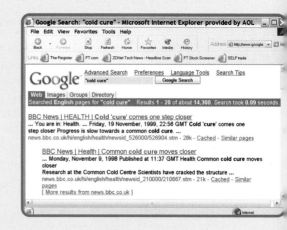

Some popular search engines:
Google
Yahoo
alltheweb

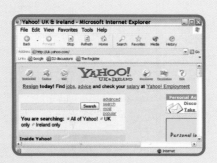

Keyword searches

All search engines include a 'keyword search' facility. This looks for words or phrases. For example, to find out more about Hampton Court in London, simply type "Hampton Court" into a search engine, complete with quote marks. Click on the search button and wait a while: a list of pages will appear that mention Hampton Court. If Hampton Court has its own website (which in fact it does), this will appear at or near the top of the list. If the list that appears is too long to fit on to a single page, you'll see links to further results at the bottom of the listing. 'Next' will show the next page. The others will show pages with further information in decreasing order of interest and relevance.

If you are looking for a single word, quote marks aren't needed. However, if you are looking for a phrase in a keyword search, use quote marks because otherwise the search engine will look for pages that include – but anywhere on the page and in any order – the words you mention. This is likely to give you a result that isn't very useful.

Category searches

Search engines such as Yahoo specialise in category searches. These are more like looking through a library where the books are arranged in groups and sub-groups. Each sub-group includes further sub-sub-groupings. Category searches are best used when you want a broad overview of the information that's available, rather than links to pages about one particular subject. For example, if you are researching a certain aspect of history, a category search will show you pages that might not appear in a keyword search. Category searches are not as precise as keyword searches and take longer, but are much better for adventurous exploration and getting an overview of the information available.

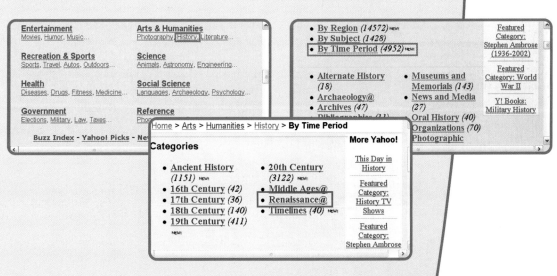

USING GOOGLE TO FIND WHAT YOU WANT

Google simple search summary

Quote marks – search for the exact phrase in quotes

'+' sign before a word – list only sites that include this word

'-' sign before a word – list only sites that don't include this word

Getting the best from any search is a process of elimination. Category searches are easy to use and understand, although it can sometimes take a certain amount of blundering around all the options that appear until you find what you are looking for. Keyword searches may need a little more practice. Over the next couple of pages we'll take you through some of the basic features of Google to find useful information. You can adapt these search techniques for yourself. The more you practise, the easier, quicker and more rewarding searching becomes.

You might expect all manufacturers to list phone numbers on their web pages. But not all do. In a recent search example, we needed to find a contact number for the film- and camera-maker Fuji. The number wasn't listed on the site. As BT's Directory Enquiries telephone service is not free, we'll use this search example to see if there's equivalent phone directory information available on the Web. We'll start by going to Google and typing "directory enquiries" in the search box, followed by the Return key to start the search.

A direct hit! We have BT's main site at the top of the list, and a direct link to the online directory enquiries service under it. But it's not all good news. BT's site asks us to register. It limits us to ten searches a day. (Adequate, but it can take a few searches to find what we want.) And it won't search for a business without knowing which town to look in. We can make a guess at London here. But if we're wrong, we won't get what we want. So although we've found a good site, it doesn't quite fit our requirements.

Further down the list displayed by the original search are other alternatives. Some of these make it clear that we'll have to sign up and pay money to find phone numbers. This isn't ideal, so we keep looking down. The ukphonebook site looks interesting.

When we click on it, we see that it's exactly what we're looking for. It's free, and in the business section we can list businesses by names without needing to know where they are. When we type 'Fuji' here and click on the 'Business' button, it shows a list of businesses with Fuji in the name, and their numbers. Among these is the number of the Fuji film company – which is what we set out to find.

More advanced search options

Here's how to use the search elimination tools in Google to filter out sites you don't want, and select sites you do. As an example, we'll look for information on home-made recipes for cold cures.

It's easy enough to get started. Just type "cold cure" into the search bar, and hit Return. You'll see a long list of sites – obviously a popular topic! But this search isn't specific enough. Included in the listing are news features, rather than recipes.

We could extend the search by typing '"cold cure" + recipe'. That would certainly work and would probably show us what we're looking for. But we'll approach this a little more creatively. Let's say we particularly like lemon. Type '"cold cure" +lemon' to show a revised search. This time we have sites that show cold cures that will include lemons, or lemon juice.

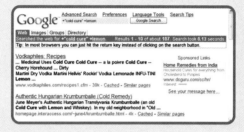

We can extend this indefinitely. This search looks for cures that include lemon and ginger but don't include cloves or coriander. No matter what you're searching for, most searches follow this same pattern – gradually homing in on the most likely sites by adding to a list of words to include and exclude, depending on what we're looking for.

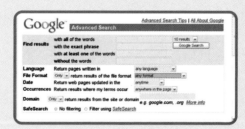

The process shown above will work for perhaps 95% of search requirements. For more advanced searches, we can use the 'Advanced Search' tool. (Click on the link at the side of the search bar.) You can use this tool to specify target dates and document types, search within a specific site rather than the whole of the Internet, and look for pages written in a given language. Experiment with the options on this page to see how they can work for you. In practice, you'll only rarely need to use advanced searches. They're most useful for limiting searches to a range of dates.

Picture and media searches

Google can also look for photos, drawings and even video clips. This sounds clever, but unfortunately it's not clever enough to recognise images directly. Instead, it searches for the names of pictures and sounds. In spite of this limitation, it can be surprisingly handy for finding Clip Art and photos. (Remember, though, that photos are often under copyright. Just because you can find them doesn't mean you can legally use them in your own work!) To use the Image search feature, click on the 'Image' tab above the search bar and type in your requirements as usual.

ADVANCED INTERNET RESEARCH

Newsgroup hints

For details of how newsgroups work, you could try searching for 'How are newsgroups organised?' or even 'How do newsgroups work?'. You'll find a large collection of explanatory articles online.

The gateway to a huge library of informally collected information

More about communities

As explained on page 140, the Internet provides a forum for various communities. You can use these to make new friends. But they can also be an almost unimaginably useful tool for research into every subject possible. At the same time, they can provide personal support while you study your favourite subjects or practise your hobbies. There are three ways to tap into this source of knowledge.

FAQs

The first is an old Internet tradition called the FAQ (frequently answered question) document. FAQs were most often created by the communities built around newsgroups, and were written as prepared answers to the most common questions asked by newcomers to each group. And because there are countless groups covering almost every subject, it's likely that if you search through the available FAQs you'll find something of value.

The newsgroup network is no longer as popular as it was, but many FAQs remain. Some are still being updated today. Because FAQs were created informally there's no guarantee that the answers in them are always correct. And many FAQs include information about group netiquette that won't interest outsiders. Still, they often provide a good starting point for a subject. A collection of FAQs is available at www.faqs.org/faqs/. You can search through it using keywords, by category, or in various other ways.

The Google and Yahoogroups archives

Postings in the most useful and interesting newsgroups (i.e. not those consisting of idle chatter or porn) have been collected and stored since the mid-1990s. This archive is now maintained as part of the Google search engine. If you go to Google (www.google.com) and select the 'Groups' tab, you can search through the hundreds of thousands of posted articles. Keyword, newsgroup, author and other searches are available. As with FAQs, it can be useful to experiment with reading newsgroups first to orient yourself among the postings that are made on almost every subject.

Asking real people

While looking through archives is useful, asking people directly can be even more effective. Both Usenet newsgroups and mailing-list communities such as Yahoogroups can be very useful to you. However, not everyone is friendly, and each group has its own culture. Blundering in and demanding that people share their knowledge with you may even make you some virtual enemies. It's a good idea to watch suitable groups for a while to see who may be able and willing to help you. In these live forums you can communicate publicly in the groups themselves, and also privately by email. While some groups are suspicious of newcomers, most will be open to someone who is willing to contribute something of value as well as asking questions.

Note that Yahoogroups seems to have replaced the newsgroup system for less technical and specialised discussions. It has its own archive system, but unfortunately it isn't as well organised or accessible as Google's. The archives of discussions in each Yahoogroup are kept separate, and there's no all-round search facility. In fact, you may have to join a group before you can even search it, because the archives aren't open to general readers. Some groups don't keep any archives at all. Even so, the discussions in the best groups can be well worth looking over. And if you join a group it's always possible to ask questions about something that someone else said, even if it was some time ago.

Meta-searches

With several search engines available, it's unlikely you'll ever try more than one or two. (In practice, most people stick with the one they're most familiar with – usually Google.) But no search engine is perfect, and one engine may find information that another misses. Meta-search tools use more than one search engine at once. They send the same query to all of them. Then they filter out duplicates in the results, and present all the remaining results on a single page. Meta-searching can be a very powerful way to look through as much of the information on the Web as possible as quickly as possible.

While there are plenty of free meta-search tools, most search only a small number of the less popular search engines. An exception to this is Dogpile, at www.dogpile.com. You use dogpile just like any keyword search engine, and results are presented in the usual way.

Commercial meta-search services include Surfwax (www.surfwax.com) and Copernic (www.copernic.com). Both provide a basic free level of service and also more advanced paid-for options which offer more powerful searches. You can even specify which engines and other information sources you want to use. Whereas Surfwax uses the Web, Copernic uses special software which you have to install. Both are highly rated with professionals who have to search for a living. Prices are reasonable, at about £50 a year. Copernic also offers a summariser tool which can automatically summarise and précis searches and other information.

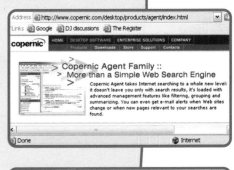

Experimental tools

Google is continually developing and trying out experimental services. Some of these are quirky, while others are genuinely useful. You can try out the latest ideas at the Google Labs page at labs.google.com. Don't expect the same level of service as you would from a fully developed search engine. These are tools-in-progress and can't be expected to work absolutely reliably. But they can offer some interesting jumping-off points, and can sometimes spark ideas for searches and investigations you might not have had otherwise.

About.com is another alternative information service. It offers a standard search engine, but also features articles written by experts and enthusiasts. The information is often good, and rivals or even betters that available in www.faqs.org/faqs/. Unfortunately, it's quite advertising heavy. It's a good idea to install a pop-up stopper (see page 163) before visiting it.

MAILING LISTS

Not just Yahoo

Not everyone likes Yahoo. Yahoogroups makes its money from advertising that is included with all emails, and the email addresses it collects are also used to send junk mail to. While you can opt out of this, the options are well hidden. Alternatives to Yahoo include Topica (www. topica.com), Cool List (www. coollist. com) and the UK-based Freeserve offshoot, Smart Groups (www.smart groups.com).

Mailing lists are one of the best ways of finding people with shared interests. While you can manage a mailing list by hand, using features built into email software (cc:, bcc: and reply to all), it's more convenient to get a special computer on the Internet to do this automatically. Special list software automates all the management, so that emails are automatically sent to everyone in the group. Messages can be bundled into a convenient daily digest instead of being sent piecemeal. And if people want to join (subscribe to) a list or leave it (unsubscribe), they can do this by sending a special email to the Internet computer that manages (hosts) the list. All of this is done with no human intervention. The list manager, known as the owner or moderator, will step in only if something goes wrong – say, if an email address no longer works and the user hasn't unsubscribed him- or herself, or, very rarely, to remove troublemakers.

Finding lists

Yahoo hosts an almost unbelievably huge collection of lists at its Yahoogroups site (groups.yahoo.com – note there's no www at the start of the URL). Yahoogroups also allows each list's members to swap files and share photos. Lists can be given varying degrees of privacy. Some are completely hidden, available by invitation only, while others are open to anyone. Most, but not all, lists keep archives. If you're looking for a list, Yahoogroups is the best place to start. You can also use it to start your own list – it's very easy to use, and won't put a strain on your PC.

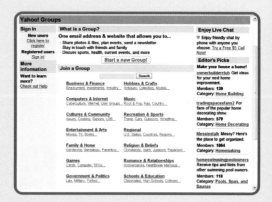

Yahoo groups includes tens of thousands of mailing lists to explore and join

More obscure lists sometimes include a web-subscription facility like this one. You will need to confirm the subscription by replying to a special email

Not all lists offer the same features as Yahoogroups. More obscure lists, typically used by professionals and academics, are often more basic. There won't be any file areas, and there may not be any web-registration facilities, so that the only way to subscribe or unsubscribe will be by email. There's no definitive directory of these more obscure lists. Catalist (http://www.lsoft.com/lists/listref.html) has a searchable index of one large group that uses one particular kind of mailing list software called Listserv. For alternatives, it's best to use a web search.

Mailing list netiquette

To join a list, you'll have to send an email like 'subscribe <name of list here>' to a special address. The details will vary and will appear on the list's website. Because subscriptions are processed by computer, you have to send exactly what's requested otherwise the computer won't be able to make sense of your request. When you subscribe, you'll be sent information on how to unsubscribe. Keep this safe. Lists are mostly fairly friendly places, although you will sometimes find communities of people whose sole aim appears to be to snipe at each other. It's always a good idea to look through any list archives that are available before joining, to see how useful and interesting you'll find the discussions, and to get an idea of the style and approach of the list's members.

Newsgroups

In spite of the name, the newsgroup network has nothing to do with news. It's actually a collection of discussion groups similar to mailing lists, but using different technology. To use newsgroups, you will need special software called a news reader. Internet Explorer includes a version of Outlook Express that can read news. Alternatively, you can buy newsreader software on the Internet. One of the best readers is called Forte Agent (www.forteinc.com). A free version is available. You will also need access to a news server. Your ISP should provide this. If not, various public news servers are available for free. Search the Web for 'free news server' for an up-to-date list. Setting up a newsreader is very easy. Simply fill in your name and email address and the name of your chosen news server.

The newsgroup network is huge, quirky and anarchic. Groups are divided into categories, which may include various sub-categories. For example, there are a few hundred sub-groups in the uk category, which is specifically for UK users, and tens of thousands in the alt category, which is the newsgroup world's 'and everything else' location. Some groups include a document called an FAQ (frequently asked questions). This includes basic information about the group and also provides a handy summary of the group's collected knowledge (see page 138).

Socially, the newsgroup world can be far more aggressive and challenging than most mailing lists. Many newsgroups include people flaming (insulting) each other, sometimes in pointless exchanges that can last for years. On the other hand, some newsgroups include experts and professionals, and the standard of humour and wit can also be higher than you'll find on a typical mailing list.

Outlook's news reader is primitive, but good enough for casual use

If you decide to use the newsgroup network regularly, it's well worth buying a good reader such as Forte's Agent

Binaries

Newsgroups can be used to exchange music, pictures and even video clips and software as well as text. Long files are posted as binaries – long strings of unreadable gibberish, split into parts. A good newsreader can automatically connect all the parts together and recreate the original file. However, the newsgroup network is not completely reliable, so not infrequently you'll find that parts are missing. Unfortunately, there's no solution to this – it's a fact of newsgroup life.

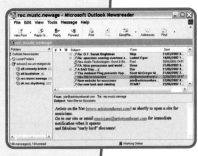

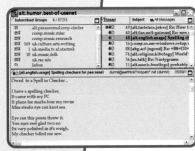

MORE WAYS TO COMMUNICATE

Email attachments

As mentioned on page 28, you can attach files to email messages. Most email tools can handle ten or so files with ease. However, this doesn't mean you can send ten full-sized video clips. ISPs usually have a limit on how large an email can be. A typical size for dial-up users is 2Mb. Text messages will never come close to this – you can send an entire book in 2Mb – but video and sound files can easily cross this limit.

One solution is to upload the files to some web space, and allow friends and family to view them or copy them from there. Another is to use a file-splitter utility to break large files into smaller chunks. Your recipients will have to use the same utility to sew them back together, but if you both agree which software to use beforehand, this is easy. There are tens of possible utilities you can use, many of them free. Search for 'file splitter' and 'Windows' to find some examples. Another approach is to compress files before you send them. Sometimes this is known as zipping them – from the name of one of the most popular compression programs. Zipping shrinks files so that they take up less space, but keeps all the information intact. Windows includes a built-in zip feature. In Windows Explorer, select the file or files you want to zip, right click, and choose Send to → Compressed (zipped) Folder. The amount of zip compression depends on what kind of file you are sending. Word files will be around 20% of the original size. The size of JPG and TIF images, and WAV and MP3 music files won't change much.

Send a fax via the Web to most places in the world, using the free TPC service

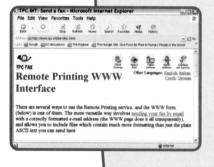

Internet and other faxing

Windows XP doesn't include fax features by default, but these can be installed from the Windows XP CD. Open the Control Panel, select 'Add or Remove Programs', and click on 'Add/Remove Windows Components'. Click on 'Fax', and the Fax tool will install. You can run the various sub-facilities from All Programs → Accessories → Communications → Fax. The software uses your fax modem. Unfortunately, it can't share your modem with your Internet connection tools. It can be coaxed into working if you install two modems and connect them so that they share one line, or if you have a stand-alone fax device with a modem that also has a PC connection.

An alternative solution is to use a free service available on the Internet. This can send faxes anywhere in the UK and most of the world. Unfortunately, it isn't particularly convenient, especially for formatted pages, and you may need to install special software to use it fully. However, as a free service it can save a small fortune if you fax regularly overseas. Details are available from www.tpc.int/tpc_home.html.

Chat and Instant Messages

Chat is a technology that allows Internet users to have typed conversations with each other. It's extremely popular with teenagers (and with their parents, who find that it can replace endless expensive phone calls). It's also widely used by adults for keeping in touch with friends, general socialising, and also dating and flirting. The standard chat format is one-to-one, although some websites and online services offer chat rooms where it's possible to chat in groups. There are a number of competing systems. Unfortunately, these aren't compatible, so instead of a single worldwide chat network there are various smaller networks. Microsoft has its Windows Messenger system, aimed at users of Hotmail and the MSN online service. AOL and Netscape use the AIM (AOL Instant Message) system. AOL also has its own internal online chat system called IM (Instant Message). This can be linked with AIM so that outsiders can chat with AOL subscribers.

Windows Messenger is included in Windows XP. To use it you will have to go through a moderately complex process that asks for some personal details and signs you in as a member of the .Net Passport scheme. There are worries about the security of the service so it's suggested you don't give your real email address, and instead use the offer of a free Hotmail or MSN address when signing up. This will distract spam away from your true email.

To use AIM, you will need a copy of the Netscape browser. This is often given away with magazines. You can also download it from www.netscape.com, but unless you have a broadband connection this may not be comfortably practical.

The features in all these tools are very similar. It is best to use a nickname when setting up these services, for reasons of confidentiality. Once signed in, you can create a list of favourite people, and the service shows you when they are online. You can start a conversation by selecting them and typing a message – although they do, of course, have the option not to respond. You can also set up 'I am away' messages, which will log comments sent to you, so you can read them when you return.

AOL's Instant Messenger showing how a typical two-way chat system works. Microsoft's Windows Messenger adds voice and video chat to text chat. If both chatters use a microphone they can talk to each other. If they use a webcam and both have a broadband link, they can see each other too

SMS and texting from your PC

There are many paid-for web-to-SMS services which charge a small amount per message. But a small number can send messages completely free. These are usually supported by advertising on the website, and perhaps also a short advert tag that is added to your free message. One example is the Cardboard Fish site at www.cbfsms.com. For others search the Web for 'Free SMS'.

FINDING AND DOWNLOADING SOFTWARE FROM THE INTERNET (I)

When is 'free' not free?

When looking for free software, you'll sometimes find that 'free' really just means a free trial. True freeware is always labelled as such. If it's free, you shouldn't have to pay anything for it, ever.

A similar scam is the idea of a 'free download'. All downloads are free. It's the software you have to pay for. Some sites advertise 'free downloads' just to attract attention, which they can convert into advertising revenue.

If you're looking for a specific kind of software product, there is a good chance that you can find what you want on the Internet. Whereas a typical computer store might hold a few hundred software products, literally hundreds of thousands of products and other software items are available online. Many of these are available for free, or at little cost.

However, the quality of online software is very variable. At one extreme there are outdated, badly designed tools that are unlikely to be of any use to anyone. At the other is software that can compete in usefulness and reliability with professionally sold products costing hundreds of pounds. In between is a vast selection of smaller tools that do a useful but perhaps unspectacular job, and aren't perfect or particularly sophisticated, but fill a niche that is too small for large companies to bother with. Although many of these tools are written by amateur or part-time computer programmers, they can be surprisingly useful, and also good value for money.

The DivX video player shown here is available only online. It plays video that uses the DivX format, which offers high video quality in small files. More information from www.divx.com

Finding software to download

There are three approaches. You can use a search engine to look for a type of software. For example, search for 'word processor' or 'photo editor' and you will see a list of sites offering programs to download. Of course, you will also see a lot of sites with information about word processors and photo editors. You can refine your search by adding the word 'download' (i.e. '+"word processor" +download').

Alternatively, you could find websites that are just collections of shareware, by doing a web search for 'shareware'. Some even have user ratings for each piece of shareware. A handful of these shareware sites can be accessed only by subscription. We suggest you ignore these, as plenty of other sites will have the same software available with open access. Most sites include search features so you can search by category or by the name of a particular piece of software.

Some sites to try include the following.
Cnet (shareware.cnet.com) Easy searching and categories
Tucows (www.tucows.com) A friendly site (pronounced 'two cows') packed with shareware
Download (www.download.com) Related to Cnet, but with user ratings
Simtel (www.simtel.net) Huge archive of all kinds of software

The final option is to use magazine listings. Monthly magazines frequently review shareware items, and always include a web link when they do.

Software types

When you buy a shrink-wrapped CD, you are always buying a finished product, often with a paper manual. Online software isn't quite so cut and dried.

Freeware is completely free. You can copy it to your PC and use it for nothing. It will keep working for as long as you want it to. If software is labelled as freeware, what you see is what you get. There are no catches or hidden payments to worry about. Variations on freeware include postcardware and emailware. 'Payment' is literally a postcard or an email. There's no penalty if you don't send these, but it's the polite thing to do and helps encourage the person who created the software.

A **demo version** is a special version of a product that has some important features disabled (i.e. turned off). These features are either absent or don't work. Typically you won't be able to save your work or transfer it to some other software. Demo versions are usually free, and are available so that you can try out the software to see if you like it enough to buy it. Some demo versions include an unlock feature. If you enter a code, the disabled features are enabled (i.e. made to work) and the software will be fully functional. To get the code you have to make a payment, usually by credit card. Larger companies tend to produce demo versions that can't be unlocked. If you want the software, you'll usually have to buy it on CD.

A **beta version** is a version of a product that hasn't been finished yet. Some features may not work fully, and the software may not be as reliable as a finished product. This might seem like a bad thing, but some smaller software writers never finish a project; their last beta version is quite good, with plenty of useful features. Beta versions are usually free. Larger companies supply beta versions so that they can be tested by users. These beta versions are less likely to work reliably. They will often also include a time-out feature, which means that they will stop working after a certain date. Very large companies like Microsoft sometimes charge for beta versions.

Shareware, also known as **trialware**, is available on the basis that you can pay for it after you have tried it and are sure it does what you want. Shareware may be available as a demo version, a fully featured product that works properly, or as a full version with an electronic reminder built-in that nags you if you continue to use it. To stop the nagging, you will have to type in a code that shows that you have paid for it. Shareware is usually produced by small companies rather than large ones. It varies hugely in quality, which is why it is important to try it before buying it.

Magazine demo versions

While this is not strictly shareware, magazines often include trial versions of software on their cover CDs and DVDs. These are either straightforward demo versions, or special offers for an upgrade, where an older version of the software is provided free and the latest version is available at a special price. You'll often need Internet access to use this software. You won't usually need to download it, but during installation you'll often be asked for a special code which will be available only on the product website. This approach is really just a way to sell software at a reduced price.

FINDING AND DOWNLOADING SOFTWARE FROM THE INTERNET (II)

Mirror sites

You'll sometimes be given a choice of sites to download from. These are called mirror sites, and are copies of the original source site held on a different computer. If one site is very busy, your software will download more quickly if you try a mirror. You may find that a site on the west coast of the USA is faster for you than one in London. The best way to find out is to experiment.

Downloading and installing software

1. Before you start, it's a good idea to create a special folder called 'My Downloads' inside My Documents (see page 102). This will help you keep any downloads organised.

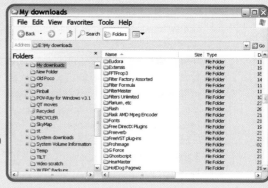

2. Find the software. Try various sites, and use the search facilities on each site to track down a range of products to try. Make sure you limit your search to Windows software. (You should see a selector somewhere on each site which lets you specify that you want to include only Windows software in your search.) Software labelled for Macintosh or Linux will not work on your PC. However, software designed for older versions of Windows, such as Win95, Win98, WinME and so on, should work.

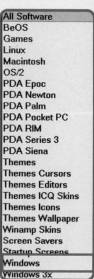

3. When you have found your shareware, it will either start downloading automatically, or you will need to right click on a link and select 'Save as'. It's a good idea to create a folder for each piece of software you download. Software files often have cryptic names such as 'wecs118v2.zip'. If you put the software in a folder with a longer and more intelligible name, you'll be more likely to remember what it was for.

4. As the software is downloading, a progress window will appear. This shows how much of the download is left to go in megabytes (or kilobytes if it's a very small download), and also how far the download has progressed, shown as a percentage.

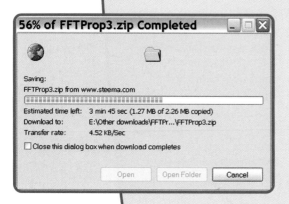

5. Once the software has finished downloading, you'll be given a choice to open the file or to save it. Opening the file will either start the installation process, or will show the contents of a folder that contains a file called Setup or Install. (Usually you'll see some other files as well.)

6. The installation process is the same as for any software. Because the installation details are on your hard disk rather than on CD, the installation will be much quicker. But the steps you follow (see page 18) will be similar.

Troubleshooting downloads

Occasionally, a software download will stall at some random point. Very rarely it will stall at the 99% mark. In the latter case it means you need to free some space on your destination disk. Windows copies downloads to the main disk first before copying them to the location you specify. If there's not enough room to copy the file, it doesn't complain, it simply stops the download.

If a download stalls earlier, you may be able to salvage it by logging off from your Internet connection, logging on again, and restarting the download. Windows will sometimes restart the download from the place at which it stalled rather than right at the beginning. If this doesn't work for you, and your downloads often stall, it's worth investing in a download manager. This is software designed to deal with exactly this problem. Examples include GetRight (www.getright.com), Go!Zilla (www.gozilla.com) and AcceleratorPlus (www.speedbit.com).

Paid-for software

The download process is the same for software you pay for as it is for shareware. But before you reach this stage you will need to pay for your software. This is usually done by credit card, and follows the usual steps (see page 50). But there are a number of points to watch out for.

Some software sellers have a hidden discount feature on their site. If you fill in all your details and hit the 'Back' button on your browser instead of confirming the sale, you'll see a message appear offering you an extra discount of perhaps 10% as an incentive to complete the trade. This feature is fairly rare, but it's always worth checking for, just in case.

Commercial software sellers often pile on plenty of electronic hard-sell on their sites. You'll be led towards buying package deals that include discounted extras you may not want, paying for advanced versions of software when cheaper – or even free – versions are closer to what you need, and asked to provide your contact details for special offers that never materialise. The only solution here is to double check everything before you confirm a sale.

Another common mini-scam is the 'protected download' option. This adds an extra pound or two to the cost of the software, and is included so that you can be sure you'll be allowed to download the software again if you lose the original download. A better option is to make sure you never lose the original. It's a good idea to regularly copy the contents of your My Downloads folder to a rewritable CD, so that you have a safety copy and can reinstall everything if you lose all the information on your hard disk.

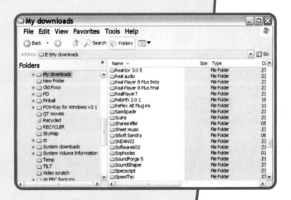

Backup your downloads folder! Otherwise you may have to pay for your downloaded software again

If you try running shareware and see an error message that says something like 'VBRUN400.DLL not found', this means that you will need to find a copy of a VBRUN file. This contains the main part of the Visual Basic system, which is used by some shareware. The easiest way to do this is to use a search engine to look for 'VBRUN'. You'll see a list of sites that hold these VBRUN files, ready for you to copy to the Windows/System directory on your hard drive.

NEWS AND REVIEWS

Amazon reviews

Don't forget that Amazon doesn't just sell books, CDs and DVDs, but also includes a public review section with each item. These are often well worth reading. Unsurprisingly, the US site (www. amazon. com) is more likely to have reviews available than the UK version (www. amazon. co.uk).

Salon is one of the Internet's leading online magazines. Some content has to be paid for, but even the free content is worth exploring

Many of the sites owned by daily newspapers are famous. But there are plenty of other sources of information and comment that are just as useful.

Broadsheets

Any or all of these newspaper sites can provide you with the usual printed combination of news, commentary and more general lifestyle and magazine-style features. There is no downside or catch. Access is free, although you may need to register. Searchable archives are usually available, and these can be a godsend for journalists and researchers or for anyone who wants to remind themselves about the details of a news story they half-remember.

The Guardian
www.guardianunlimited.co.uk
The Telegraph
www.telegraph.co.uk

The Times
www.timesonline.co.uk
The Independent
www.independent.co.uk

TV, foreign and other news

For a more varied selection, try these other news sources. The BBC site is very well respected; the others offer different perspectives and more social and cultural coverage. Moreover and News Now are news summary services. Use them to customise your own newsfeed to reflect your interests.

BBC News
news.bbc.co.uk
Channel 4
www.channel4.com/news
CNN
europe.cnn.com

New York Times
www.nytimes.com
Moreover
www.moreover.com
News Now
www.newsnow.co.uk

Alternative sources

If you'd prefer your news less pre-packaged, try these sites. The Paperboy site is not attractive, but it appears to link to every newspaper everywhere in the world. Newsday and Newslink (note the lack of 'www') are US-oriented national and local newsfeeds. Reuters is the famous news agency. Salon provides intelligent debate and magazine-like articles. Anorak collects dubious, unlikely or just plain impossible stories from the tabloids.

The Paperboy
www.thepaperboy.com
Reuters
www.reuters.com
Newsday
www.newsday.com

Newslink
newslink.org
Salon
www.salon.com
Anorak
www.anorak.co.uk

Film news and reviews

The IMDB (Internet Movie Database) site is the definitive resource for film fans and historians, and lists almost every film ever made, with cast and crew details and individual viewer ratings. IoFilm is a smaller-scale review site. Scoot is a well-known film-finder, which lets you find out what's playing locally. Information and booking sites for the various cinema chains are also available. The Virgin site includes links to other kinds of entertainment. Of course, if you're a fan you can find information about your favourite stars by typing their name into a search engine. Anyone even moderately famous will have a range of fan websites, and very probably an official site of his or her own.

IMDB
www.imdb.com
IoFilm
www.iofilm.co.uk
Scoot
www.scoot.co.uk/cinemafinder/default.asp

Odeon
www.odeon.co.uk
UCI
www.uci-cinemas.co.uk
Virgin
infospace.com/uk.vnetuk/ent/index.htm

Music and music reviews

There's an almost endless collection of music and music resource sites available online, covering every style. Classical Net includes thousands of CD reviews and links. GMN offers classical and other news and information. Jazz Nights and Hit The Decks are respectively jazz and dance music information sites. Piano Nanny is representative of the many sites online that offer free music lessons. As with film artists, your favourite song-writers, performers and composers will almost certainly have their own official and fan websites. They may also have their own discussion groups and mailing lists.

Classical Net
www.classical.net
GMN
www.gmn.com
Jazz Nights
www.jazznights.co.uk

Hit The Decks
www.hitthedecks.co.uk
Piano Nanny
www.pianonanny.com

Books and book reviews

While famous sites such as Amazon may have stolen the show, there's still plenty to explore away from the large online bookshops. Book Browser bills itself as 'the guide for avid readers' and offers exactly that. Bibliofind is a rare- and antiquarian-book-finding service that puts buyers and dealers in touch with each other. Art and Culture is a unique online magazine that crosslinks artists and their interests. Bloomsbury Magazine includes news, discussion areas for writers and hints for anyone who wants to set up a reading group.

The Bloomsbury Magazine offers a mine of information about books, reading, writing and book people

Book Browser
www.bookbrowser.com
Bibliofind
www.bibliofind.com

Art and Culture
www.artandculture.com
Bloomsbury Magazine
www.bloomsburymagazine.com

THE WORLD'S BIGGEST REFERENCE LIBRARY

eBooks and PDFs

eBooks are books supplied in various electronic formats. The most popular is PDF (portable document format), created by Adobe. Although eBooks aren't likely to replace print publishing any time soon, PDF files are still widely used for advertising flyers, data sheets, lecture notes and other information. Adobe's PDF reader is available for free. You can download it from Adobe's website (www.adobe .com). Many magazines also give it away on their monthly cover CDs or DVDs.

Literature

Finding out just how much reference information is available online can be a surprise. All of the following books, dictionaries and encyclopaedias are free. While it remains true that reading books on your screen is less pleasurable than reading them in print on paper, it's still useful to know that these are available for when you want to check a fact or a look up a quote.

Ancient classical literature

classics.mit.edu
The Internet classics archive includes copies of works by a total of 59 Greek, Roman and Chinese writers from the classical period, including Julius Caesar, Lao Tzu, Sun Tzu, Plato and others. In some cases you can read the original Latin, Greek or Chinese text as well as an English translation.

Modern classical literature

www.literature.org/authors
With nearly 200 complete works online, this is one of the largest collections of literature on the Internet. You can find works by Aesop, H.G. Wells, Jack London, the Brontës, Voltaire, Bram Stoker, Arthur Conan Doyle (including the Sherlock Holmes stories) and others.

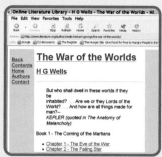

Classics for children

www.ucalgary.ca/~dkbrown/storclas.html
Many classic children's stories are now out of copyright, and so can be made available freely. This site includes works by Beatrix Potter, Lewis Carroll, Victor Appleton (famous for the Tom Swift stories) and Oscar Wilde.

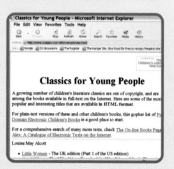

Quotations

www.quoteland.com
Hundreds of quotes arranged by author and topic, and also selected by occasion. Very useful for public speakers and writers, and for those looking for a thoughtful or amusing quote to suit a family occasion.

Dictionaries, maps and encyclopaedias

Encyclopaedia Britannica

www.britannica.com

Once available only in print form at sizeable cost, the Britannica – a summarised version, at any rate – is now available for free online. If you want all the details you'll need to buy the still-expensive paper version, or the CD (see page 123).

Multimap

www.multimap.com

One of the best mapping tools. It includes searches by postcode and place name, and you can even look at aerial views of your house. The UK has the most detailed maps, but simpler maps are available for the rest of the world.

Dictionaries

www.freewaresite.com/onldict/fre.html

There are hundreds of dictionaries online. This freeware dictionary offers basic translations for a number of popular languages. About 10,000 words are listed – enough for everyday conversation, but not for more specialised use.

www.dictionary.com

You can find English definitions at this site.

Searching for more?

To find more, use a search engine. For example, if you are looking for a Latin dictionary, use Google and search for '+latin +dictionary'. Whatever your subject interest, you'll find there are literally thousands of pages of all kinds of reference materials available.

5.9

The world's biggest reference library

Language translation

www.freetranslation.com

This site, like others, attempts automatic language translation. If you're expecting perfectly fluent and elegantly crafted results, you're going to be disappointed, because machine translation is still clumsy and very imperfect. But the service is useful for those times when you see a website in a foreign language and would like some idea of what it's trying to say.

FINDING PEOPLE ONLINE

More on finding people

An excellent list of online people-finding resources and tips is available at www.journalism net.com/people/

Finding friends past and present

Friends Reunited (www.friendsreunited.co.uk) remains the prototype friend-finder site. At £5 a year it's cheap, and the site lists contacts for almost every primary and secondary school, university and college in the UK. Contact is made by email request sent via the site. Naturally, wanting to talk to someone doesn't guarantee that he or she will want to talk to you – and vice versa.

Apart from contact information there are also nostalgic reminiscence areas where you can read comments about your old school and old teachers – although, after a number of embarrassing incidents and at least one libel case, these have been toned down in recent years. The service is now international and has recently been extended to include old work contacts.

Variations on Friends Reunited include Find A Shipmate (www.findashipmate.com) for sailors, Find A Workmate (www.findaworkmate.com), The Forces Reunited (www.theforcesreunited.co.uk) and Friends Faraway (www.friendsfaraway.com) for expatriates. Friends Reunited succeeded because it reached a critical mass. Not all the alternatives have reached that point yet. But they can still be worth investigating.

Find an old friend, with Friends Reunited

Finding phone numbers

If you're looking for someone's contact details in the UK, one of the most useful, if not necessarily friendliest, resources is 192.com (www.192.com). The service isn't free. There's a range of subscription options, which vary from a blanket annual payment of £19.99 for 100 searches, to a small number of free searches in exchange for providing your contact details to advertisers. It's a very ad-heavy site and also rather aggressive with its marketing. If you can tolerate these distractions, it's perhaps even more useful than BT's 192 telephone line. The information is also available on CD (see page 123).

While competition does exist, it's rather sketchy. BT's own web service and the UK Phonebook have already been mentioned on page 136. Services such as 192 Directory (www.192directory.co.uk) and 192 Enquiries (www.192enquiries.com) are free but list only businesses. As BT's original 192 service is phased out in August 2003, expect a rash of variations on the number 118, which will become part of the replacement. For an up-to-date listing of sites, try searching for '+"directory enquiries"+118'.

Finding email addresses

There's no single email directory for the Internet. But there are websites which try to make it possible to find people's contact details. Unfortunately, most are useful only if you're trying to find someone in the USA. Some examples include Bigfoot (www.bigfoot.com), WhoWhere (www.whowhere.lycos.com) and US Search. All of these have drawbacks. Bigfoot is free but not very reliable, and at about $10 a search, US Search is expensive.

Begin your Search - Enter the last known information on the person you are searching for:

First Name	Middle Initial	Last Name (req)	Search Type
			⊙ People Locate
City	State	Approx. Age (req)	○ Background Search
	Select all States ∨		Search

The search feature on US Search – good for US searches, but costly

Other online sources

A quicker and cheaper way to try to find someone's email address is to use a search engine. You can simply search for their full name or surname. If the name is popular and common, you can limit the search by including an associated word such as a known hobby. This approach can hardly be guaranteed to work, but it shouldn't take more than a few moments and costs nothing.

If someone is or was a Usenet user (or if you think he or she may have been, but aren't sure), it's a good idea to search through the Usenet archives on Google (see page 138). You may find his or her email address included in postings. There are two potential problems here. First, if he or she hasn't posted for a while, the email listed may be out of date. Second, Usenet users often disguise their email addresses to hide them from spammers – look for words like 'no spam'. You may need to reconstitute the address by hand before you can use it.

Services like AOL include their own internal search tools. These are for subscribers only – they're not available to other Internet users. Because they're based on user profile information, they can't be used for postal addresses or phone numbers – just email information. Moreover, because people rarely use their real names in profiles they're not hugely useful, but may be worth trying as a last resort.

'Whois' and other services

If someone owns his or her own domain, you can sometimes find a contact address, phone or email from the domain records. DNS Stuff (www.dns stuff.com) is a page full of useful domain-related search tools. Use the Whois ('who is') search if you know the domain name, and IPWhois if you know just the IP number of the domain or website.

The author and other search option in Google's newsgroup archive advanced search

Find messages	with **all** of the words		10 messages ∨ Sort by relevance ∨
	with the **exact phrase**		Google Search
	with **at least one** of the words		
	without the words		
Newsgroup	Return only messages from the **newsgroup**		(Example: rec.games.misc, comp.os.*, *linux*)
Subject	Return only messages where the **subject** contains		
Author	Return only messages where the **author** is		

GENEALOGY ONLINE

Genealogy with Microsoft Power-Point

If you have a version of Microsoft Office, you'll find that PowerPoint's Organisation Chart feature turns out to be perfect for home-made family trees. Go to Insert → Picture → Organisation Chart. The jargon used (subordinate, co-worker, assistant and so on) is, of course, designed for business use, but it's easy enough to change it for genealogy. It's also easy to add as many generations to your tree as you need.

Getting started

With the help of a PC and the Internet, you can trace relatives far more quickly than one could in the past. In fact, genealogy is an interesting example of an activity that ties together many essential Internet and PC skills – creating and maintaining documents, using search engines, email and the Web, and keeping your own detailed archives. You could start by buying special genealogy software. But we recommend that you begin by researching the websites listed opposite. You'll find everything you need online, and the information will be more comprehensive and easier to sift through than the pre-packaged genealogy tools you can buy on CD.

Essential tips

1. Work backwards. Just because you find someone from the 17th century who shares your surname doesn't mean you're directly related. If you trace back chronologically you'll be able to say definitively who your ancestors are.
2. Contact relatives. Email can be invaluable here. You can ask distant relatives in other countries to search their local records for you – and make some new social and family contacts at the same time.
3. Compare notes. It's likely that at least one other person in the network of people you will be making contact with shares your interest, and will have done some useful research of his or her own.
4. Remember the wars. War records can be an unusually comprehensive source of information. Try www.kcl.ac.uk/lhcma/top.htm, or search for 'Liddel Hart' – one of the definitive military archives.
5. Cheat if you have to. It's possible to buy basic pre-researched genealogy tools on CD. This can save you time if you have a fairly common name. But you're unlikely to get a very full picture, and if your family name is fairly obscure there's no alternative to a proper search.
6. Get organised. You could draw your family tree on paper, but it can be more informative and more interesting to rely on the extra features available in software. Web links, a database and even a PowerPoint presentation (see the sidebar) are all valid and useful ways of displaying the fruits of your efforts. You can use these tools to include all the background information you have collected.

Are you related to Elvis? Probably not, but this genealogical sample from One Great Family will show if you might be

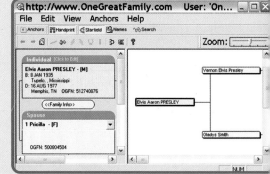

Genealogy resources

www.familysearch.org
The famous Mormon records library, including ancestral searches and US-specific census information. Also a good starting point for beginners.

www.sog.org.uk
The website of the Society of Genealogists. Includes Boyd's Marriage Index, which lists marriages by county. Otherwise rather severe and technical, but possibly of interest to more experienced genealogists.

www.englishorigins.com
A compendium of various UK parish and other listings. Access costs £6 for 150 searches, which must be made within 48 consecutive hours. But many of the listings are available only on this site, so it may be worth it.

www.genuki.org.uk
A huge collection of all kinds of resources, from ancient parish and other records, to relatively recent phone directory listings provided by BT. An essential resource, and one you can lose yourself in for hours.

www.ancestry.com
Access to both US and UK records, but at the fairly steep cost of $80 a year. Apart from an ancestral database there's also a news story database, and various message boards and discussion areas. A very basic guest account is available if you want to browse what's on offer.

freebmd.rootsweb.com
Free access to UK birth, marriage and death records between 1837 and 1901. This might sound like a limited resource, but it is free, and there are 40 million unique records to search through.

www.pro.gov.uk/index.htm
The official site of the UK Public Record Office. Includes a digital version of the 1901 census, and assorted other records – some of which are buried quite deep, so you'll need to do some exploring.

www.familyrecords.gov.uk
A related government site that includes old census information – very useful, and easy to use.

www.cyndislist.com
A huge directory of Internet links for genealogists. More than 175,000 sites are listed. Many are geographical, but others include more specialised information including old diary listings, notes about DNA research, and emigrants' stories.

www.rootsweb.com
Another vast listing of free resources. An essential starting point for beginners, and also the home of the ROOTS-L mailing list.

www.onegreatfamily.com
Yet another huge listings and search site, with a useful seven-day free trial offer.

The Public Records Office holds all kinds of information of interest to historians and genealogists

Cyndi's list – the best all-round collection of genealogical links on the Web

Newsgroups and mailing lists

On Usenet, there are over 20 groups in the soc.genealogy series. Unfortunately, they're no longer being archived by Google, but you can read the last few hundred postings on Google's website (see page 138). It's also worth searching Yahoogroups for genealogy mailing lists – type 'genealogy' into the search box on the main page. Many lists are inactive, but you can find some useful leads and contacts among those that aren't.

ESSENTIAL MAINTENANCE FOR WINDOWS

Essential maintenance for Windows

Cleanup options

When your disk is nearly full – Windows prefers to keep at least 200Mb free on each disk – you'll see a message appear on the bottom right of your screen. You can start Cleanup by clicking on this message.

Although Windows should work reliably, it can benefit from some routine housekeeping. Each of your disks should be checked and maintained regularly. Windows itself can also be automatically updated with small changes, known as patches, which are supplied by Microsoft and downloaded over the Internet.

Disk maintenance tools

Select 'My Computer' to see a list of the disk drives in your PC (a typical PC may have fewer disks than are shown here).

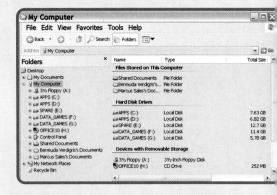

Right click on one of the disks and select 'Properties'. You'll see this window appear. The pie chart shows you how much space there is free on your disk. You can also change the name here. If your disk is full, or nearly full, clicking on the 'Disk Cleanup' button shown here will start a clean-up process.

Select the 'Tools' tab and these three maintenance options will appear.

Using the defragmentation tool

When you first start using your PC, there will be a lot of empty space on your hard disk. As you use it more and more, it becomes harder and harder for Windows to use this space efficiently. Gaps appear when small files are deleted, and eventually files become scattered across the whole disk. Defrag fixes this problem by gathering all the scattered parts together. It also tries to move software to the most easily accessible parts of the disk, so that it will start more quickly.

So using defrag regularly – say, at least once a month – will help speed up your PC. The tool is very easy to use – just click on the 'Defragment' button. But it's important to understand that it works only on one disk at a time – the one you right clicked on to reach this page. The process can take a very long time, so you may need to leave your PC running overnight. You can carry on using your PC while it defrags, but you will get much better results if you don't.

Using Scandisk

Sometimes the information on a disk can start to unravel. Untreated, this can lead to files disappearing, although this happens only rarely. Scandisk prevents the unravelling. Windows runs Scandisk automatically if you ever reset your PC by hand, or if the power fails without a proper shutdown sequence. You can also run it manually if you are worried there is a problem. It is a good idea to do this regularly, just in case.

Like Defrag, Scandisk works on one disk at a time. There are only two options, and you choose either or both. 'Automatically fix file system errors' is the most useful option. 'Scan for and attempt recovery of bad sectors' should be used only if you suspect there is a physical problem with your hard disk. It literally checks the whole of your disk, and takes a very long time.

If you try to check your system disk, you will probably see the following message:

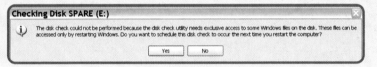

Scandisk can't check a disk while it is being used. To solve this problem, select 'Yes' and then restart your PC immediately. Scandisk will now fix any problems before Windows starts.

Other maintenance options

Windows update

By default, Windows is set up to notify you of any updates that are available. The software that does this is called Windows update. It can be seen working in the 'system tray' at the bottom right of the screen. For more details, see section 6.2.

Removing old software

If you decide an old piece of software is taking up space and you will never use it again, it's a good idea to remove it. Just deleting the desktop icon or the entry in the Start menu won't remove it from your disk. The Control Panel 'Add or Remove Programs' option shows a list of your installed software. To get rid of an item, click on the 'Remove' button. This will delete all mention of it and you won't be able to use it again, unless you reinstall it.

As software is being deleted, you will sometimes be asked to confirm the removal of certain files. You can usually select the 'Yes to all' option here, to delete these files automatically. Very occasionally, this will cause a problem. Windows XP will deal with this by asking you to insert your master Windows CD so it can repair any files that have been removed or damaged.

Partial deletion syndrome

6.1 Essential maintenance for Windows

If you have created files using a piece of software, they won't usually be deleted when you remove the software. Often this is a good thing, but sometimes it can leave you with files you no longer want. The best approach here is to try automated removal first, and then do any extra cleaning up by hand only if you need the disk space.

ESSENTIAL MAINTENANCE – KEEPING WINDOWS UP TO DATE

Windows Update

Microsoft tries to update parts of Windows regularly. The usual reason for an update – sometimes called a patch – is because a security problem has been reported, and Microsoft wants to fix it before hackers can take advantage of it.

Windows includes an auto-update feature to take care of these updates. When you connect to the Internet, it checks if an update is available. When the warning appears, you can decide to download and install it. Installation is completely automatic: you don't need to specify folders or start the installation by hand.

You can control the update feature using the update icon in the system tray at the bottom right of the screen. It looks like a blue sphere with a small Windows logo hovering over it. Click on this at any time and you can see which updates are waiting. In the window that appears, you click on 'Settings' to set up how you want to handle updates. Windows can add them fully automatically, or you can decide to allow updates only when you want them to happen.

Finding Windows Update on the system tray

Windows Service Packs

Every year or so, Microsoft creates a Windows service pack. This includes all the previous patches that were included in each update, and also some new patches that address other problems and issues. There are three ways to get a service pack.

1. You can buy a new PC or an upgrade copy of Windows XP. (This makes sense only for new users.) New PCs are almost always supplied with the very latest version of Windows XP.
2. You can get it on CD. Microsoft is making Service Pack 1 available on CD free to UK users. (The same CD costs $9.95 in the USA.) For details, see the Microsoft UK website. The URL for SP1 is http://www.microsoft.com/uk/windowsxp/servicepacks/sp1.asp This may change for future service packs.
3. You can download it. The express version is 30Mb, which will take around two hours to download over a dial-up link (a matter of minutes over broadband). The full version is nearly 200Mb, which may be possible for broadband users. The URL above includes a download link.

Do you need a service pack?

Windows XP is missing support for a new and potentially very useful technology called USB2. Moreover, a system called Bluetooth, which is used to connect mobile phones and other mobile items to PCs and to each other, is also not supported. Unfortunately, SP1 does not include Bluetooth either, but it does have USB2 and hundreds of other minor changes. Windows XP won't look any different with SP1 installed, but it should work slightly more reliably. There isn't usually any good reason not to install a service pack.

The Java Virtual Machine

Java is used on many web pages to make them more interesting than is possible with standard HTML. It can create animated special effects, and often appears on shopping pages. To use Java in Internet Explorer, you will need to install a piece of software called a Java Virtual Machine (JVM). For various legal reasons this was not included in the first version of Windows XP. If you try to view a Java-enhanced page without this software, you will see an error message.

An alternative source of Java – the current Java download page on Sun's website

XP SP1 includes a full Java Virtual Machine, and future service packs are likely to do likewise. However, it's possible that at some point in the future Microsoft will again stop supporting Java features in its web browser. If this happens, you could try a competing JVM available for free elsewhere on the Internet. Sun, the company which created Java, is a likely source. Since specific URLs may change, it's best to find their current location with a web search for "Java Virtual Machine". This also applies if for any reason you are planning not to install SP1 and run into the Java problem.

Remote assistance

If you are having maintenance and other problems with your PC, you can ask a friend to help you remotely over the Internet. This feature, called Remote Assistance, recreates on your friend's PC a copy of what is on your screen. Your friend can start software and make changes as if he or she were sitting right next to you (allowing for transmission time across the Internet).

To start Remote Assistance right click on a blank area of the Start bar at the bottom of the screen and select 'Show desktop'. This hides all your open windows. Now hit the F1 key. Under 'Ask for assistance' you'll see the 'Invite a friend to connect to your computer with Remote Assistance option'. Click on the button shown and it will lead you through the rest of the process. If the other person hasn't used Remote Assistance before, he or she will be shown what to do through a link to the details on Microsoft's website which are included with the message. Note the connection is one way: your friend will be able to use your computer, but you won't be able to see his or hers.

Setting up a Remote Assistance request

VIRUS CHECKERS AND FIREWALLS

Attachments and email viruses

Email viruses propagate through attachments. Never open an unexpected attachment, even if it has been sent by someone you know and trust. Images, photos and plain text emails without attachments are always safe. Video clips are usually safe, but some kinds of video include web links, and these can't be guaranteed. WAV and MP3 sound files are also always safe. But beware especially of attachments with the following file extensions: .swf, .scr, .vbs, .pif, .exe and .com.

Viruses and how to avoid them

Viruses are malicious pieces of software that hitch a ride to your PC. Unlike most pieces of software, they can install themselves automatically. There are two aspects to a virus. The first is that it tries to reproduce itself. The most effective viruses use email, and can even search through your address book and send themselves to everyone listed.

The second aspect of a virus is the payload – or what it is programmed to do. This varies from nothing to destroying your PC. Most viruses are relatively harmless, but a few take extreme action, including deleting everything on your hard disks, and even destroying your PC's motherboard.

Anti-virus software

Not all anti-virus tools are equally powerful. Cheaper versions lack advanced features, such as protection from Office macro viruses, instant message and chat viruses; and intelligent virus-scanning, which can trap new viruses even though they haven't yet been included in the definition library. These more powerful products are typically labelled 'professional' and cost about £100, as opposed to 'family' or 'standard' products which cost between £30 and £40. Some anti-virus tools, such as Norton, are available in value 'bundles' with other related products.

Infected CD software

Instant messages

Floppy disk

Email attachments

Document macros

Norton anti-virus www.norton.com
Not quite perfect performance, but easy to use and widely available in stores

McAfee anti-virus www.macafee.com
The most obvious competitor to Norton, with similar features

Kaspersky
www.kaspersky.com
A less-well-known product, with powerful virus-scanning, but also rather slow

eset NOD32 www.nod32.com.au
An extremely fast and powerful anti-virus product, with an outstanding success rate, but not very easy to use. If you are a more experienced user, you may find it worth investigating

Keeping out hackers with a firewall

A firewall monitors your Internet connection and makes sure that all the traffic in and out of your machine has been authorised by you. Without a firewall it's possible for a hacker to look inside your PC, install viruses and programs that spy on what you are doing, and even send spam through your PC.

Windows XP includes a firewall, but it isn't sophisticated enough to keep out a serious hack attack. Open the Control Panel, select 'Network and Internet Connections', then 'Network Connections'. You will see one or more ISP names listed under the DialUp heading. Right click on each, select Properties → Advanced. To turn on the firewall, make sure the box in the Internet Connection Firewall box at the top is checked. Repeat for any other ISPs you use.

Using a firewall

To get the best from a firewall you will need to understand how Internet connections work. The two most important concepts are ports and IP numbers. An IP (Internet protocol) number is literally the Internet equivalent of a postal address. It's sometimes known as an IP address and looks like four numbers separated by dots, e.g. 123.17.0.89. Every computer on the Internet has a unique IP number. When you make a connection to your ISP, you are assigned an IP number of your own. If a hacker knows your IP number, he or she can begin to mount an attack on your computer.

Ports are the doors in and out of a computer. Every Internet service, including web browsing, email, file transfer and instant messaging, uses a port number. There are literally thousands of them. Firewalls work by blocking Internet traffic coming to or from certain IP numbers, and on certain ports. Some ports need to be open because without them your web browser and email won't work. Some IP numbers need to be open too, especially those that manage the connections to your ISP and to other PCs on your home network, if you have one. Traffic from the remaining ports and IP numbers should be blocked.

If you don't use a network, you can simply install a firewall and it should work immediately. If you do use a network, you will need to let the firewall know the IP numbers of the other PCs on your network (see below). IP numbers on a network are set up by Windows automatically.

Different firewalls handle networked PCs in different ways. Some ask you if you want to allow a PC access through the firewall. As a worst case, you will need to find the IP number and type it in by hand. To do this, use the Windows Command Prompt feature. Start the PCs on your network and open the Command Prompt window (under Start → Accessories). Type 'ipconfig' into the box that appears, and hit return. The IP address will appear. You'll also see other technical information about your Internet connection, although this will be of interest only to expert users. The IP number of your main PC isn't needed. The firewall will already have it worked out.

Firewall information and links

Norton Firewall
www.norton.com

The product is also available in large computer stores

Black Ice
www.iss.net

Look under Products → Home and small offices protection

ZoneAlarm
www.zone labs.com

Note that the free indefinite trial version of ZoneAlarm seems rather unreliable

All of these will show that your PC is being tested by hackers tens of times a day. While this is alarming, it's also entirely normal! Any of the above should be able to stop hack attacks before they can do real damage.

```
Microsoft Windows XP [Version 5.1.2600]
(C) Copyright 1985-2001 Microsoft Corp.

H:\Documents and Settings>ipconfig

Windows IP Configuration

Ethernet adapter Network Bridge (Network Bridge):

        Connection-specific DNS Suffix  . : mshome.net
        IP Address. . . . . . . . . . . . : 192.168.0.1
        Subnet Mask . . . . . . . . . . . : 255.255.255
        Default Gateway . . . . . . . . . : 192.168.0.
```

PESTS AND POP-UPS

Rogue's gallery

Here's a list of adware and spyware sources. Some of them include adware as part of an apparently innocuous and useful piece of software: Gator, GAIN, NetZero, BearShare, iMesh, Cydoor, BonziBuddy, Ezula, Trickler, Common Name.

This list isn't comprehensive – names change all the time – but if you see any of these on your PC, it's worth checking for installed and hidden adware. Another tell-tale sign is ad pop-ups appearing on ad-free sites, such as the BBC's.

Unwanted advertising

Banner ads are added to websites as a source of income for the website owners. While they may or not be interesting – usually they're not – few Internet users realise that they also greatly slow down their browsing.

Pop-ups are pages that appear automatically. Some sites produce one or two, while others create a web blizzard. There are also pop-unders, which hide behind other pages and aren't revealed till you try to close your web browser.

Adware makes pop-ups appear everywhere, even on sites that wouldn't normally show them. Adware often disguises itself as an innocuous or even a useful piece of software that asks for permission to install itself when you look at a web page. You won't be warned about what it's really for, and you won't be allowed to uninstall it. You can get rid of it only with special software.

Email spam is sent directly to your mail box. The content is rarely interesting and often obscene, and deleting spam by hand soon becomes an irritating distraction.

Cookies and spyware

Spyware is another challenge to your privacy. Commercial spyware tracks your browsing trail on the web and uses this to contribute to a statistical database. Personal spyware can be installed on your PC by relatives or visitors. It tracks your actions in detail, including websites you visit, emails you write, your chat sessions, and even your passwords.

Cookies were originally built into web browsers as a convenience. Some pages can be set up to work differently according to a user's choice – for example, the BBC news site will provide different news according to whether visitors choose the UK or overseas summaries. With cookies, this selection can be made once and remembered. But cookies are now often used by spyware to track your browsing trail.

Dealing with pests and pop-ups

Removing spam

It's possible to buy software that attaches to Outlook Express and filters spam after it has arrived at your PC. Some examples also work with other email packages. While this method is effective and is affordably cheap (the software rarely costs more than £30 or so), the removal is a not entirely convenient two-step process, where email is first downloaded and then scanned.

An alternative is to sign up for a spam-busting mail service. This collects your mail for you online and filters and forwards it automatically. Most of these services operate in the USA, but this makes no practical difference for UK users. The spam-busting potential is greater, because the list of active spam sources and the spam vocabulary can be updated continually.

Two suggestions for plug-in email filters are McAfee's SpamKiller (www.mcafee.com) and Contact Plus Corporation's Spam Buster (www.contactplus.com). For online filtering, two possibilities are SpamCop (spamcop.net) and Email Filtering (www.email-filtering.com). A web search will turn up many alternatives.

Pop-up stoppers and adbusters

There are countless products available online that block pop-ups and stop ads. They start working as soon as you install them and need little or no setting up. The best refer to a list of ad sources – most online advertising comes from relatively few ad suppliers.

Pop-ups are more problematic, because occasionally they can be legitimate and useful. So it's worth checking to see what indication you get when a pop-up has been eliminated, and whether you can take control manually and look at a pop-up if you think it might be genuine and useful.

As with spam killers, there are many products to choose from. Ads Gone (www.adsgone.com), StopZilla (www.stopzilla.com) and Ad Subtract (www.adsubtract.com) are all popular choices. Free trial versions are usually available.

Spyware killers, pest controllers and cookie busters

For more serious spyware killing, you'll need commercial software. Try either PestPatrol (www.pestpatrol.com) or LavaSoft's AdAware, which is a tiny download (less than 1Mb) and is available in a simple and free form, or as an enhanced paid-for version (www.lavasoft.com).

Cookies in Internet Explorer

You can control cookies using a feature built into IE. Select Tools → Internet Options and then the 'Privacy' tab. Set the slider to 'High'. While this isn't a foolproof method or one that offers perfect safety, it will eliminate many unwanted cookies.

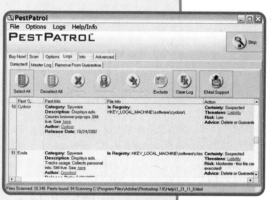

PestPatrol shows you exactly where spyware lurks, no matter how deeply it's buried

AdAware – and a message you don't want to see

CUSTOMISING WINDOWS

Create your own desktop

An interesting trick is to use a very tiny file for the desktop and use the stretch function to make it fill the screen. Each individual pixel is smoothed out to a soft star-like cross. Open Microsoft Paint (Accessories → Paint), create a new file, set the size with Image → Attributes, then use the magnifying glass to zoom in so that you can paint your pixels. Save the image as a .bmp file in My Pictures, then select it using browse.

Windows isn't quite infinitely customisable, but you can do more to change almost every aspect of it than many users realise. The more extreme changes require specialised software, but it's possible to change the basics quite a bit by using features that are built into Windows itself. Here are some examples.

Change the desktop background ('wallpaper')

The default Microsoft meadow is certainly relaxing, but you can replace it with any photo or image, including photos you have taken yourself. Open the Control Panel and select 'Appearance and themes' and then 'Change the desktop background'. You can now browse Microsoft's own collection of alternative photos, or you can load one of your own. The Center/Tile/Stretch option controls how the image appears. Use Center if the image is exactly the same size as your desktop (i.e., 800 x 600, 1024 x 768, 1280 x 1024, or one of the other standard resolutions). Use Tile for a tiled effect when the image is much smaller. Stretch will stretch any size of image to make it fit. This may distort it. If the image is a lot smaller than the desktop size, stretching it will blur the details.

Use a different theme

Select Control Panel → Appearance and themes → Change the computer's theme to pick a different visual scheme. A theme changes the background image, the look of the computer's main icons (My Computer, Recycle Bin, etc.), the colour scheme of the windows and sometimes also the sounds that are used. Windows XP comes with two themes – a blue default, and an optional theme that can be either silver or olive green. If you want more themes, you can buy them in the Windows Plus Pack (available from computer stores).

Create your own look

If you click on the 'Appearance' tab that appears to the right of Themes, you'll see a different window. Here you can make some crude changes to the look of Windows, including changing the colour of the window frames. For finer control, click on the 'Advanced' button. Now you can change the size of each element in a window, change the fonts that are used and the size of the letters, and so on. The background colours apply to all windows. You may want to change these if pure white is too bright for you. If you're wondering why the windows that appear here look different to the others, it's because the colours shown here are different. You won't see title colours like these unless you use software that was written for older versions of Windows. If you want to completely customise these colours too, and more besides, you'll need extra software (see page 179).

Change how folders work

Open Windows Explorer and select Tools → Folder Options and you'll see a list of choices you can make about how files and folders work. If you find double clicking difficult, you can set up Explorer so that a single click opens files. With this option selected, right clicking still works in the usual way.

On this page you can also decide whether to open separate windows for each folder you look through, or to keep a single window for all of them. The latter is usually more convenient. The 'Use Windows classic folders' option hides certain folder features. It affects only a few specialised folders, and is usually best left as it is.

Change how folders appear

Explorer offers different ways of presenting the list of files in a folder. If you click on the box with a blue line at the top (at the far right of the icons at the top of the Explorer window), you'll see a list appear. **Thumbnails** shows very small previews of the photos in the folder. It also shows mini-previews of what's inside each sub-folder. **Tiles** shows smaller preview images. Unfortunately, neither works with every kind of image file. For example, Tiles doesn't preview files in the very common .jpg format – the one used by many digital cameras. But there's also a **Filmstrip** option that appears for just this purpose. This shows all the images in a line, with a built-in full-size preview feature.

The **Icons** option shows files by type. Each icon indicates which piece of software will start when you open it. For example, .mpg video files will appear with a Media Player icon, because they play in Media Player. .rm files will show a RealPlayer icon. **List** and **Details** show a list of the names of files. They're often the most useful, as they provide the most information in the smallest screen area. List provides a simple list that includes a small icon that works as above, and also the file name. Details also shows other information including the time when the file was created or modified. If you click on each column header, you can sort the list. For example, clicking on 'Date modified' will sort the files by age. Clicking a heading again reverses the sort order. If you right click on any column header, you'll see a list of all the possible details that can appear. Tick the ones you want to see, untick the ones you don't. To change the width of each column, click and drag the small grey divider lines that appear between each heading.

Select how files are displayed in folders using this highlighted button. When there are photos from a digital camera, the Filmstrip option will also appear

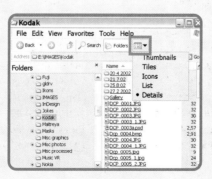

Make all folders the same

If you prefer a certain folder view option, go to the View tab in the Folder Options window, and make sure the 'Remember each folder's settings' button is ticked. Click 'OK'. Find a typical folder, perhaps one with letters or other documents in it, and then set up the view option – list, details, etc. – you like best. Select 'Folder Options' and 'View' again, and click on the 'Apply to all folders' button. If you change the view in some folders, the new view will be remembered for all the folders.

CUSTOMISATION – DIGGING DEEPER

Alternative web browsers

The main reasons for using an alternative to Internet Explorer (IE) are speed and security. Pages appear more quickly in an alternative such as Opera. All of these possible alternative browsers include email and newsgroup facilities in addition to basic browsing. Netscape also offers the AIM Instant Message system.

Netscape (www.netscape.com)

The most popular alternative to IE, and the most comprehensive. It includes a simple web-page editor, and can load multiple pages simultaneously. Free.

Opera (www.opera.com)

Popular with advanced users, Opera comes with some useful features, including new kinds of mouse control. A free version has advertising. To get rid of the ads, you'll have to pay $29.

Mozilla (www.mozilla.org)

A non-commercial alternative, Mozilla has been created entirely by volunteers. It's free but lacks some of the more advanced features of other browsers and isn't quite finished yet.

Alternatives to Windows Explorer

Alternative file explorers aren't the most glamorous of applications, but if you use your PC a lot they can offer a huge boost to productivity by making it easier to copy and preview files. All of the following are available from shareware libraries such as Tucows (see page 144).

2x Explorer

Free, very simple, and a very small download. No frills and no image previews, but useful for file copying.

The Opera browser is supplied with a huge selection of places you may want to visit

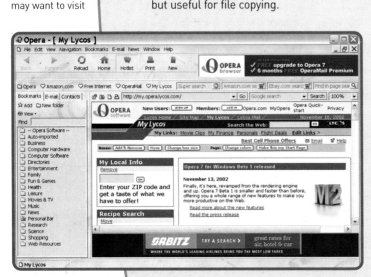

Directory Opus

Very possibly the most sophisticated, but also most expensive, alternative to Windows Explorer, with some interesting enhancements. Costs £50 to register.

AccelMan

Large, sprawling and feature-packed, this alternative file browser can do almost everything. It takes a little while to get used to after Explorer, but the results can be worth it.

Special effects

By default, Windows XP displays menus with an animated flourish. If you'd prefer a simpler display – and also a quicker one – you can turn off these effects. Right click on the desktop, select 'Display Properties' and then Appearance → Effects. Uncheck the 'Use the following transition...' box. There are other settings you may want to change here. The shadow feature for menus is barely noticeable, so it can be left as it is. Of the others, the font-smoothing feature is the most important. Use Cleartype if you have an LCD monitor. It makes text on the screen slightly easier to read.

Tweak UI

It's possible to go far beyond these simple changes. Tweak UI (UI is short for 'user interface', which is computer jargon for the part of Windows you can see and use) is a free tool available from Microsoft. It's often included on magazine cover disks – or to download it search for +'Tweak UI' +XP – and gives you extra control over Windows. You can turn off error sounds, control various other animation options, and make Windows XP work more as you'd like it to.

Tweak-XP Pro

For the dedicated tweaker, there are shareware tools that are more powerful than Tweak UI. Tweak-XP Pro from Totalidea (www.totalidea.de) is one of the most comprehensive. It costs about £35 to register, and includes a vast range of Windows XP tweaks, as well as other useful options including a pop-up and ad stopper.

More for Tweakers

Here are some alternatives to Tweak-XP Pro that are worth trying out. Customizer XP is freeware. The rest are available on a trial basis.

X-Setup (www.xteq.com)

MagicTweak (www.magic tweak.com)

Customizer XP (www.tweak now.com)

Optimizer XP (windows x.idz.net)

6.6 Customisation – digging deeper

Some advanced tweaks with Tweak-XP Pro. On this page you can:

- Log on automatically
- Get the most from your PC's memory
- Remove unnecessary files
- Make the taskbar translucent
- Hide and show special folders
- Move special folders
- Hide items on the Start menu
- Speed up your network

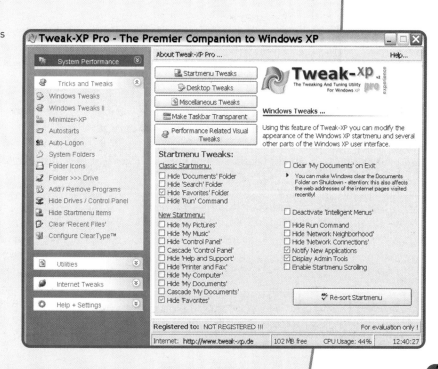

CUSTOMISATION – SOUNDS, FILE TYPES AND SPEED-UPS

Shortcuts: speed tips

Shortcuts can also be created within folders – drag your target file to a folder instead of to the desktop. You can delete shortcuts just like any other file. You can also edit them by right clicking on them and selecting 'Properties'. This shows the file that the shortcut represents. Click on 'Change Icon' if you want to customise the shortcut's icon.

Shortcuts all in a row. Shortcuts are shown with the shortcut arrow at the bottom left of the icon, and (not shown here) also the words 'Shortcut to...' in the name

Changing the sound scheme

You may not appreciate the dinks, clonks and clicks that Windows XP produces while you work. You can remove these sounds or replace them with others from the Sound control panel. Select Control Panel → Sounds, Speech and Audio Devices → Change the Sound Scheme. To turn off the sounds, select 'No Sounds' in the selector near the top. Otherwise you can turn individual sounds on and replace them with others in the sound selector below. To change a sound, select it and browse the disk for your favourite alternative. Click on 'Save as...' at the top to give your new sound scheme a name when you have finished. You can change one sound, or all of them. To turn off one sound while keeping the rest, click on it and select 'None' in the sound selector.

The list of WAV sounds included in Windows XP is quite long. But you can browse the disk for others, or even make your own recordings and use those (Start → All Programs → Accessories → Entertainment → Sound Recorder will start the simple Windows sound recording tool)

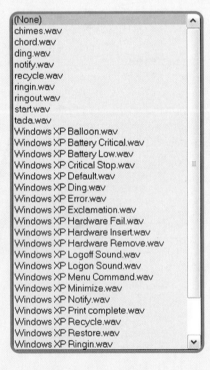

Using shortcuts

You can start software from the Start bar (see page 14). But when you install software, it will often create a shortcut on the desktop. A shortcut is a link to the software – it works much like a web link – and double clicking on it will start the software in the usual way. You can also create shortcuts to files. When you double click on one, the file will open ready for you to edit it.

Shortcuts are easy to create, and very useful. First, clear the desktop by right clicking on a blank part of the task bar and selecting 'Show the desktop'. Now open Windows Explorer, and find the file or program you want to create a shortcut for. Drag it to the desktop and hold down the Alt key. The mouse will change into the shortcut indicator – a curved arrow that points up and to the right. When you let go, the new shortcut will appear as an icon.

Changing file associations

In Windows XP, programs are automatically associated with different types of file. There's no point trying to edit a photo in a program designed to work with sound. So photo files (.jpg, .gif) will be associated with an image editor such as Photoshop or Paint Shop Pro. But sometimes these associations become broken. This often happens when different programs compete over file associations when you install them. Occasionally, a file type will lose all its associations. Or you may decide you want to edit a particular file type (such as a .dat general data file) using a text editor such as Wordpad. Here's how to fix the problem.

If you click on the 'Advanced' button in the File Associations Setting box, you can change the icon that's associated with a file type – click on 'Change icon'. You can also set up associations so that double clicking on a file does something other than opening it – although there aren't many situations where you'll ever want to do that.

The error message that appears when you try to open a file type that isn't associated with software

In Windows Explorer, click on Tools → Folder Options → File Types. Scroll down the long list that appears till you find the file type you want (in this case it's a WAV audio file)

Click on 'Change', and 'Select a program' from the list that appears. If there's no list, you can browse for the program by hand. Click on 'Apply' when done

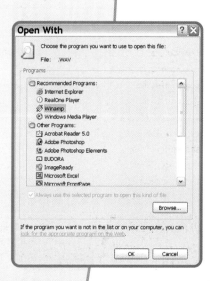

You can also change existing file associations by clicking on 'Change'. This will remove the connection to a piece of software and replace it with the new one you specify.

INSTALLING NEW HARDWARE

Will DIY invalidate my warranty?

Different manufacturers and computer dealers have different rules about this. Some allow simple upgrades, but others have a much stricter and less friendly policy and state clearly that any work needs to be done by an approved dealer. Some even use special screws to attach the case which won't work with a standard Phillips screwdriver. Check which tools you need and whether your manufacturer allows upgrades before starting!

Unlike cars, washing machines and microwaves, PCs are designed so that it is easy for almost anyone to add new hardware. You don't need advanced computer skills or any tool more complex than a screwdriver. With some hardware extras you don't even need to open the case at all. With others, some work inside the case is required, but the installation process is so easy it shouldn't take more than 10–15 minutes. The example here shows how to remove an old soundcard and replace it with a better one. Similar steps apply when adding a video/video capture card, a network card, or some other extra.

Step 1 Unplug everything (see page 7 for precautions) and remove the case

The screws you need to remove to take off your case could be anywhere on the back panel, the underside or even the top. (Some PCs don't have screws at all, and use simple clips, but these are rare.) Make sure you locate the correct screws carefully. Avoid those that hold other parts, such as the power supply, in place. Do not lose the screws.

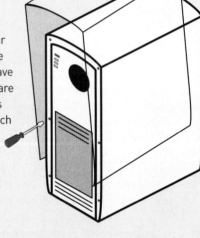

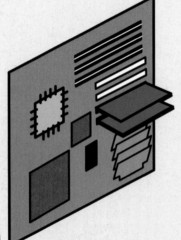

Step 2 Find the expansion slots

These expansion slots are designed for easy access. Once you remove the PC's case they are easy to find. The cards slot into them in a way that forces any connectors to appear on the back panel of the PC. If slots are not being used, they may be hidden behind blanking plates. These keep dust, mice and insects out of the PC.

Step 3 Remove a blanking plate, if necessary

If you are replacing an existing card, you can reuse the slot it fills. If not, you may need to remove a blanking plate, which will either be screwed on to the back panel, or be made of thin metal that bends when you push it. If it is screwed in place, undo the screw and remove the plate. If it is not, push the bottom of the plate to flex it backwards and forwards till it snaps off, and then remove it.

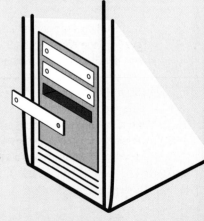

Step 4 Remove the existing card, if necessary

To remove an existing card, remove the screw that holds it in place. Then carefully tug at both ends to lever it out. If there are connectors on the back, you can sometimes push them with a screwdriver to pop out the card. Try to hold the card only by its edges and avoid touching the metal circuit tracks. Avoid especially touching any chips on the card. (Chips are sensitive to static, and even tiny amounts can damage delicate circuitry.)

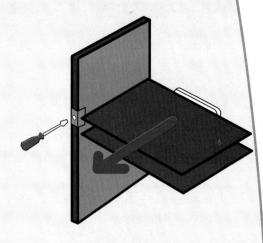

Step 5 Fit the new card

To fit a new card, align it so that the metal connector tracks are at the bottom and the connectors fit into the blanking plate slot, and push it carefully into one of the expansion slots. Make sure the slot is holding the card tightly, and that the card is pushed all the way so that it is level and doesn't stick up at either end. Be careful not to miss the slot with the bottom of the card. You may need to push quite firmly, but don't resort to extreme force or try to use a hammer – the card should slot in easily without them.

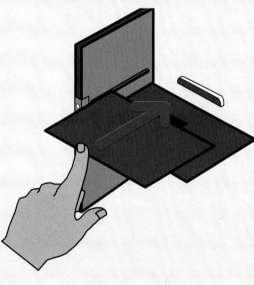

Step 6 Screw the card in place

Once the card is seated in the slot you must screw it in place so that it doesn't fall out. Not doing so may destroy the card or even damage your PC. Use the same screw as the one that held the original card or blanking slot in place. Once the card is fitted, reassemble the case, reconnect everything, start the PC and insert the CD or DVD with the driver software. This will install the drivers. You may need to restart the PC before the card is ready to use. For details of software settings, refer to the card's manual.

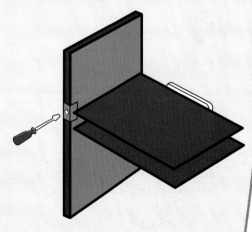

On screws

If you are replacing a card, make sure you don't lose the screw that holds it in place. If you need spare screws, your local, small PC store will often supply you with a handful at nominal cost, or even for nothing. (Larger stores are likely to be less helpful.) Explain you need expansion slot screws rather than case screws – the two types are different.

Torches, desk-lamps and other tools

The most useful tool is a simple Phillips screwdriver. An electric version is very handy and will noticeably speed up any work you do. Also useful is a good source of light, such as a desklamp or torch.

OTHER UPGRADES

Buying spares and upgrades

Probably the best all-round list of suppliers of upgrade parts is a weekly magazine called *MicroMart*. Some suppliers have their own websites, so you can order parts online. Of these, Dabs (www.dabs .com) has one of the most comprehensive ranges. Your original manufacturer should be your last choice. Most companies, except for a few very large names like IBM, use standard parts. So you may well save money if you buy your spares elsewhere.

More memory

It's easy to tell if your PC needs more memory. If you find yourself waiting a long time when you switch users, or you regularly work with large photos, or you find that your PC is taking a long time to respond while its disk activity light is flashing, you don't have enough memory. Adding more will make your PC respond more quickly. It's sometimes also useful if you plan to work with video.

Memory chips are supplied as long, very thin wafers which slot into long, thin slots next to the processor chip. There are many different types of memory, and you will need to buy exactly the right one. Unfortunately, the types can't be identified merely by looking at them. You will also need to open up your PC to see if there are any slots free. If not, you will need to remove the current memory and replace it with a larger capacity. If there are free slots, you can slot new wafers into one of them. However, sometimes if two slots are filled out of three, it's still easier to remove the memory that's there and replace it than add a new one.

To find the type of memory you need – this will be described with a cryptic acronym such as SDRAM, and usually a number such as PC2100 – phone the technical support line of your PC's manufacturer. As a rough guide, 256Mb is adequate for Windows XP, and 512Mb is recommended for more demanding users. 1Gb is overkill for almost everyone. Prices vary constantly, but you should be able to upgrade to 512Mb for less than £100.

To remove memory, undo the clips at the side and pull upwards. To fit new memory, place the wafers into a slot and apply firm, even pressure along the length. The clips will move into place. Once they are fitted, give them a further push from the side to make sure they're locked. Make sure the location cut-out holes on each wafer are aligned with the tabs in each slot. Making a mistake here can destroy the memory and damage your PC.

Master *vs* slave

You can fit up to four disk drives inside a PC. Two ribbon cables ('primary' and 'secondary') leading to the motherboard connect to two drives each. On each cable, one drive must be the master and the other the slave, otherwise your PC won't start. Your first hard disk, the one with Windows installed, should always be the primary master. The red edge of the cable should always be inserted nearest the marked corner (look for a '1' or an arrow) on the motherboard. To set master/slave operation for a disk drive, you will need to move some jumpers – tiny clip-on connectors at the back of the drive. Refer to your disk's manual, or a diagram printed on the drive itself. Use pliers, not your fingers, to pull out and replace the jumpers.

A spare hard disk

There are many uses for a spare hard disk, including extra space for games, music and video, and also backups and archiving. Disks are now relatively cheap, and you can double your disk capacity for much less than £100. Huge disks of 120Gb, which are useful for video-makers and computer musicians, are available for less than £200.

The hardest part of fitting a new disk is installing it physically. Your existing disk will usually be fitted inside a drive cage. On a small PC you may find, when you open up the case, that there's a CD or DVD drive already in the cage, and no room for anything else. If so, there's nothing more you can do, short of transplanting your entire PC into a new case – which is certainly possible, but not recommended for beginners. If there is room, you may need to unscrew the back of the PC and slide out a plate, which has the motherboard fixed to it, to gain access. To fit the drive, screw the drive into the slots cage and connect it with the long flat cable to the original drive. Change the jumpers first (see the diagram). Attach the cable to the back, and also attach a spare power connector. Copy the way these are attached to the first drive.

For gaming, replacing your video card will give you much better animated graphics. Note that Windows usually starts in an ugly 640 x 480 16-colour mode until you install the new card's drivers. Most soundcards will work without drivers, but you will need to install them to use any advanced features.

An advanced upgrade is to replace the motherboard and processor. This can give you a much faster PC and will cost between £300 and £600 depending on the parts you use.

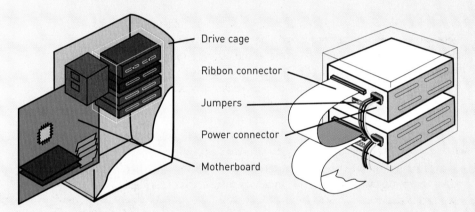

Drive cage
Ribbon connector
Jumpers
Power connector
Motherboard

Replacing a CD drive with a DVD drive, or a CD-writer

CD-writers and -readers and DVD-writers and -readers are all a standard size. Replacing one with another is simply a case of removing the connectors on the back, undoing the holding screws, slotting the old drive out, slotting the new drive in, and replacing screws and connectors. Don't forget to copy the master/slave setting on the back. You may also need to update your CD/DVD-burning software from the manufacturer's website. If your new drive is a very recent model, the software may not work with it properly until you do this.

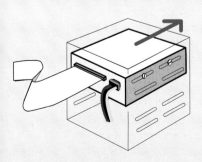

1. Slot the old drive out. It will often slide out of the front of the PC.

2. Slot the new drive in, and reattach the ribbon and power connectors.

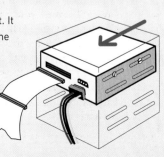

BUILDING A NETWORK

10/100 Ethernet?

Ethernet comes in two speeds – 10Mb/s and 100Mb/s. Any hardware marked '10/100' should work at the higher speed automatically. Make sure you check the speed of a hub before buying it: the slower speed is still sold, but the faster speed isn't usually any more expensive. You'll also see descriptions such as '10Base-T' and '100Base-TX'. The number here tells you the speed. You can ignore the words and letters around it – they have specific technical meanings that are relevant only to professionals.

If you have more than two PCs in your house – perhaps a laptop and a desktop machine – the easiest way to transfer information between them is by means of a network. A simple but clumsy alternative is to write information to CD-Rs or CD-RWs and carry these physically from one machine to the other. This will do the job, but for most kinds of work and play it's far more convenient to link the machines directly, because with a network you can:

- **share files** Photos, music and other information can be loaded into one PC and viewed/listened to on others on the network
- **play multi-player games** Games such as Half Life and the Quake/Doom family can be shared
- **share an Internet connection** Everyone can use the same connection, which will be shared among every PC
- **synchronise useful information** If you use both a laptop and a desktop PC, it's possible to make sure that names, addresses, emails and other details are always updated and identical on both machines.

Networks were once very complicated, expensive and difficult to set up. Windows XP makes building a network much more straightforward.

Step 1 Choose your network hardware

There are two types – a wireless system known as WiFi, and a cable-based system known as Ethernet. The latter is much cheaper and is typically faster, but the cables are less convenient and potentially ugly in a home setting. WiFi is much neater, but is currently still far more expensive. It is also less secure. Unless you are careful, your neighbours may be able to see inside your PC as easily as you can.

Internal Ethernet network card – as little as £10

The plug on a network cable is known officially as an **'RJ45 connector'**. In spite of the name, there's nothing complicated about it – it simply clicks into place in the corresponding socket in a network card or hub

Laptop Ethernet card – about £35

You can sometimes buy all the separate parts for a small network as a kit that will save you money on buying the parts individually.

Cables – from £5 to £15 depending on length. Ask for 'Cat 5 uncrossed' cable

Network hub – the central exchange for a small network. Not needed if only two PCs are linked. Between £40 and £100

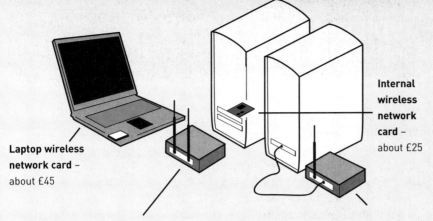

Laptop wireless network card – about £45

Internal wireless network card – about £25

A 'wireless access point' connected to a PC – This is a radio receiver and transmitter, the wireless equivalent of a hub; about £100

External wireless network unit (connects via USB. Use as an alternative to an internal card if your PC is already full, or you don't want to open it up) – about £70

802.11a and 802.11b?

The wireless networking system is known (rather unhelpfully) as the '802.11' standard. There are two main types: 802.11b hardware, which is slow (around 10Mb/s) but cheap and widely available, and 802.11a, which is faster (up to 50Mb/s) but much more expensive, and usually only available on special order from specialist suppliers. The two types are not compatible, so 802.11a cards and extras won't work on an 802.11b network (and vice versa).

An experimental 802.11g standard has also been suggested. This is as fast as 802.11a, but is compatible with 802.11b. It is not available yet, but may – perhaps – appear around 2004–05.

A wireless network needs no cables. A connection is made automatically as soon as each computer is within range of the central wireless access point. The reliable range within a house is around 50m, at a speed of around 10Mb/s. This means you can use your laptop in your study, kitchen or living room. It will connect to the main PC in your home automatically. You can also connect your laptop to the Internet through the main PC's own Internet connection. If you have another desktop PC, that can join the network too.

Step 2 Run the network wizard

Once you have your hardware installed (including all the drivers), start the Windows XP network wizard. This sets up your network for you. You need to specify:

● whether this PC connects directly to the Internet
● which ISP you want to use for the connection
● a name and description for the PC. The name will appear on the network
● the name of your entire network. The default is MSHOME. You'll probably want to change this to something more personal. Every computer has to use the same network name.

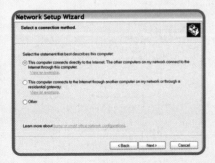

If you have a Firewire card, it will appear in this list of network connections as if it were an ISP! Ignore this when it happens. The true Internet connections are the ones that use your modem or broadband hardware

If your PC is connected to the Internet via a modem or broadband link, select the top option here

BUILDING A NETWORK – ADVANCED OPTIONS

FTP

The system used to copy files from the Internet to your PC is called FTP (file transfer protocol). An 'FTP site' is a library of files for you to copy. Simplified FTP features are built into all browsers, so you can use a browser to copy files without needing to understand FTP's technical details. Windows Explorer's Network Places includes similar simplified features. Experts sometimes prefer specialised FTP software (search for 'FTP software').

Sharing files and folders

By default, Windows XP is set up so that other people on a network can access only the Shared Documents folder on your PC. This is often inconvenient – for example, if you have a laptop and want to be able to copy files to and from it.

But Windows XP includes a feature called folder-sharing. Everyone on the network can read the files in a shared folder. You can also give them permission to change the files, or create new ones. You can even share an entire disk, with all the folders in it.

To share a folder, open Windows Explorer, right click on the folder and select 'Sharing and Security...'. You'll see a box appear with a warning message. Click on the message, and then tick the bottom two boxes. If you want others to read the files but not change them, leave the bottom one unticked.

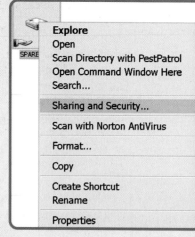

Right click on a drive to show the sharing options

Network drives

To make it easier to navigate around a network, you can map drives or folders so that they appear like hard disks inside your machine, with their own drive letter (D:, G:, etc.). You can also map folders on a single PC. This is a simple trick, but a very useful one. If there's a folder you use over and over, map it and save time when opening or saving files.

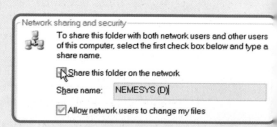

Check these boxes to turn on sharing

To map a drive, open Explorer and select Tools → Map Network Drive... Drives are created in reverse order, starting with Z:. Browse for the disk or folder you want, and select 'OK'. Your new disk is ready. To rename it, right click on the drive and select 'Rename'. To remove the mapping, first make sure you're not working with any files in the disk or folder. Then right click on the drive in Explorer and select 'Disconnect'. Ignore the warning message that appears.

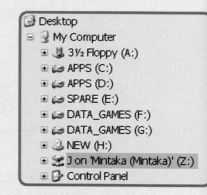

Here's a DVD writer on a remote PC mapped to a networked drive. Now it looks as if it's directly attached to this computer

My Network Places

If you click on 'My Network Places' (it appears in Windows Explorer), it will expand to show all the disks and folders that are connected. It also appears in file selector boxes – which is very handy, because it means you can save and open files anywhere on the network directly (as long as they are set up for sharing).

My Network Places can also be used to store links to Internet locations. A small advertising link to the Microsoft Network (MSN) appears there by default, but you can add your own links as well. When you are in your web browser, click on the tiny Explorer icon to the left of the URL, and drag it to My Network Places. It's immediately added to the list as a network place. This is very useful indeed for Internet sites that use the FTP file-copying system (see the sidebar).

Name	Comments
Electra (Electra)	
apps (d) on Electra (Electra)	\\electra\apps (d)
SharedDocs on Electra (Electra)	\\ELECTRA\SharedDocs
apps (c) on Electra (Electra)	\\electra\apps (c)
f on Electra (Electra)	\\electra\f
g on Electra (Electra)	\\electra\g
spare (e) on Electra (Electra)	\\electra\spare (e)
ftp.simtel.net	
ftp.simtel	
Mintaka (Mintaka)	
SharedDocs on Mintaka (Mintaka)	\\MINTAKA\SharedDocs
video (e) on Mintaka (Mintaka)	\\mintaka\video (e)

The Simtel shareware FTP site included in My Network Places. Clicking on the site creates a direct link for file copying

Synchronising files

Use the Windows Briefcase to keep files on a laptop and PC up to date with each other. To create a briefcase, right click on your laptop's desktop and select New → Briefcase. Before you leave home, copy the files you will be working on from your PC into the briefcase. You can then work on them while you are away. Back at base, connect the laptop back into the network, open the briefcase folder and select Briefcase → Update All. If you want to update only some of the files, highlight them with the mouse and select Briefcase → Update Selection.

Advanced hardware

If you have two Firewire-equipped PCs, run a cable between them, then run the Network Setup wizard in the Control Panel. Windows XP will create a Firewire network. You won't need to buy or install any network cards. If your PC has only one Firewire socket, you will need to buy a Firewire Hub – a box that adds more sockets. Firewire Hubs cost about £40 and are very easy to install. Just plug them in.

This appears in My Network Places. While it looks interesting, it's not very useful except on big networks. If you select 'Microsoft Windows Network', you'll see your workgroup. Open it and you'll find all the computers that are part of it. The other two icons, Web Client Network and Terminal Services, are intended for very specialised applications and can safely be ignored.

ADVANCED WINDOWS (I)

Pinning and removing on the Start bar

To pin software to the Start bar, right click on either the software file in My Program Files, or on its name in the All Programs listing (Start → All Programs). Then select 'Pin to Start menu'. To remove pinned software, right click on it and select 'Unpin from Start menu'. (As a rule, it's a good idea to try right clicking elsewhere too. You'll find all kinds of other useful options.)

When things go wrong

Ctrl + Alt + Delete is a magic key combination that can kill a piece of software that refuses to die. It opens a list of the software running in your PC. Most of this is obscure – it includes everything that Windows XP is doing automatically behind the scenes. But you can usually pick out the errant software from the list by name. To kill it, select it and then click on 'End Process' at the bottom right.

Removing software that starts automatically

You'll sometimes find that after you install some software, it insists on starting itself whenever you start your PC. To prevent this, look at Start → All Programs → Startup. If it appears in that list, select it and delete it. If it doesn't, select Start → Run and type 'msconfig' into the box that appears. Click on the 'Startup' tab, and see if it's listed there. If it is, untick it. If not, click on the 'Services' tab and tick the 'Hide All Microsoft Services' box. If it appears in the list, untick it. If it doesn't, unfortunately that means it can't be removed without expert-level skills.

Find out what's running behind the scenes with msconfig – the Windows configuration tool

The registry, and restore points

Windows XP has a central library of settings called the registry. You can edit this by hand by using a tool called regedit (Start → Run → Regedit), but you should never do this unless you know exactly what you are doing. The wrong tweak can break Windows permanently.

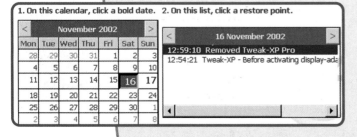

Set restore points and avoid potential trouble when you change drivers or add new software

However, there is a safety fall-back feature called System Restore. Before you install new software or a new driver, you can set a restore point. If there are problems, you can roll back your changes, and Windows will be restored to full working order. You'll find the tool in the Help and Support Centre. Close all windows and hit F1 to make this appear. The restore feature appears under Pick a Task.

More Windows XP tweaks

Tweaking Windows XP is a popular pastime, and there are plenty of websites devoted to ways you can change, improve or customise XP.
Here are some of the best.

www.tweaktown.com

Plenty of information which can take a beginner to intermediate level and beyond

www.xp-erience.org

Windows XP news updated daily. Also includes drivers and freeware utilities

www.tweakxp.com

Plenty of tricks and tips and also forums for Windows XP users

www.windows-administrator.com

Tweaks and tips for those with experience of Windows

www.windowsxpforums.com

Free forums where you can ask questions and get answers from other Windows XP users

Extreme customisation tools

Not everyone likes the standard blue, silver and green colour schemes that are supplied with Windows XP. Shareware is available that lets you change these. You can even change the initial ('boot') screen which appears if you have set up Windows XP to ask you for a password. If you want a quick and easy variation, it's possible to download themes that other people have created. But you can also create your own from scratch. This takes more time and artistic ability than most people have, so you can compromise by making small changes to someone else's work to give you exactly the design you want. You can even create extreme effects, such as making unused windows transparent.

Windowblinds (www.windowblinds.net) attaches itself to Display Properties. You can create your own themes from scratch

StyleBuilder (www.tgtsoft.com) – change absolutely anything and everything about Windows XP

6.12 Advanced Windows (I)

More themes and customisation software

Themes and artwork

www.deviant art.com

www.belchfire.net

Logon screen customisation tools

XP Logmod

www.sub-seven.com/ logmod

Chameleon XP

www.geocities .com/outer softinc

Logon Loader

www.rad files.com/ logonloader

ADVANCED WINDOWS (II)

Fun with dual displays

Try the following:
● in Photoshop and other image editors, keep the various palettes and controls on one monitor and the image you are working on on the other

● keep email and other low-priority software on one monitor away from your main work focus

● set up the spare monitor channel as a video output and connect it to a TV for games and watching DVDs.

Dual displays

With Windows XP, you can plug in more than one graphics card and use two monitors to create either one large split display or two independent displays. This is a better idea in theory than in practice, because most PCs are designed so that you can fit only a single card. But some cards include a dual-head feature, and can work with two monitors at once. Some, such as the Matrox Parhelia range, can even work with three to create a wrap-around effect.

When installing a dual-head card, make sure you first remove all the software for the old video card, including the drivers and any desktop management tools. It's also essential to ensure that you have the latest drivers. Otherwise, two cards work very much as one. Features for splitting and combining the available displays in various ways will appear in Display Properties → Settings → Advanced.

Power management

Instead of switching off your PC, you can leave it in standby or hibernate mode. Standby turns off the disks and monitor, but leaves any working information in memory; if there's a power failure, you'll lose your work. Hibernate is safer. It saves your current work to disk. But it's available only if there's enough disk space. The big advantage of both is that your computer will restart very quickly – in a matter of seconds instead of the minute or two that it normally takes. You can set up these power options by going to Control Panel → Performance and Maintenance → Power Options and exploring the tabs that appear in the power options window. Note that you may need a special keyboard with Sleep and Power buttons for these to work properly.

Faster start-ups

There are two other ways to speed up your PC while it's starting. The first is to defragment your disks (see page 156). The second is to use a utility tool called BootVis available from Microsoft. It profiles how much work your computer does while it's starting up. But it also has an optimisation feature. It's not particularly friendly, but you need to run it only once and select Trace → Optimise System and it will do the rest. You can find it by searching for 'BootVis'.

Instead of powering down, why not try standby mode?

BootVis – a simple and free way to make your PC start faster

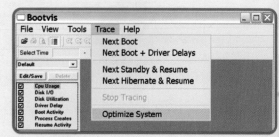

Disks, partitions and filing systems with Partition Magic

Windows XP uses two different filing technologies. FAT32 is an older system used in earlier versions of Windows. NTFS (new technology filing system) is an improved system developed for professional use. Your PC may be set up to use either system. NTFS offers some advantages, so it can be worth converting from one format to another.

Windows XP includes a conversion tool, but it's hard to use. A better option is PowerQuest's Partition Magic, mentioned on page 103. Partition Magic can also split a very big hard disk so that it appears as two smaller ones. (Each split is called a partition. It appears in Windows Explorer with its own drive letter just as if it were a separate disk.) In fact, Partition Magic can create and destroy partitions, change their size and even merge them together. It's not essential for beginners, but if you plan to start adding extra disks to your PC, or customising it to an intermediate level, it's a very useful tool to have.

Multi-boot systems

If you have an old PC with an old copy of Windows, it's sometimes possible to transplant this version into your new PC by installing the old disk. Partition Magic includes a feature called a boot manager, with which you can decide which version of Windows you want to use. This will also work if you regularly clone your main Windows XP disk to a spare drive. If your main disk dies, you can use Partition Magic to start your PC using the backup copy of Windows on the spare disk. This is known as a dual-boot system. ('Boot' is short for 'bootstrap' – an old piece of computer jargon.) It's simple to set up and is a very simple but effective way of keeping all your information and Windows settings safe.

Another use for Partition Magic is preparing a blank disk so that Windows XP can use it – if you buy a blank hard-disk drive and install it in your PC, it won't work right away. This preparation process is called partitioning and formatting the disk. Windows XP includes a format tool (right click on a disk, select 'Format'), but there's no built-in way to partition a disk.

Partition Magic makes disk management easy. It also comes with a tutorial primer that explains the jargon and all the different things you can do

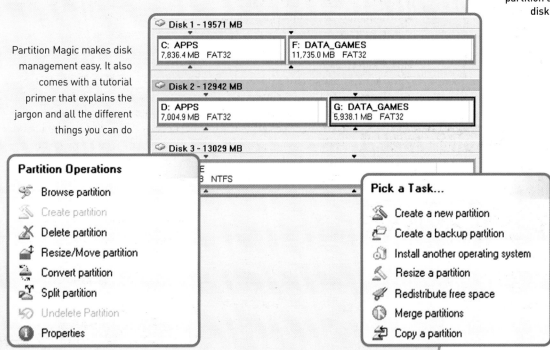

LOOKING BACKWARDS, LOOKING FORWARDS

Windows archaeology

You'll often find older versions of Windows at work. Windows NT remains popular with business users, and occasionally you'll even find office computers that are still using Windows 3.1. However, given that it is unlikely you will have permission to install your own software at work, it should not matter to you if what you have in the office is older than what you have on your home PC.

Looking backwards

This book has been written for users of Windows XP. But what if you have an earlier version of Windows (see page 13)? Many of the ideas covered are similar, although the details are often different. Earlier versions of Internet Explorer (IE) are very similar to the version used in Windows XP. The basics – the forward, back, home, refresh and stop buttons, the history list, and favourites/bookmarks – are the same for absolutely all the most common web browsers. But there are differences too. If you have version 4 of IE, you may find that some sites don't quite appear the way they should. Later versions, including 5, 5.5 and the current 6, are almost identical.

It's a different story with Windows Explorer, which has changed significantly over the years. With Windows 98 it took on many of the qualities and features of a web browser. Put simply, the earlier the version, the more features it will have missing. Other Microsoft software has been through a similar process of evolution. Versions of Office, including all its component parts (Word, Access, Excel, etc.), have been available for at least a decade. Earlier releases lack the sophisticated file selector that the most recent version has, and are also more prone to errors and crashes. Also missing are some of the more complex features included in Office XP, particularly the taskbars which provide quick summaries of the things you can do. Publisher lacks many of the pre-set templates that are available now, although the basic editing features remain the same.

In terms of other software, you'll find that plenty of commercial products available today will still work on older versions of Windows. If you have no plans to upgrade to Windows XP, you should always check for compatibility before buying any new software product to make sure that it will work with your older Windows version. Shareware is another mixed bag. Some of it is so old that you can use any version of Windows, perhaps even Windows 3.1. But as with commercial products, some will work only with Windows XP. Again, you should check carefully before trying or buying.

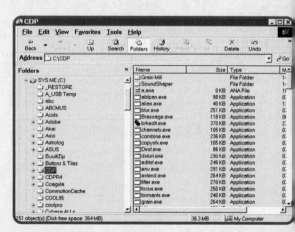

Windows Explorer from Windows ME – cosmetic differences, but otherwise very similar

Looking forwards

Some time in 2003 Microsoft will introduce a new product called Windows XP Media Centre. This will be almost identical to Windows XP, but will include a new and improved version of Media Player. Microsoft's plan is to create PCs that can replace a home CD player, VCR, DVD player and photo album with a single unit with a familiar remote control. In the longer term, Microsoft is planning a completely new product, which will run on a completely new kind of PC. Currently this is codenamed Longhorn, and has a provisional release date of 2005/06. Almost everything will change, including the look, and also the filing system, which will be designed to work more intelligently, almost like a huge database. Security will also be improved. This will make viruses much less likely, but will also close current loopholes that make online music piracy possible.

Alternatives to Windows

Windows XP is still not a perfectly secure piece of software. And it's also rather expensive – accounting for up to 50% of the price of a new PC. The main alternative is a system called Linux. Versions of Linux are sold in larger computer stores by companies such as Red Hat, Suse and Mandrake. The big advantages of Linux are that it's supplied with a veritable mountain of free software (albeit of variable quality), it's more secure and robust, and at about £60 it's also much cheaper. The big disadvantage is that you can't use most Windows software with it. If you mostly use your PC as an office tool and don't care about playing the latest games, then it can be worth considering a change. You can set up a PC so you have Windows XP and a version of Linux installed at the same time, choosing one or the other when your PC starts. Linux isn't recommended for beginners. But it's almost infinitely customisable, which makes it an interesting playpen for people who enjoy computer DIY. In fact, it's completely open to tinkering, so someone with programming experience (and not a little free time) can change any or all of it, to any extent.

Lindows

One of the more unusual variants of Linux is called Lindows. Originally created to run Windows software on a Linux PC, it seems to have settled for being compatible with the most popular file formats. Lindows is sold with an annual licence that gives you access to a website with hundreds of programs to download. It's making slow inroads into the budget-PC market, especially in the USA. It hasn't taken off in the UK yet.

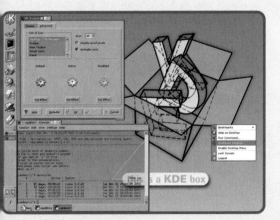

Linux gives you a choice of look. You can choose between a look called KDE, shown here, or an alternative called Gnome, which looks and works slightly differently

Lindows is available on CD and also as a download. But the download version is rather huge, and not recommended unless you have broadband

GLOSSARY

Application Any piece of software

BIOS (basic input output system) The special software built into your PC's motherboard that controls how the hard disks, CD-ROM drive, memory and other extras work

Boot Short for 'bootstrap'. The automatic sequence a PC goes through while it's starting up

Browser Short for web browser. A piece of software used to look at web pages

Bug A mistake in software that causes it to work improperly, or not at all. *See also* crash

Button A control that appears on the screen and does something when you click on it with the mouse

Byte The smallest unit of storage in a PC. Roughly the same as a single letter. *See also* kilobyte, megabyte and gigabyte

CD-ROM Software and other information supplied on a CD

CD-ROM drive The slot in your PC which can read information on a CD-ROM

Chat A tool used to have instant typed conversations with over a network or the Internet

Click Move the mouse cursor so it's over something on the screen, and push down the left mouse button to make something happen

CPU (central processing unit) Another name for the processor chip at the heart of a PC

Crash When your computer stops working. Usually caused by a bug. *See also* hang

Database A collection of organised information

Default A standard setting in a PC that applies unless you change it

Defragment A regular housekeeping process that's needed to rearrange the information on a disk drive so it's stored more efficiently

Desktop The main window inside your PC. Shows wallpaper, icons and the Start bar

Directory A list of files and folders

Disk drive Or just 'disk'. The main storage inside a PC. Keeps copies of all your information even when a PC is turned off. There are hard disks and floppy disks

Disk space The amount of space that a file or folder takes up on a disk drive or the total amount of space available on a disk drive

Document Any piece of information you create – a picture, a music recording, a spreadsheet, or an ordinary letter

DOC A file type used to store text documents that include extra information about fonts, page layout, etc.

Double click Two rapid clicks with your finger on the left button of a mouse. Used to open a file or start a piece of software

Download To copy information from the Internet to your PC. *See also* FTP

Drive letter A single letter followed by a colon ':' that specifies a disk drive in a PC's file system

Driver A specialised piece of software that links Windows XP to a specific item of hardware so that Windows can make full use of all its features

Email (electronic mail) Sending and receiving messages and other information over a network, and especially over the Internet

Explorer The main tool used to look through and organise files in Windows XP. *See also* Internet Explorer

FAQs (frequently asked questions) A collection of common questions with answers used in various Internet discussion forums

File Information stored in a PC. A file can contain software, a document or any other information

File extension A three-letter code that specifies what kind of information is kept in a file, and links the file to the software needed to work with it

File name The name of a file, in two parts – a long descriptive name which can be anything, and a file extension

File selector A box that appears on the screen when you open or save a file so you can tell your PC where the file is, or where it should go

File system The system used to organise files inside a PC. A combination of drive letters, each of which contains many folders

File type A description given to a file according to the kind of information inside it – e.g. letter, music, video, etc. Windows keeps track of the file type using the file extension

Floppy disk A small plastic wafer that holds around 1.4 megabytes of information. Very slow, very old, now almost obsolete

Folder A way of dividing up a disk drive so you can keep related information organised together. Like files, folders have unique names

Font A lettering style

FTP (file transfer protocol) A way of copying files between the Internet and a PC

Gigabyte (Gb) A billion bytes. A unit of storage used to describe the disk space taken up by very large files

Hang When your PC freezes and stops working, usually because of a bug or more rarely because of a hardware problem

Hard disk A spinning metal disk inside a box. A PC uses one or more hard disks to store information. Each has a capacity of many gigabytes

Hardware The parts of your PC you can see and touch, including any extras you connect to your PC. Also known as peripherals

Hibernate Used to power down your PC overnight so it starts quickly the next day, instead of going through a full boot

Icon A small picture that appears on the desktop. When you double click on it, it will open a file or start a piece of software

IM (instant message) A variety of chat

Install To copy software to your PC so you can start to use it

Internet An international network of computers supplying access to all kinds of information, and also making services like email and the Web possible

Internet Explorer The browser built into Windows XP that makes it possible to look at information on the Web

ISP (Internet service provider) A company that sells an Internet connection, usually for a monthly subscription

Kilobyte (Kb) 1,024 bytes. About the size of an email with only a few lines of text in it

LAN (local area network) A network that connects PCs that are physically close together, as in a home or an office building

Load With respect to software, similar to run – i.e. to start using a piece of software. Also to open a file

Megabyte (Mb) Approximately 1 million bytes. About the size of a small photo

Memory Also known as RAM, the working space inside a PC that loses all its information when the PC is turned off. Usually hundreds of megabytes in a typical PC

Menu A list of things you can do in a piece of software, often presented as a selection of headings at the top of a window, with lists that drop down when you click on them

Mouse A small plastic device with buttons used to point at information on a PC's screen

Mouse cursor An arrow or other shape that moves as you move the mouse, and indicates where on the screen the mouse is pointing

MP3 A file type used to store medium-quality music and sound recordings

MS-DOS (Microsoft disk operating system)
A much-simplified way of accessing the files inside a PC that uses typed words instead of mouse control

MS-DOS prompt The typing tool used to tell MS-DOS what you want it to do. For experts only

Network Two or more computers connected together so they can share information. *See also* LAN and Internet

Open To look at a file or document from your PC's hard disk so you can make changes to it. *See also* save

Partition A subdivision of space on a hard disk that has its own drive letter and is made to look like a separate disk for reasons of speed or convenience

Processor The master chip inside a PC that does the most important work

RAM (random access memory) The memory inside a PC

Reboot To restart your PC deliberately. Sometimes necessary after you install software or because a bug has made your PC crash or hang

Registry The central store of settings for all the software in your PC. Can be edited by hand, but this isn't recommended for beginners

Reset switch The switch at the front of your PC that will cause a reboot. Not to be used except in emergencies – otherwise you will lose all your work

Run Software that is loaded into memory and working is said to be running

Save To copy a document or file to disk after you have finished working on it, so any changes become permanent. See also open

Shortcut A file that links to another file or application, often used on the desktop

Software The tools inside your PC that work with information and make your PC useful to you

Start bar The Start menu that appears at the bottom left of the screen, and the list of software you are using that appears next to it towards the right. Sometimes also known as the taskbar

System disk A floppy disk used to start Windows XP when it won't boot otherwise

System tray The area at the bottom right of the screen in Windows XP that shows the clock and various other useful software that's always working in the background

Task Any piece of software currently running inside your PC

Titlebar The area at the top of a window that shows the title

Web (World Wide Web) The simple system used on the Internet to display information from computers all over the world

Window A box on the screen that includes all the menus, information and other details needed to use a piece of software

Windows XP The version of the Windows software described throughout this book

FURTHER READING

Magazines

There are many different PC magazines available, aimed at a range of readers, from absolute beginners to serious PC professionals. Here's a selection of those more suitable for beginners.

Computer Active (VNU)

Good, basic how-to features for beginners, written in a friendly and accessible way, and also reviews of both hardware and software, and news. For web users there's an alternative called **Web Active**, which follows the same successful format.

Computer Shopper (Dennis Publishing)

Cheap and often cheerful, this long-running title includes a blend of material for both beginners and more experienced readers. A suitable choice for beginners looking for a taste of a slightly more demanding PC experience.

Internet Advisor (Future Publishing)

A very beginner-oriented magazine concentrating almost exclusively on simple how-to features for Internet users.

PC Basics (Paragon Publishing)

Very easy-to-follow guides to upgrading, troubleshooting and using PCs. An ideal starting point for beginners.

PC First Aid (Paragon Publishing)

A guide to sorting out the problems associated with a misbehaving PC. Includes information for both beginners and more advanced PC users.

PC Format (Future Publishing)

Aimed at younger readers, this includes a jokey and rather irreverent mix of practical information, news and other features. A useful source of information about games and games reviews.

PC Gamer (Future Publishing)

Everything about games, including news, reviews and previews. Surprisingly, some of the information may be a little advanced for beginners, but it's an essential read for anyone interested in PC gaming.

PC Home (Paragon Publishing)

Simple PC tips and projects ideas, suitable for general family reading.

Practical Internet (Paragon Publishing)

Written with a view to time-saving and money-saving features, this is another friendly Internet-oriented title. A companion title called **Practical Web Projects** provides useful hints and tips for both beginning and more advanced web designers.

Microsoft Windows XP (Future Publishing)

Hands-on ideas and suggestions for projects at beginner, medium and advanced levels. The content is mostly good but the magazine is heavily supported by Microsoft, so some of the features have tendencies towards advertorials.

Also watch for shareware collections on CD. Most magazines include at least some shareware on their cover CDs and DVDs. But you'll see occasional one-off specialised titles that offer hundreds of free and trialware programs to try out.

Books

Microsoft Windows XP Step by Step
Microsoft Press
ISBN 0-7356-1383-4
Windows XP for beginners from Microsoft's own publishing division. A good resource for beginners looking to improve their practical knowledge of Windows XP and how it works

Microsoft Windows XP Inside Out
Ed Bott & Carl Siechert
Microsoft Press
ISBN 0-7356-1382-6
A more advanced guide to Windows XP. Beginners may find it a challenge, but it's an excellent reference for more advanced users

Windows XP in a Nutshell
David Karp et al
O'Reilly
ISBN 0-5960-0249-1
O'Reilly Publishing is better known for its professional computing titles, and this book continues that professional approach but aims it at both beginners and experienced users looking for a definitive Windows XP reference guide

The Which? Computer Troubleshooter
Robin Davies
Which? Books
ISBN 0-85202-881-4
An excellent and fully illustrated guide to dealing with computer problems

The Which? Guide to Computers
Richard Wentk
Which? Books
ISBN 0-85202-877-6
The definitive reference guide for information about buying and upgrading a PC

The Which? Guide to Money on the Internet
Jonquil Lowe
Which? Books
ISBN 0-85202-873-3
All about online and TV banking; arranging loans, mortgages and other services; trading in shares; and how to vet the good dealers from the cowboys

Information from Which?

You'll find a wealth of consumer and shopping information available direct from Which?. *Which?* magazine provides definitive consumer reviews. *Computing Which?*, published every two months, covers PC hardware and software (see www.computingwhich.co.uk for details).The online services include:

Which? Online
The complete online information resource for consumers, with thousands of reports from the Which? range of magazines, plus an interactive product picker and searchable guides like *The Good Food Guide*

Which? Extra
Free to magazine subscribers, this offers a huge archive of hundreds of *Which?* reports and Best Buy listings

For more details see www.which.co.uk

INDEX

about.com 139
Access 106, 121
Act! 120
ADSL (asymmetrical digital subscriber line) 25
adware 162
AIM (AOL Instant Message) 37, 143
AIT/DLT/DAT tape drive 104
Alt Gr key 16
Alt key 16, 17
Amazon 50, 53, 58, 59, 148
AOL 24, 27, 37, 96, 143, 153
applets 101
archiving 95, 138
auction sites 53, 56-7

backups 104-5
    hardware 104
    incremental backups 104
    project/document backups 104
    scheduling 105
    software 105
    system backups 104
BACS 133
banking online 126-7
blogs (online diaries) 99
Bluetooth 158
books
book reviews 149
buying online 58, 149
    classical literature 150
broadband 25, 26
Bryce 87

'C:' drive 103
calendar-creation tools 95
cars
car fraud checks 61
    discount sites 61
    private sales 61
CD drive 11, 102, 104, 173
CD-R disks 104, 174
CD-RW disks 104, 174
CD-writer 11, 173
CDs 64
    buying online 59
    cloning 76
    copy protection 76
    playlists 76
    ripping (copying from) 66, 74-5, 77
CHAPS 133
Chat 37, 143
children

online security 34, 35, 36-7
    software for 38-41
Cleanup 156
Clip Art 92, 93, 95, 113
cloning
    CDs 76
    disk drives 103, 105, 181
    photos 72, 73
    codecs 89
computer-aided design (CAD) 46
contact managers 120, 123
Control Panel 20, 164
cookies 162, 163
copyright 81, 93
Ctrl + Alt + Delete 17, 178
Ctrl keys 16, 17
customising Windows 164-9
    advanced tweaks 167, 178, 179
    alternative web browsers 166
    changing the desktop 164
    changing the sound scheme 168
    dual displays 180
    files and folders 165, 169
    menus 167
    power management 180
    shortcuts 168
    themes 164, 179

databases 106, 121, 123
desktop 14-15
    customising 164
    shortcuts 168
Desktop folder 103
desktop publishing (DTP) 90-1
    brochures 112-13
    professional printing 91
    software 107, 113
    templates and page layouts 90-1
dictionaries 151
digital cameras 8, 12, 42, 69-71
    connection system 69
    memory 69
    picture quality 69
    professional printing 94
discussion boards 99
disk drives
    AIT/DLT/DAT tape drive 104
    'C:' drive 103
    CD drive 11, 102, 104, 173
    cloning 103, 105, 181
    defragmentation 156
    DVD drive 11, 102, 104, 173
    failure 104
    Firewire drive 104
    fitting extra drives 103, 104, 172-3

floppy-disk drive 11, 102, 104
hard-disk drive 11, 102, 104, 173
    maintenance 156-7
    master/slave operation 172
    partitioning and formatting 181
    Travan tape drive 104
domains and domain names 100, 153
Drag and Drop editing 111
drivers 18
dual displays 180
DVDs
    backups 105
    buying online 59
    DVD+R/RW 104
    DVD burner 83, 89
    DVD creation 89
    DVD drive 11, 102, 104, 173
    DVD-R/RW 104
    player software 64, 67

eBay 56-7
eBooks 102, 150
educational software 38, 40-1
email 28-9, 180
    addresses 24, 153
    alternatives to Outlook 109
    attachments 29, 142, 160
encryption 29
    mailing lists 140-1, 155
    smileys and emoticons 28, 29
    spam 24, 37, 143, 161, 162, 163
    viruses 28, 160
encyclopaedias 123, 151
Esc (escape) 16, 17
Ethernet 174
Eudora 109
Excel 106, 116-17, 125
    expansion slots 10

F1 key 16
FAQs (frequently asked questions) 138
faxes 14, 142
files 20-1
    binaries 141
    changing options 165
    deletion 20, 105, 157
    file associations 21, 169
    file extensions 21, 96
    file-recovery tools 105
    finding 21
    folders 19, 20, 102-3, 165, 176
    Hide feature 36, 103
    saving 21
    sharing 174, 176
    sizes 20

synchronising 177
zipping 142
film news and reviews 149
financial planner 124-5
financial services 128-9
    banking online 126-7
    comparison and listing
    services 128
    ethical investment 129
    general help 129
    money transfers 133
    mortgages 129
    stocks and shares 130-1
firewalls 161
Firewire 11, 69, 83, 84, 86, 88, 177
Firewire drive 104
Flash 101
floppy-disk drives 11, 102, 104
folders 19, 20, 102-3, 165
    mapping 176
    options, changing 165
    sharing 176
fonts 92-3, 95, 111
    fonts online 92, 93
    installing 93
    professional fonts 92
Fonts folder 93
freeware 48, 144, 145
FrontPage 100, 107
FTP (file transfer protocol) 97, 176
function keys 16

games 48-9
    cheat features 48
    film and TV tie-ins 48
    freeware 48
    hardware 49
    Internet gaming 49
    multi-player games 174
    puzzles and plotlines 48
    role-playing and fantasy 48, 49
    shoot 'em ups 48, 49
    sims (simulators) 48
    soundcard game support 79
    traditional games 48
garden-design software 44-5
genealogical sites 154-5
GIFs 99
gifts, buying online 59
Google 136-7, 138, 139, 151, 155
government services online 132
GPS (global positioning system)
    122
grammar and spelling check 29,
    114
graphics card 10, 49
graphs, charts and tables 114, 116

hackers 161
hard-disk drives 11, 102, 104
    spare drive 103, 104, 173
hardware
    backups 104
    games 49
    installing new hardware 170-1
    MP3 players 77
    networks 174-5, 177
    warranties 170
help, accessing 16
hibernate mode 180
holidays, flights and travel 54-5
    bargains 55
    courier travel 55
    flight bookings 55
    maps 122, 151
    road travel 54
    route planners 122
    specialist travel 55
    survival guides 54
home-design packages 42, 46-7
HTML (hypertext markup
    language) 97

image-editing software 70-1, 180
Ins (insert) 16
interior design 42-3
Internet
    faxing service 142
    games 49
    ISPs 24, 26-7
    music and video 65, 66
    newsgroups 138-9
    online software 18, 144-7
    radio stations 64, 67
    research 138-9
    shopping online 50-63
Internet connections 12, 14, 25
    broadband 25, 26
    dial-up connections 25
    manual installation 26-7
    sharing 174
Internet Explorer (IE) 182
IP (Internet protocol) number 161
ISDN (integrated services digital
    network) 25
ISPs (Internet service providers)
    24, 26-7

Java 101, 159
Java Virtual Machine (JVM) 159
Javascript 99, 101
job-centre listings 132
joystick 9, 49, 79

keyboards 8
    shortcuts 16-17

Keystroke recorder 37

language translation 110, 151
laptops 9, 174, 177
Lindows 183
Linux 146, 183
literature sites 149, 150
Longhorn 183

macros 115
mail-merge feature 115
mailing lists 140-1, 155
    etiquette 141
    newsgroups 141
maintenance
    disks 156-7
    Remote Assistance 159
    Windows 158-9
    maps 122, 151
Media Player 64-7, 80, 88, 183
    alternatives to 67
    creating and finding media 66,
    74-5
    customising 65
    drawbacks 67
Media Library 66, 76
MP3 format 77
    playlists 76
    ripping facility 66, 74-5
    setting up 65
    skins 65
    visualisations 65
memory 11
    digital cameras 69
    games 49
    upgrades 172
Menu key 16
menus 15, 17, 110
    changing the display 167
    navigating 17
MIDI (musical instrument digital
    interface) 79, 80, 99
MIDI files 64, 67, 80
MIDI sequencer 80
modems 8, 26
    fax modem 142
Money 124-5
monitor 8
motherboard 10, 173
mouse 8, 14
MP3 files 64, 66, 67, 74-5, 76, 160
    file-sharing services 74, 75
    hardware 77
    legal implications 75
MP4 (MPEG4) 81
multi-boot systems 181
music
    composing 80, 81

copyright restrictions 81
DRM (digital rights management) 77
MP3 files 64, 66, 67, 74-5, 76, 160
playlists 74, 76
sample-based music 81
web sites 149
see also CDs; Media Player; MIDI; soundcards; speakers
music keyboard 8
My Computer 14, 20, 103
My Documents 20, 34, 36, 102, 103
My Downloads 102, 146
My eBooks 102, 150
My Music 20, 102
My Network Places 14, 20, 103, 177
My Photos 102
My Pictures 20, 70, 102
My Videos 102

Netscape 143, 166
networks 174-7
advanced options 176-7
cable-based system 174
hardware 174-5, 177
mapping drives or folders 176
network wizard 175, 177
wireless networks 174, 175
newsgroups 138, 141, 155
newspaper sites 148
newsreader software 141
NTFS (new technology filing system) 36, 103, 181
Num lock (number lock) 16

office suites 106-9
Office XP 106-7, 182
alternatives to 108-9
educational edition 107
versions 106
Optical Character Recognition (OCR) 68
Organizer 120
Outlook 28, 107, 120
Outlook Express 28, 107, 120

P2P (peer to peer) services 74
Page Setup 22
Paint Shop Pro 70, 71, 72
parallel port 11
Partition Magic 103, 105, 181
passwords 34, 36
PayPal 57, 101, 133
PC Suite 108
PCs
inside a PC 10-11
organisation 102-3

PDF (portable document format) 150
peripherals 8-9
sharing 34-5, 37
types 9
people-finders 123, 152-3
phone number sites 136, 152
photos
cloning 72, 73
digital cameras 8, 12, 42, 69-71, 94
image-editing software 70-1
professional printing 94
retouching old photos 72-3
Photoshop 70, 180
plug-ins 33, 71
PocoMail 109
pop-ups and pop-unders 162, 163
blocking 139, 163
pornography 37
ports 161
PostScript 92
power failures 114, 157, 180
power management 180
PowerPoint 107, 118-19, 154
Premiere 82, 83, 86
Print Preview 22
printers 14, 22-3
colour printing 8, 22, 23, 94
dye-sublimation printing 94
giclee printing 94
inkjet (bubblejet) printer 22
large format and specialised printing 94
laser printer 8, 22
printing options 22, 23
professional photo printing 94
processor 10, 49, 173
Program Files 19, 20, 39, 103
property
overseas property 61
property listings 60
researching the area 60
PrtScrn (print screen) 16
PS/2 ports 11
Publisher 90, 107, 113

Quicken 124

Real Player 67
Recycle Bin 20, 105
reference information 150-1
registry 178
rescue disk 105
route planners 122
royalty-free art 93
Run 15

Scandisk 157
scanners 9, 68, 70
SCSI ('Scuzzy') 69
SDSL (symmetrical digital subscriber line) 25
Search 14
search engines 134-7, 139, 151, 153
category searches 135, 136
indexes 134
keyword searches 135
meta-searches 139
picture and media searches 137
quote marks 135, 136
refining searches 137, 144
spiders 134
security
advanced PC user protection 34
backups 104-5
banking online 126
car fraud checks 61
childproofing a PC 34, 35, 36-7
digital certificates 132
file protection 36
passwords 34, 36
shopping online 50, 51, 56
serial ports 11
Shared Documents folder 103
shareware 48, 144, 145, 147, 182
Shift keys 16
shopping online 50-63
auction sites 53, 56-7
books, music, videos and gifts 58-9
cars 61
customer rating sites 53
ethical trading 53
food and drink 62-3
free-ad sites 53
holidays, flights and travel 54-5
PayPal 101
price-comparison sites 52
property 60-1
security 50, 51, 56
selling online 53, 57
shopping portals 52
SSL server 100
shortcuts 16-17, 168
SmartSuite 108
software 14, 15, 18-19
anti-virus tools 160
backups 105
beta versions 145
children 38-41
compatibility 39, 182

deletion 157, 178
demo versions 145
desktop publishing (DTP) 107, 113
educational software 38, 40-1
freeware 48, 144, 145
games 48-9
garden design 44-5
home-design packages 42, 46-7
image-editing software 70-1
installation 18-19
interior design 42-3
killing 178
licensing agreements 18
magazine demo versions 145
newsreader 141
online software 18, 144-7
plug-ins 33, 71
registration 19
shareware 48, 144, 145, 147, 182
video 82, 86-7
web-editing software 97
soundcards 11, 49, 79, 80
    replacing 170-1
spam 24, 37, 143, 161, 162, 163
    filtering 24, 163
speakers 8, 78
    power and sound quality 78
    subwoofers 8, 78
    surround sound 49, 78
special characters 115
spreadsheets 106, 125
spyware 162, 163
standby mode 180
StarOffice 109
Start bar 14, 178
start-ups 180
stocks and shares 124, 130-1
supermarket shopping 62-3
synthesisers 79, 80
System Restore 178
system unit 8

tablets 9
taskbar 14, 110
tax returns 132
texting 143
thesaurus 115
toolbars 110, 111
    customising 115
Travan tape drive 104
TV sites 148

upgrades
    disk drives 172-3
    hardware 170-1

memory 172
motherboard and processor 173
suppliers of parts 172
video cards 173
USB connectors 11, 69
USB2 158
user accounts 34
    changing accounts 34
    creating a new user 34
    guest accounts 34
    logging on and off 35
    passwords 34, 36
    switching users 35
user pictures 35

VBRUN files 147
video 59, 64, 82-9, 160
    3D scene design 87
    adding clips to your website 89
    computer animations 87
    corrective effects 86
    creating 82-5
    DVD-ready format 89
    publishing 88-9
    saving a video file 89
    software 82, 86-7
    sound editing 86
    special effects 86, 87
    streaming 64, 65
    tape copies 88
    titles 85, 86
    transitions 85, 86
video cameras 8, 11, 83, 88
video cards 88
    upgrading 173
viruses 28, 107, 160, 183
    anti-virus tools 160
Visual Basic program 115
voice recognition 115

WAV files 77, 160
web browsers 30-3, 166, 182
web design 96-101
    free resources 98
    gremlins and horrors 99
    tools 96-7, 101, 107
    video clips 89
web pages/web sites
    banner ads 162
    blogs (online diaries) 99
    copying to web space 97
    discussion boards 99
    educational sites 41
    Favorites 30, 32
    filter tools 37
    guest books and hit counters 99

History feature 30, 33, 37
links 30, 31, 99, 177
mirror sites 146
pop-unders and pop-ups 162
text size 33
web design 96-101
web hosting 100
Whois 153
WiFi 174
Winamp 67
Windows 95 12, 13, 39
Windows 98 12, 13, 182
Windows 98SE 12
Windows 2000 13
Windows Explorer 105, 166, 182
Windows folder 103
Windows key 16
Windows ME 12, 13
Windows Movie Maker 83, 84-5, 86
Windows NT 13, 182
Windows operating system 12-13
    customising 164-9
    Home and Professional versions 13
    service packs 158, 159
    update feature 156, 158
    upgrading 12-13
Windows XP 12, 13, 182, 183
Windows XP Media Centre 183
Word 106, 110-15
    document templates 112-13
    features 114-15
    menus 110
    taskbar 110
    text editing 111
    toolbars 110, 111
    translation features 110
Works (WorkSuite) 108, 121

Yahoo 138, 139, 140

Zip files 93, 142

Which? Books are commissioned and researched by
Consumers' Association and published by
Which? Ltd, 2 Marylebone Road, London NW1 4DF
Email address: books@which.net

Distributed by The Penguin Group:
Penguin Books Ltd, 80 Strand, London WC2R 0RL

Design: Paul Sands
Original cover concept: Sarah Harmer
Editorial and production: Robert Gray, Nithya Rae

The author and publishers would like to thank Max Fuller, Jonquil Lowe and Jo Saxton for their help in the preparation
of this book.

First edition March 2003
Copyright © 2003 Which? Ltd

British Library Cataloguing in Publication Data
A catalogue record for this book is available from the British Library

ISBN 0 85202 910 1

For a full list of Which? books, please call 0800 252100, access our website
at www.which.net, or write to Which? Books, PO Box 44, Hertford SG14 1SH

Text reproduction by Saxon Photolitho, Norwich
Printed and bound in Spain by Bookprint, S.L., Barcelona